MAKING THE NEW CLASSICS

Other books by Leslie Linsley

Decoupage, A New Look At An Old Craft
Decoupage Designs
Scrimshaw
The Decoupage Workshop
Wildcrafts
Decoupage On . . .
Air Crafts
The Art of Acrylic Crafts
Fabulous Furniture Decorations
Decoupage for Young Crafters
Custom Made

MAKING THE NEW CLASSICS:

How to Transform Ordinary Objects from the Basement, Hardware Store, Tag Sale, and Surplus Outlet into Useful and Elegant Home Decorations and Accessories

(formerly Army/Navy Surplus)

BY LESLIE LINSLEY

PHOTOS BY JON ARON

DELACORTE PRESS/NEW YORK

A BETTER HOMES AND GARDENS
BOOK CLUB EDITION
of A Delta Special
Published by
Dell Publishing Co., Inc.
1 Dag Hammarskjold Plaza
New York, New York 10017

Manufactured in the United States of America

Better Homes and Gardens Book Club Edition

First printing

ISBN: 0-440-05682-9

CONTENTS

MAKING THE NEW CLASSICS

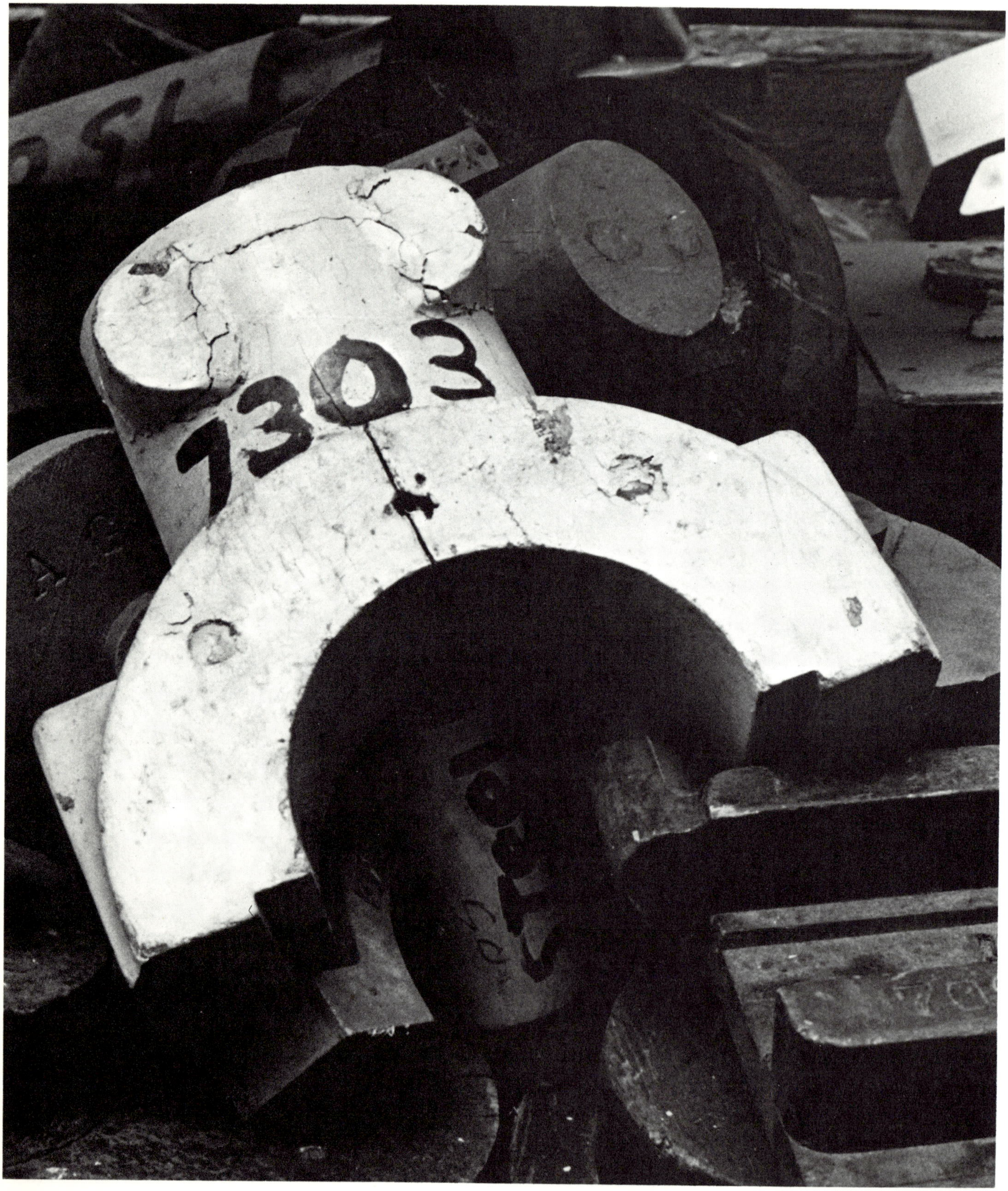
7303

HUMBLE BEGINNINGS

Army/Navy surplus, restaurant, industrial, and institutional supplies conjure up images of basic, sturdy, functional items that the individual doesn't usually buy. Yet when we do see clunky coffee-shop chinaware or an oversized pot in a magazine we are often attracted to it. Industrial packing materials made into storage units, coffee-table bases, or plant pedestals are admired for their uniqueness. Inexpensive molding used to frame maps or refurbished street signs is another example. A young couple design their apartment around stenciled Army cots and stuffed duffel-bag bolsters and we say, "How clever."

Our country produces "surplus" at an amazing—to some an alarming—rate. Surplus is something that is in excess of what is needed, something leftover and therefore reasonably priced since it has no value for its original purpose. Ever since World War II the military has been a prime source of surplus materials. Other sources include industry, second-hand shops, junkyards, and school, hospital, beauty parlor, and restaurant supply houses. Actually, much of what

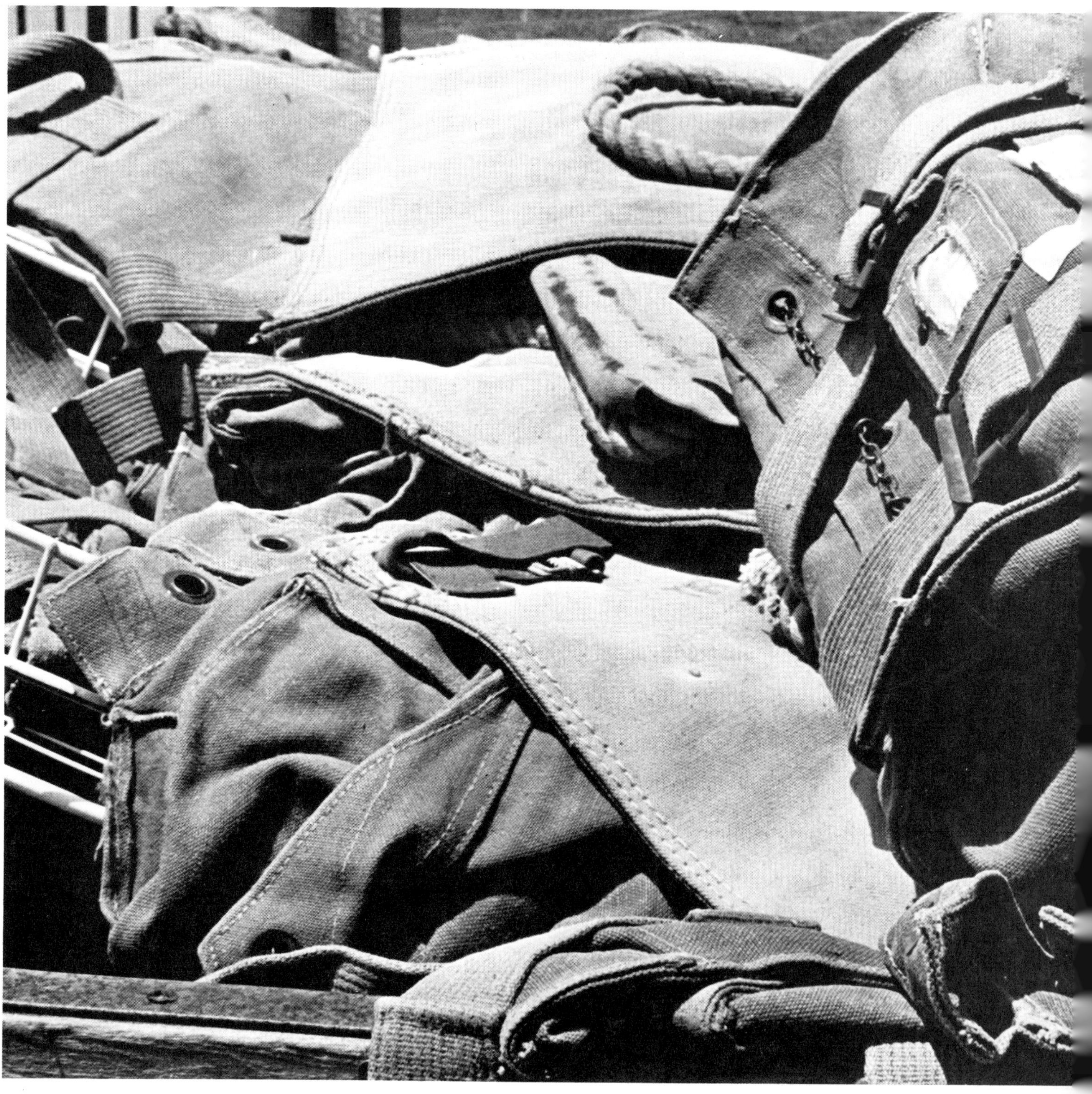

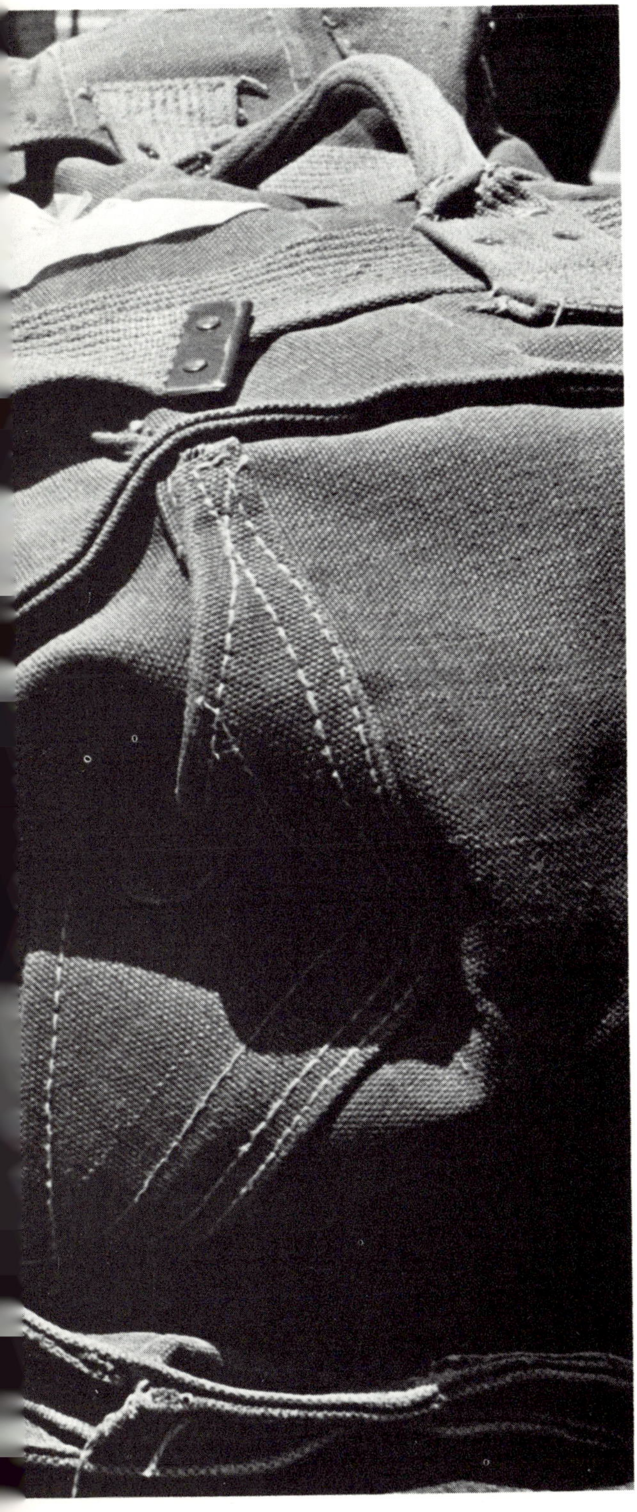

we call industrial surplus is not really surplus at all. Although some of the items are outdated, most are commonplace, manufactured in quantity, and still in use. In this book, however, the term Army/Navy surplus is an all-inclusive one covering all those materials used for a functional purpose that have the potential to be refashioned and converted cheaply and easily into good-looking, unusual accessories for the home.

Not long ago, I was in the local Army & Navy store for the third time in a week with the seemingly endless list of supplies for my daughter's two-week camp outing. "I'm working on your kind of book, Frank," I told the owner. "It's a craft book of Army/Navy surplus ideas." He looked at me quizzically. "There isn't any surplus around," he said. "Oh, yes, there is," I answered, "and plenty of it. As a matter of fact, it's all in my house right now. Wall-to-wall surplus."

There is indeed plenty of good, sturdy, reliable, durable, basically well-designed material around for the poking,

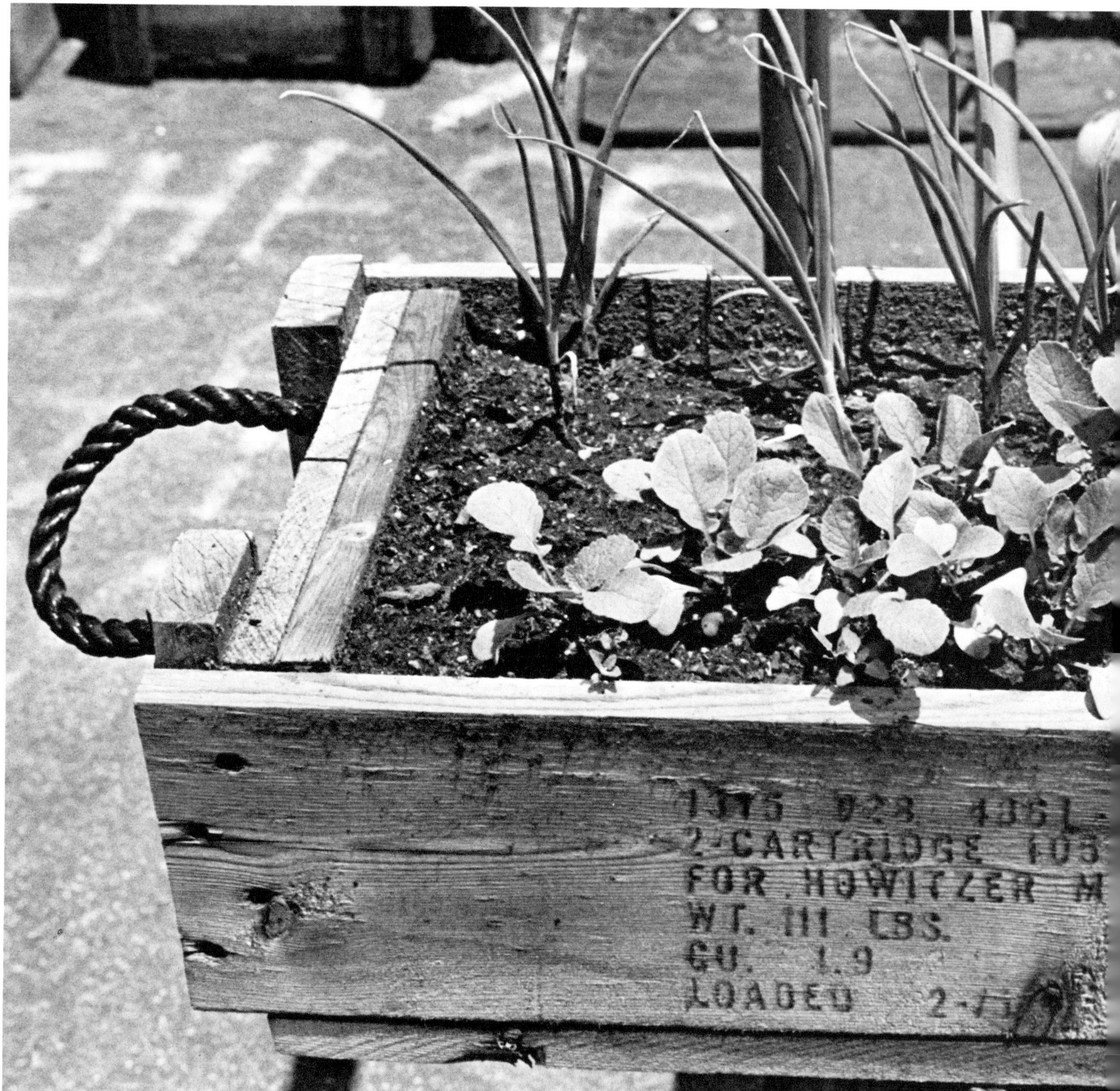
2-CARTRIDGE 105
FOR HOWITZER M
WT. 111 LBS.
CU. 1.9
LOADED

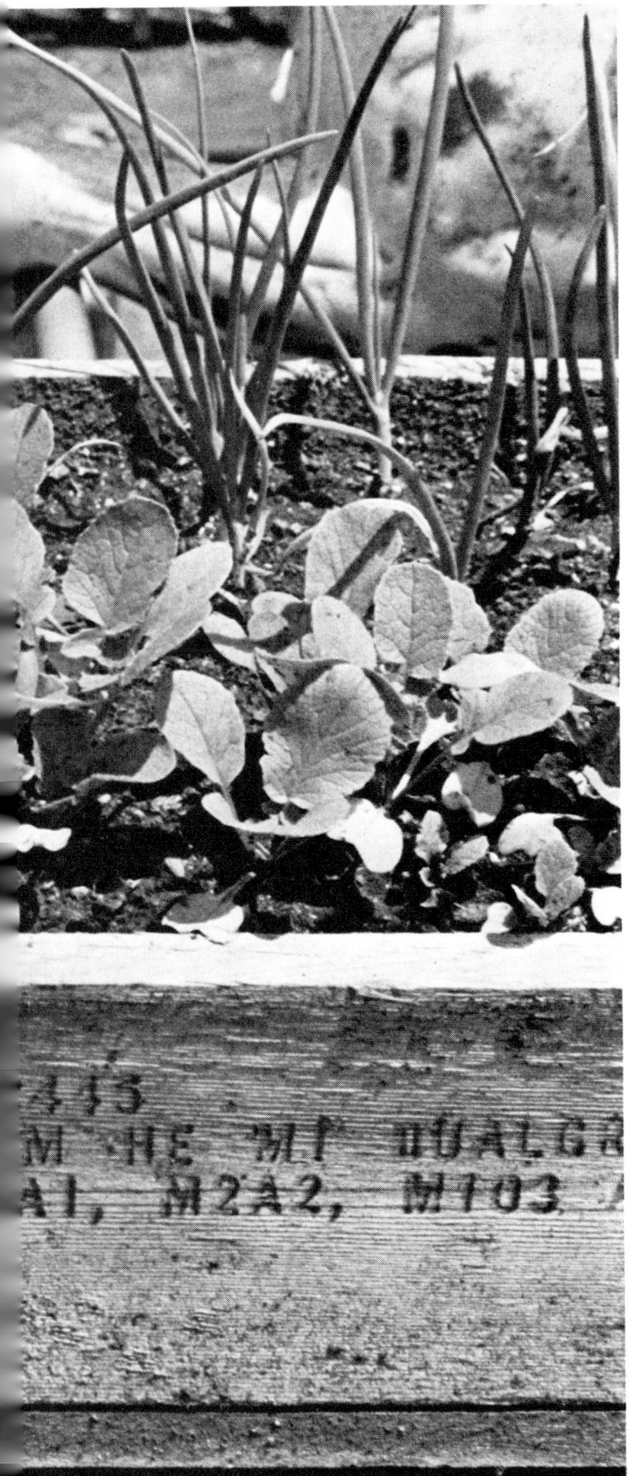

picking, scavenging, retrieving, and finally transforming into home decorating use. This is not a new idea. We have always been exposed to basic, inexpensive, nuts-and-bolts living. And in the past we accepted a certain crudeness about these ideas. But our tastes are more refined today—no longer does orange-crate furniture seem very appealing. Also, everything costs a great deal more now. So while we are knowledgeable about well-designed objects that enhance our living spaces, we cannot always afford them. We have been exposed to new building techniques and plans for making our own furniture, but we are becoming more selective about our leisure time and space is becoming limited. Not everyone has access to a home workshop. Women are working in greater numbers than ever before and families want to enjoy their free time together. In short, we all want our homes to be well designed and up-to-date. We also want to individualize our space whenever possible. But if it is a do-it-yourself project, we only want what can be done easily, with a minimum of time and money invested. Basically, I think most of us want and

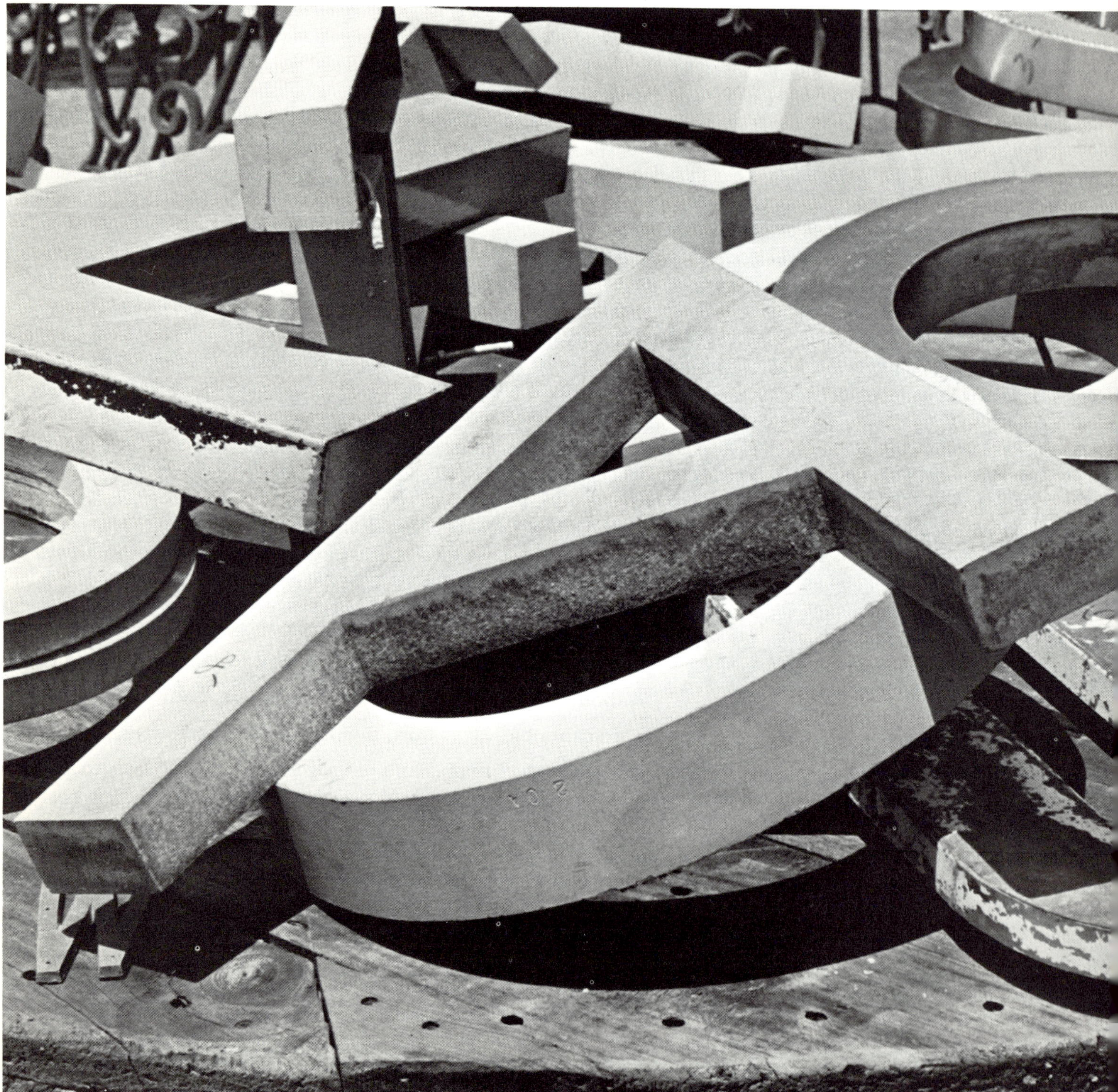

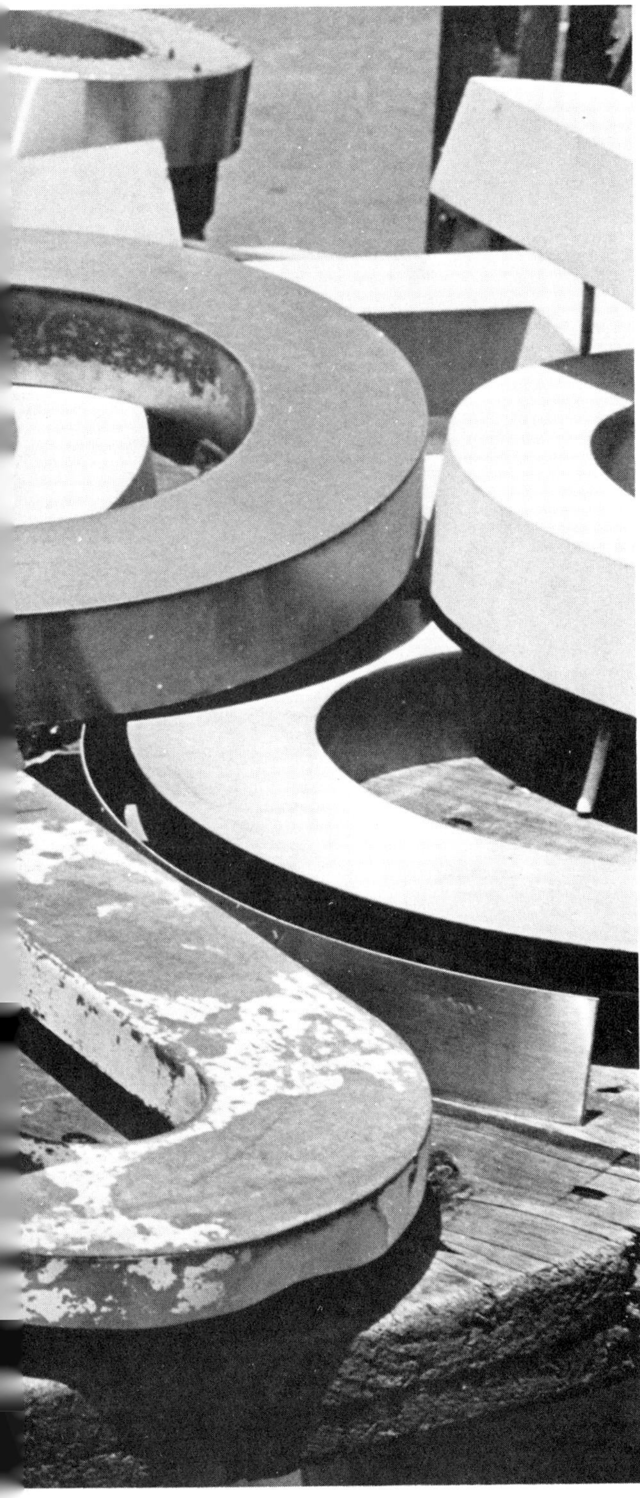

will pay for furniture that is comfortable and good-looking. It is in the area of accessories that we tend to put our creative efforts and have some fun.

Army/Navy Surplus is chock full of objects from the world of surplus. They are not hard to find if you look around. Poking in junkyards can be a source of tremendous enjoyment. You never know what you will find so there is the element of excitement and anticipation. A lot of things can turn up in out of the way places you may never have thought of going to before. Industrial sections, for instance, are worth investigating. However, all the items that are used in the book can be bought by mail and a complete source list is at the end of the book. Accompanying the descriptions of the various items are a multitude of ideas and suggestions as to how they can be used in your home, either as is, or with a minimum of refurbishing. I hope you will discover, as I have, that there is great enjoyment and satisfaction in finding and creating smart, attractive, decorative accessories from Army/Navy and industrial surplus.

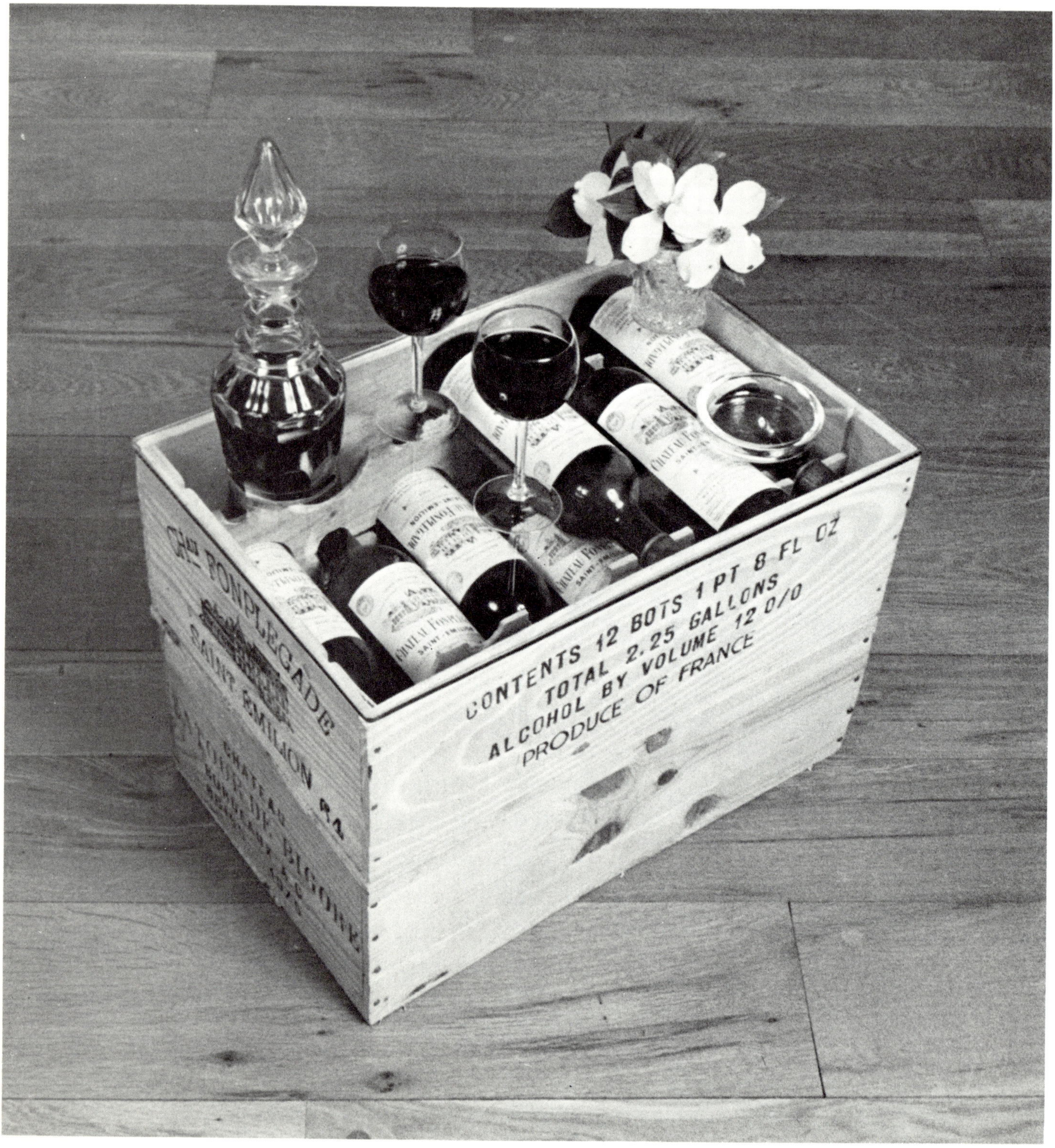
CONTENTS 12 BOTS 1 PT 8 FL OZ
TOTAL 2.25 GALLONS
ALCOHOL BY VOLUME 12 0/0
PRODUCE OF FRANCE

SENSATIONAL MAKE-OVERS

JUST IN CASE

If you can beg, cajole, or in any way talk your favorite wine seller out of two wooden cases made to hold wine, do so. These wooden boxes, which hold twelve bottles of expensive French wines, are becoming scarce and desirable. At The Purple Feet, a wine store in Westport, Connecticut, the owners have taken several boxes apart and nailed them to the top and front portion of their counter. The wood has been sanded smooth, and it makes a unique counter top that looks as though it is an assemblage of wine cases.

In order to make an occasional table you will need two cases. If you can't get them without buying the wines they contain, doing so may not bother you. The two empty cases are glued together, one on top of the other, with epoxy, then left to dry. You obviously can store wine bottles only in the top case. Measure the top case so that you have the exact width and length of the outer dimensions. Sometimes these cases are not perfectly rectangular, and it is best to measure all four sides. Take these measurements to a glass cutter and have ½-inch-thick plate glass cut and finished around the edges. Plexiglas can also be used. Set this on top of the case, and you have a rustic, good-looking, glass-top table, as well as a wine holder.

If you want to stain the boxes, this can easily be done with oil-base wood stain (such as Minwax). Select the wood color of your choice at a hardware store. (It will have sample chips of stained wood showing the various colors.) After staining, let dry and then give the cases a coat of semigloss polyurethane for a glossy finish. It will make even this crude wood look sensational.

CRAZY CORK COLLECTION

If you're a wine drinker, you might begin assembling a cork display that will surely be talked about. This bottle full of corks is a collection of the owners of The Purple Feet. Here the bottle is simply displayed in an old pine box surrounded by plants. It could be placed in a hallway to attract attention or on top of a box that can also serve as a table. This pine box is another junkyard find with many, many uses.

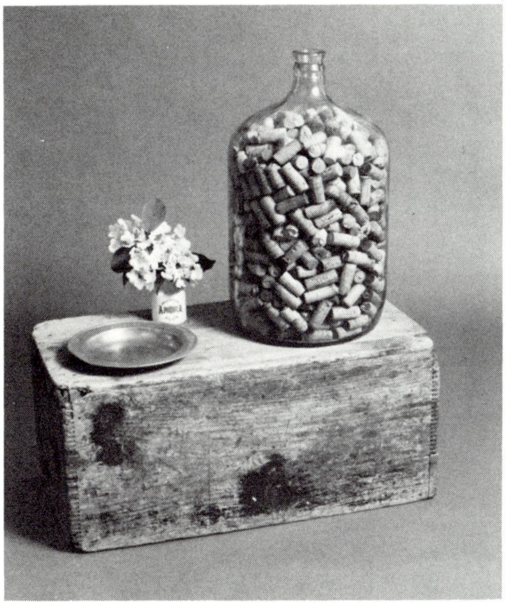

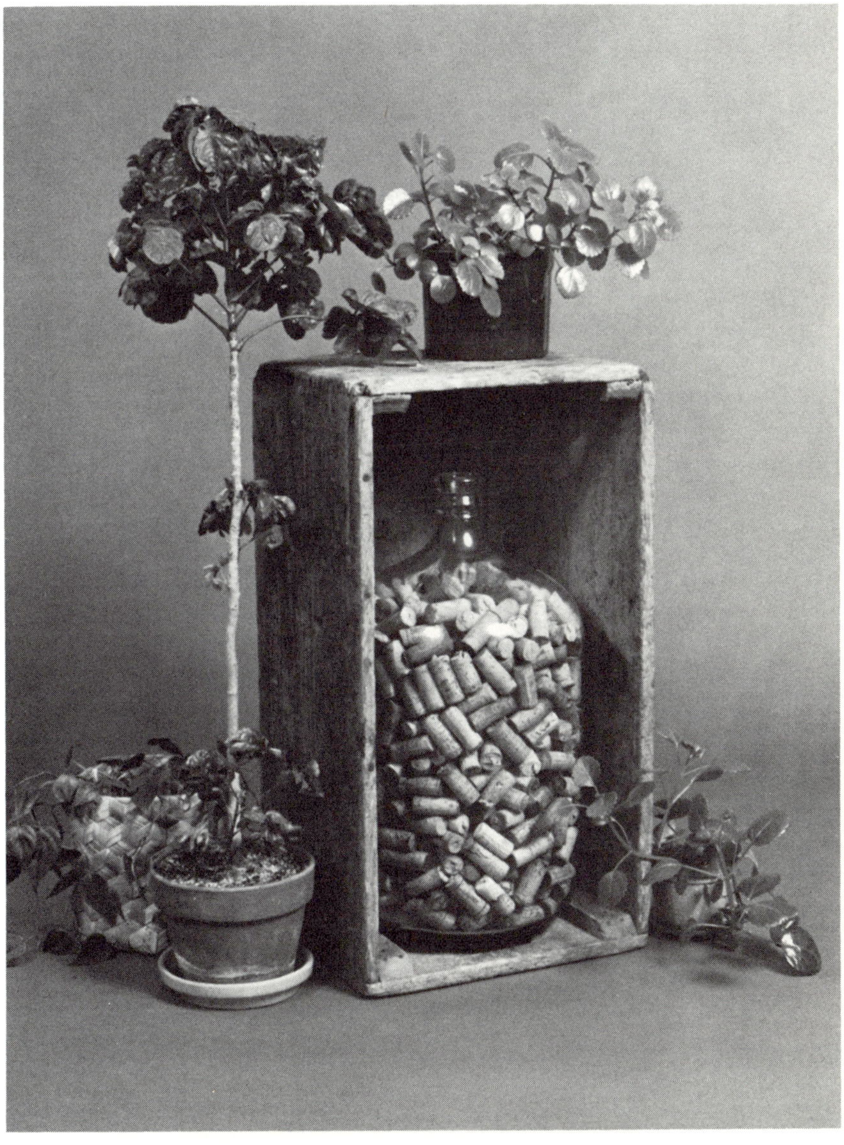

TRIVET

If you don't want to wait to fill a bottle with corks, try using just a few. A cork trivet will cost nothing to make. Since the wine names are stamped on the corks, you will have a record of the wines you like. Lay the corks end to end in several rows, using as many as you want to make the desired size. Glue each one to the others with an epoxy. Or you might want to glue them to a tile, rubber backing, or similar material. A very large cork assemblage could even be used as a bathmat next to the tub.

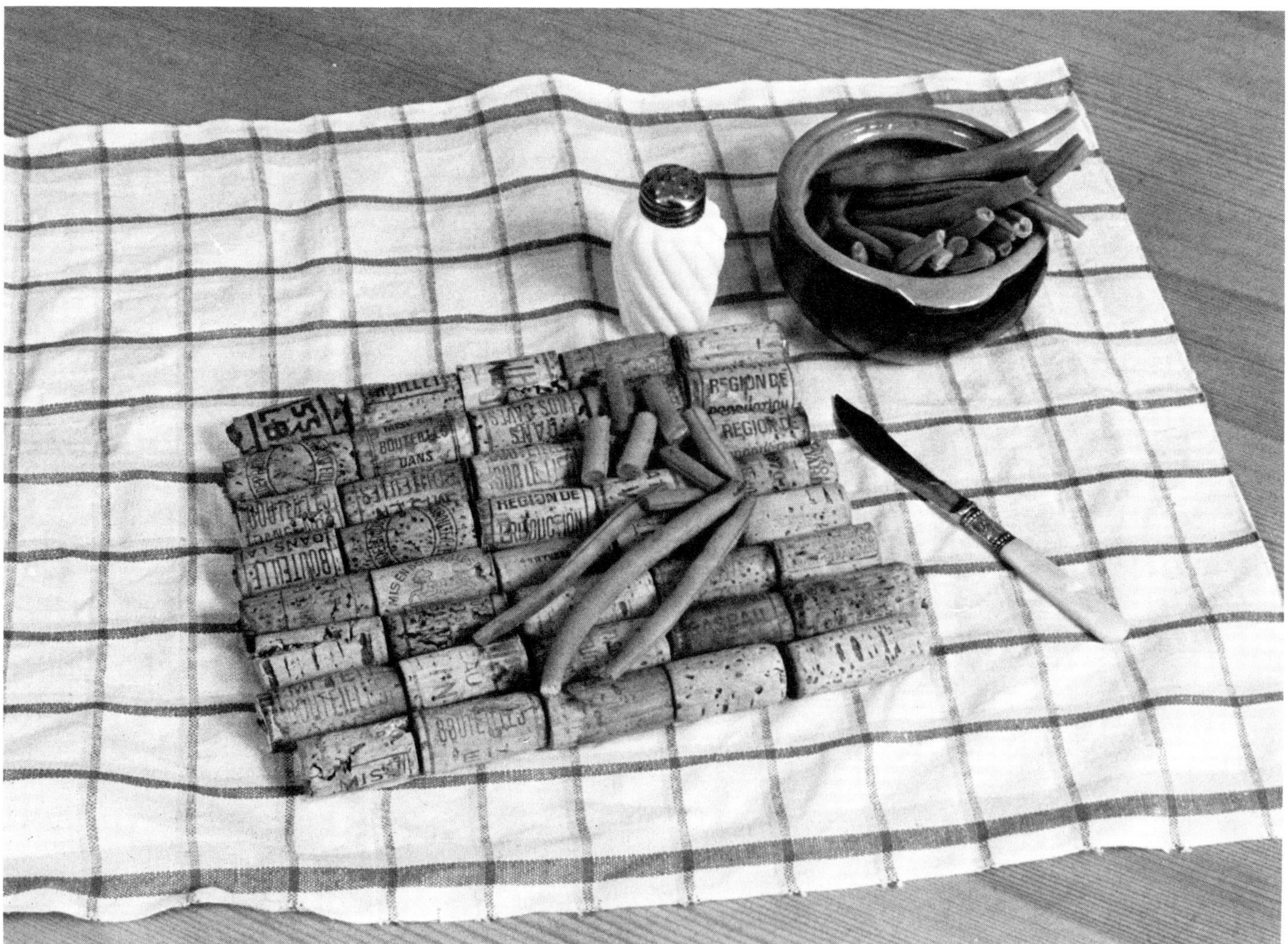

NICELY SPICED

While we rarely, if ever these days, see wooden crates filled with soda bottles, these containers have become surplus. They are often rather beaten up, but there is something so appealing about anything made of wood that we seem to treasure it as a reminder of the past.

Begin by sanding the crate so that it is smooth. A wood or plastic sanding block will make this job easier. Select a dark oil stain such as walnut or ebony and brush it over the wood. A 1-inch, inexpensive sponge brush is good for this and can be thrown away when the job is finished. Apply the stain liberally to the outside as well as inside sections so that no area is left exposed. Let the stain sit for fifteen minutes before wiping away the excess with a clean rag. Let this dry overnight.

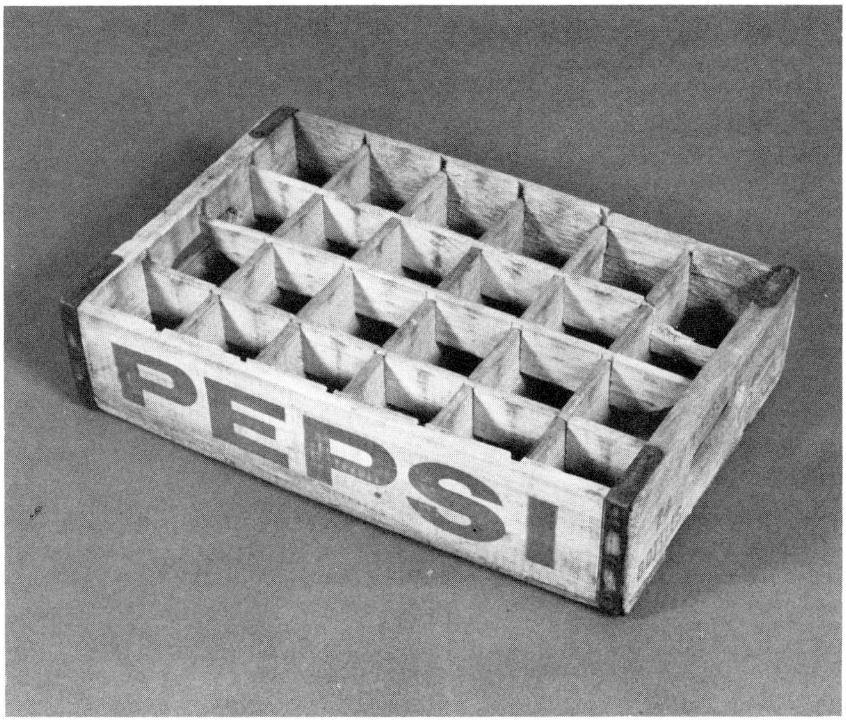

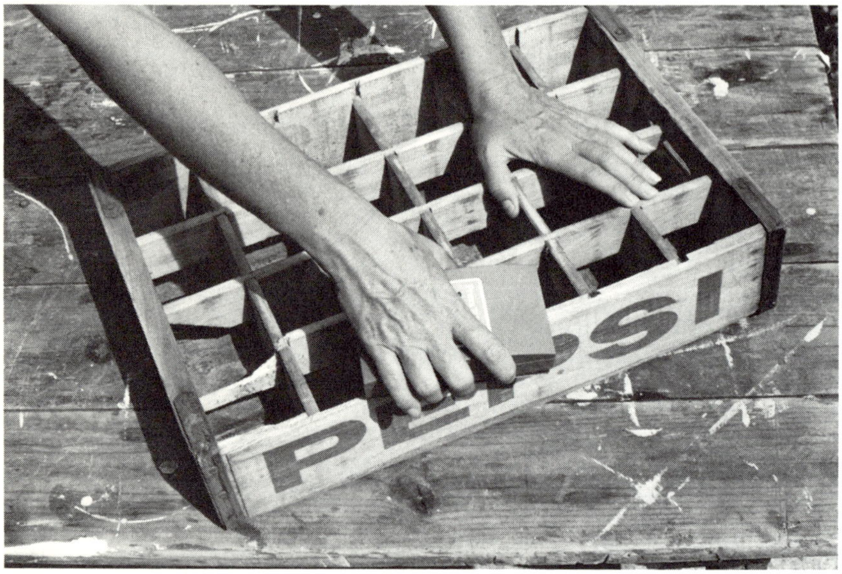

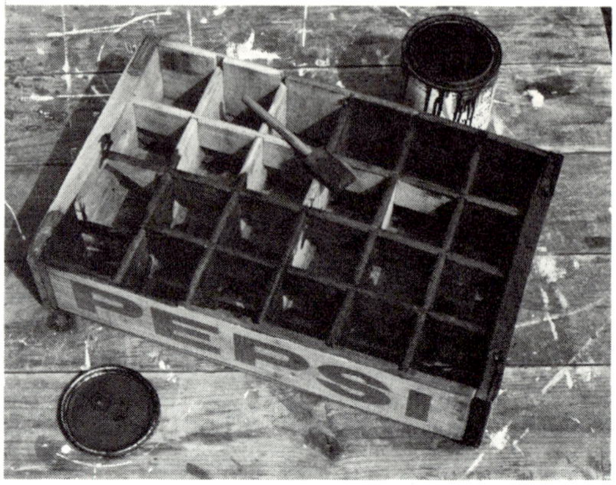

Coat the crate with high-gloss polyurethane varnish. This will give the stained surface a glossy sheen. The polyurethane should dry overnight before you apply another coat. Rub the finish with very fine steel wool to eliminate any bumps or imperfections in the varnish. Apply a coat of furniture paste wax (such as Johnson's or Butcher's) to the sides and top for added luster. The crate will suddenly be transformed from an ugly duckling into a handsome display rack.

The small-sized spice cans found in the supermarket fit perfectly into the spaces and form an attractive, colorful wall display. When you are cooking, the spices will be readily available and visible. Stand a potted plant on the top or use this space for more spices. The rack is easy to hang on two nails through the back.

The soda crate could also be used to display a miniature collection. Line each compartment with fabric or wallpaper for more interest.

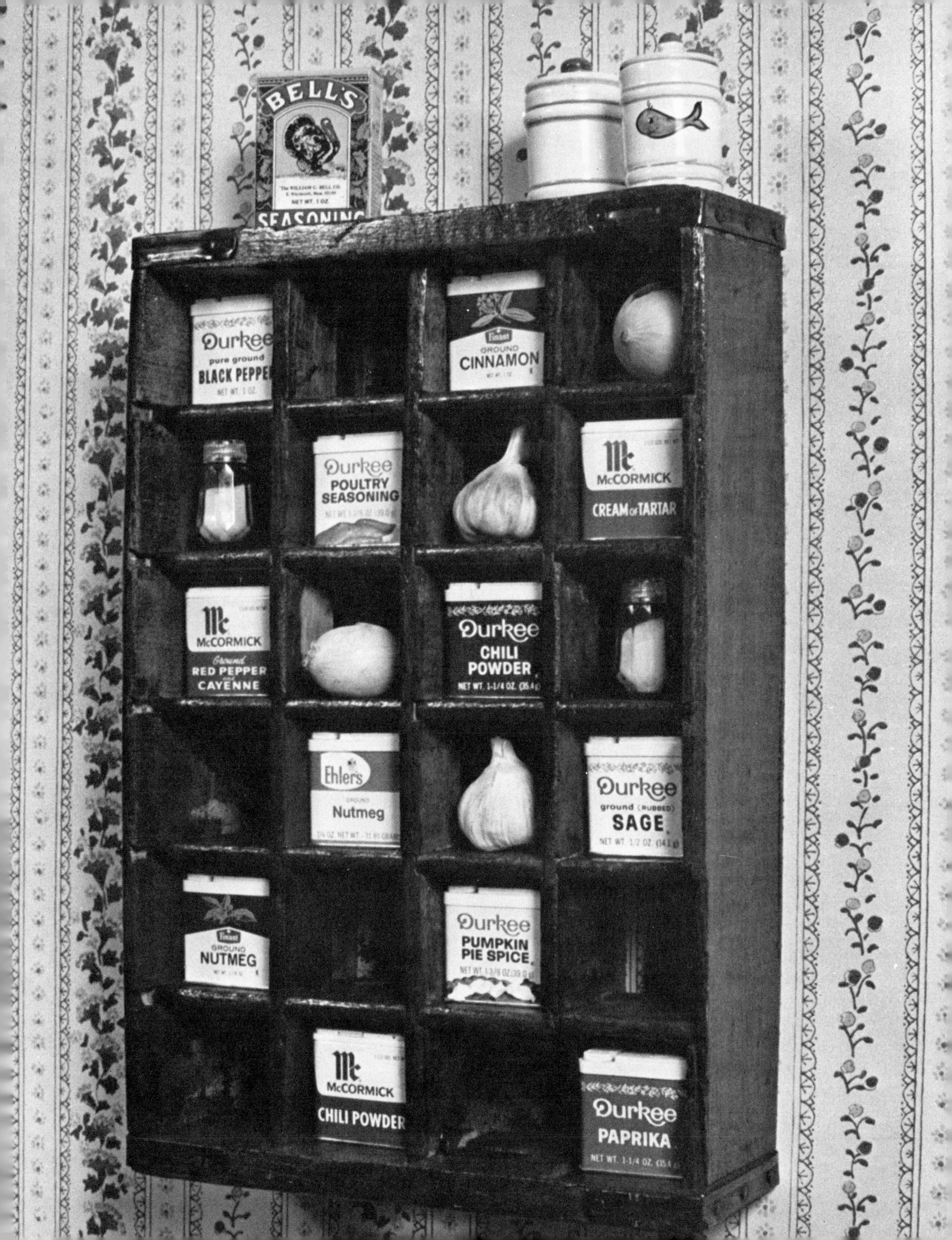
BELL'S
SEASONING
Durkee
pure ground
BLACK PEPPE
GROUND
CINNAMON
Durkee
POULTRY
SEASONING
McCORMICK
CREAM OF TARTAR
McCORMICK
Ground
RED PEPPER
CAYENNE
Durkee
CHILI
POWDER
NET WT. 1-1/4 OZ.
Ehler's
GROUND
Nutmeg
Durkee
ground (RUBBED)
SAGE
NET WT. 1/2 OZ.
GROUND
NUTMEG
Durkee
PUMPKIN
PIE SPICE
McCORMICK
CHILI POWDER
Durkee
PAPRIKA
NET WT. 1-1/4 OZ.

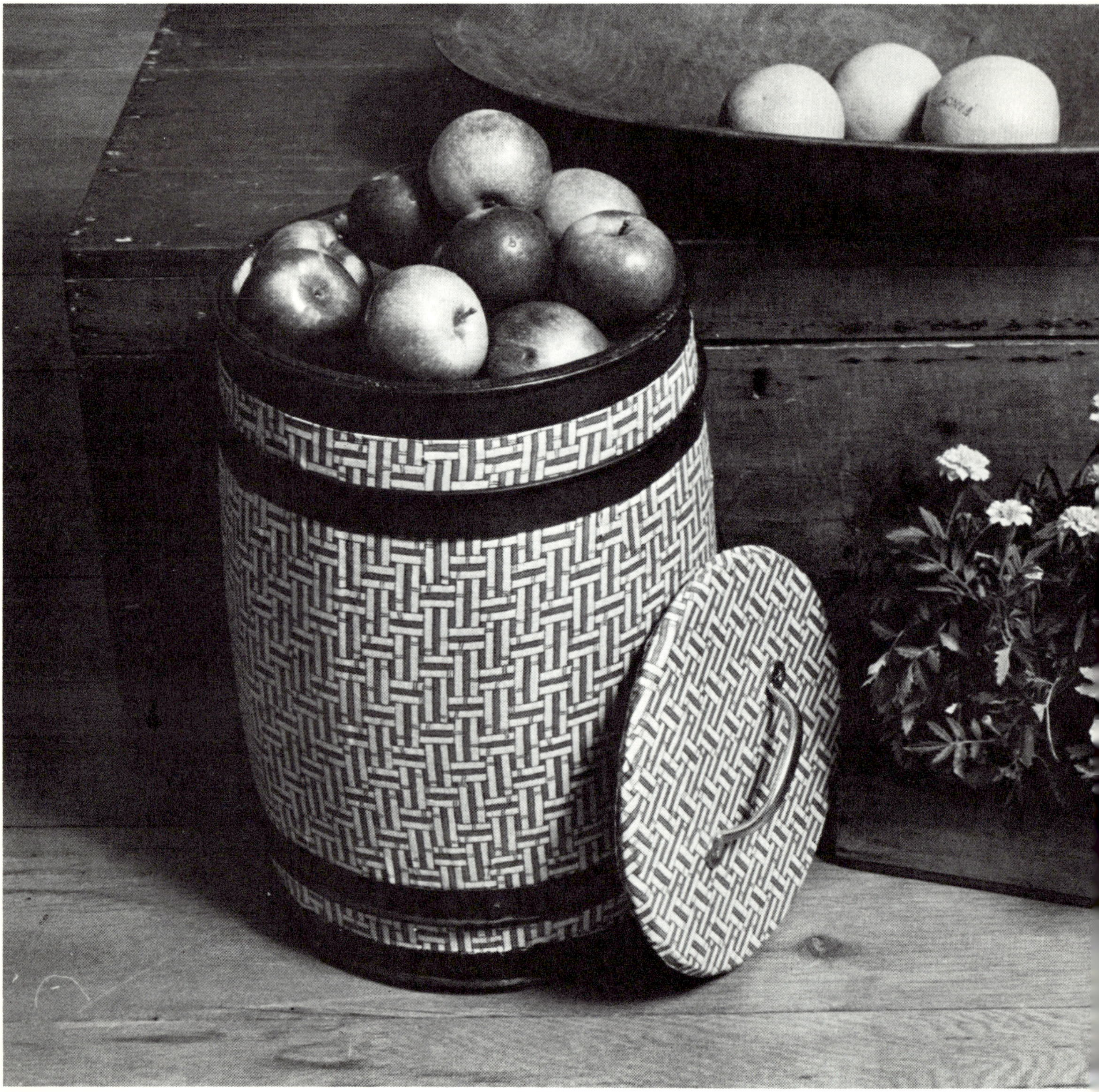

ROLL OUT THE BARREL

Kegs, barrels, buckets, and tubs have always come in a wide variety of sizes. Some were once used to carry fish, others, firewood. Small buckets were used at the well for hoisting water and others were used when milking the cow. Fruit buckets, wine kegs, sap buckets, ice buckets, and salt boxes are long-forgotten household necessities. Such containers have always been considered inexpensive throwaway items and could be picked up in dump yards or found in flea markets for practically nothing. Nails were almost always shipped in small kegs, and hardware stores were happy to give them away once emptied of the contents. Usually made of wooden staves bound together with cylindrical metal hoops, they have a flat top and bottom of equal diameter. The barrels are sturdy, usually made of pine, and are therefore popular items for creative ideas. They have become increasingly stylish as chairs, table bases, ice buckets, hampers, and cookie jars.

Over the years as the barrels were replaced with more practical substitutes, they became sought after for use as storage bins. Several companies have responded to this need by manufacturing them for consumer use. Any size is easily obtainable by mail. They can be ordered finished with a wood stain and varnish, or can be purchased in their rough, crude state. This affords you the opportunity to be creative.

If you like the natural wood, sand the barrel until it is smooth, then finish with a coating of polyurethane varnish. However, there are so many ways to cover the wood that it is a shame not to experiment with a few ideas. Remember that the inside is as rough as raw wood can be and should therefore be sanded before using. By selecting a fabric as a covering, you will have many options. The fabric might match the room curtains or perhaps the wallpaper. A basketweave pattern was chosen here because it suggested multiple uses. It seems to look well in the kitchen as an apple barrel, but at another time will be handsome as a hamper for clothes. A paper covering can be applied, but is much more difficult to work with. Because the barrel is cylindrical, but is wider in the middle than top and bottom, it is hard to avoid wrinkles and creases when wrapping with paper.

Begin by measuring your barrel to determine how much fabric will be needed. I used a polished cotton that had been treated with Scotchgard for soil resistance. If you can remove the metal hoops, do so before covering the barrel. If not, work around them. These hoops can be painted with spray paint or acrylic. Use the color that best accents the fabric you use. When dry, replace the top and bottom hoops, but not the middle ones.

Cut the fabric so that the top and bottom edges can be folded in for a neat finished edge. There should be enough to wrap around the barrel and overlap the fabric ends. It will be necessary to make cut lines every three or four inches around the top and bottom in order to wrap the fabric smoothly. These will not show if you are using a print pattern. With a solid material you will have to be more careful when glueing it to the barrel.

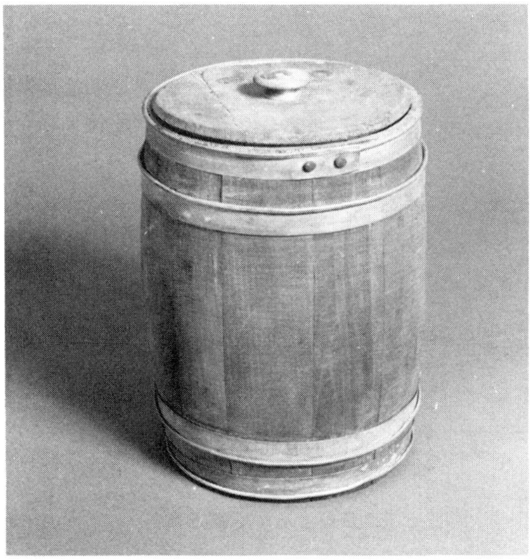

Spray fabric adhesive is used to apply the fabric. It is quite easy to do. Simply lay the fabric wrong side up on a sheet of newspaper. Coat the entire piece liberally with the spray adhesive. Be sure to cover the edges and corners well. Turn down the top edge in order to form a hem. It will stick to itself. Repeat this on the bottom, then respray the top and bottom hems.

Carefully lift the fabric, holding it at the corners. Place the top edge of the fabric on the barrel so that it butts up against the metal hoop. Press down along the side edge of the fabric and smooth it onto the barrel with your hand. Continue to align the top edge as you pull the fabric taut with your other hand. Clip in from the top and bottom as needed to avoid unevenness or wrinkling as you wrap the material around the cylinder. Overlap the material where it is clipped and take extra care to smooth this down while matching the pattern.

Once the material has been attached, the center hoops can be reapplied. Drop them over the top and the bottom, and hammer down so they are secure. Tap lightly around the edge of each rim, at the same time making sure not to pull the fabric.

Next, remove the knob handle from the lid. Place the top on the fabric and cut a circle that is approximately 1 inch larger all around. Cut another circle to exactly fit the inside of the lid. Spray the adhesive on the larger circle of fabric and place it on the outside of the lid. Smooth the material down over the edge to the inside. Coat the smaller circle of fabric with adhesive and place it onto the inside, creating a finished cover for the barrel.

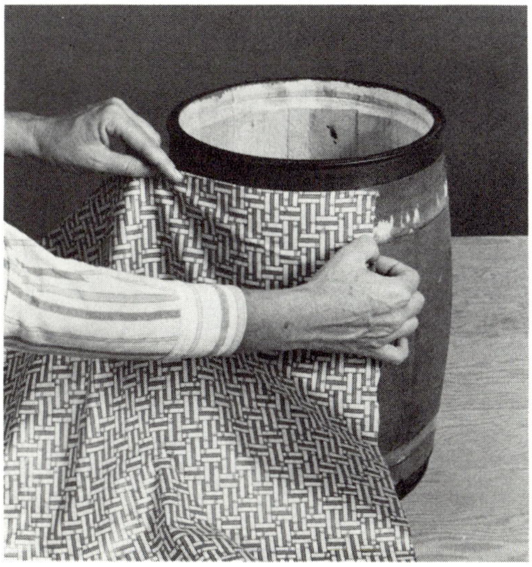

If you want to replace the knob, it can first be painted or covered with fabric. I found an inexpensive, sturdy, brass-colored handle that I felt was better looking than the original. You might look around for an unusual item for this purpose. Porcelain drawer pulls come in a variety of sizes and shapes. Marine supply outlets yield interesting hardware. Old doorknobs can substitute for handles. These are often found in antique shops, at auctions, tag sales, junk shops, and so on. Perhaps an old bathroom fixture can be recycled for this use.

To finish the inside of the barrel, go over the exposed wood with heavy-grit sandpaper. You might like to repeat the fabric on the inside, or spray paint it with a matching or complementary color. If left exposed, seal the wood with a coat of polyurethane varnish. Shiny vinyl paper could also be used, but it will require a bit of patience to apply.

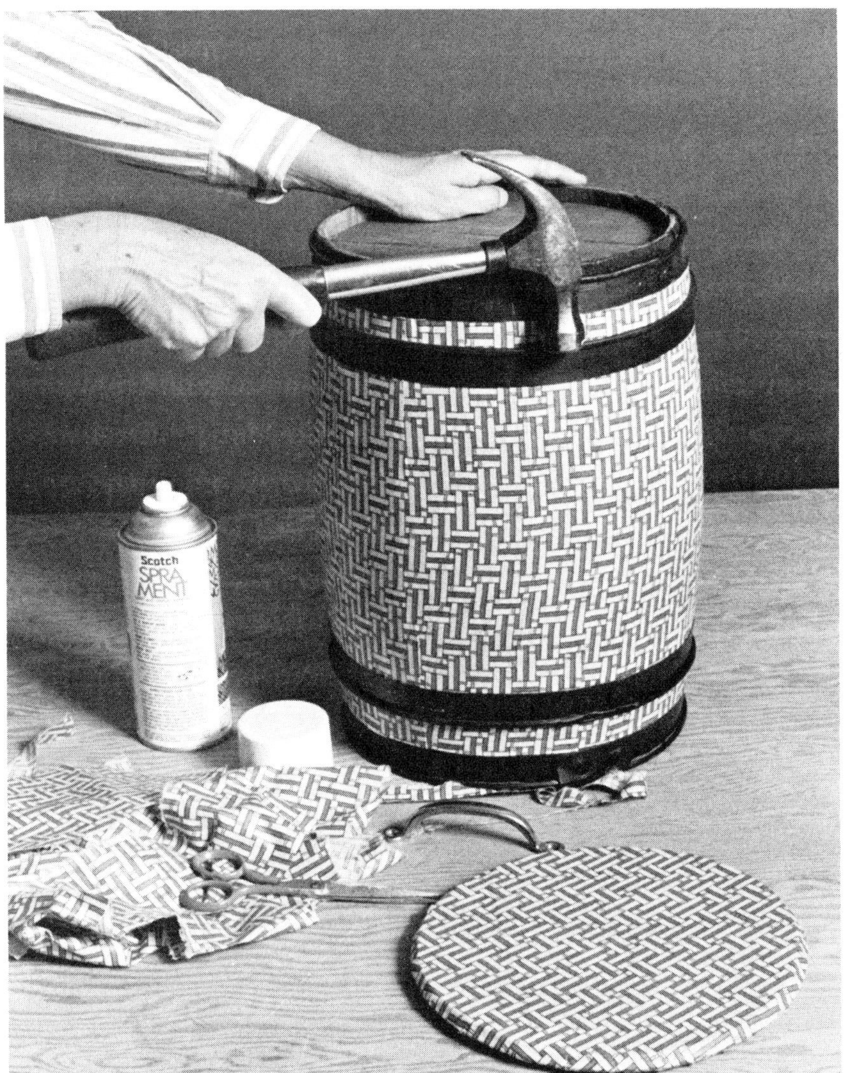

Hammer repainted metal hoops back onto barrel.

TYPE CAST

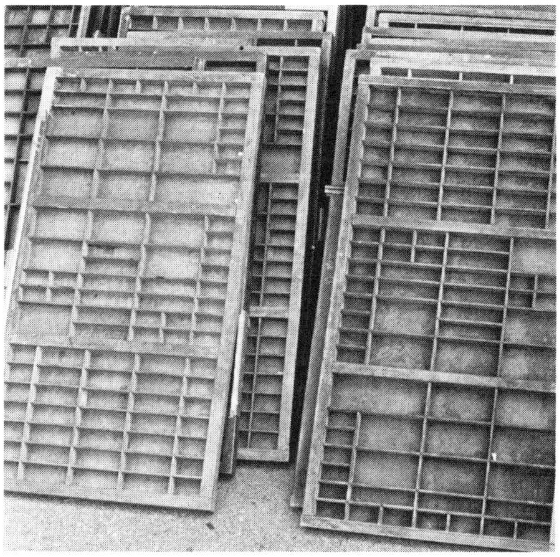

When handsetting type for printing typesetters always kept the individual letters in compartmented drawers, or type trays. These trays held all the characters of a particular type font, and since each typeface is different in size, the number and size of the compartments would differ to accommodate the contents. Today new technology and equipment in typesetting has made handsetting practically obsolete. Now the wooden trays are used primarily as collector's display boxes to hang on the wall or to convert to coffee tables.

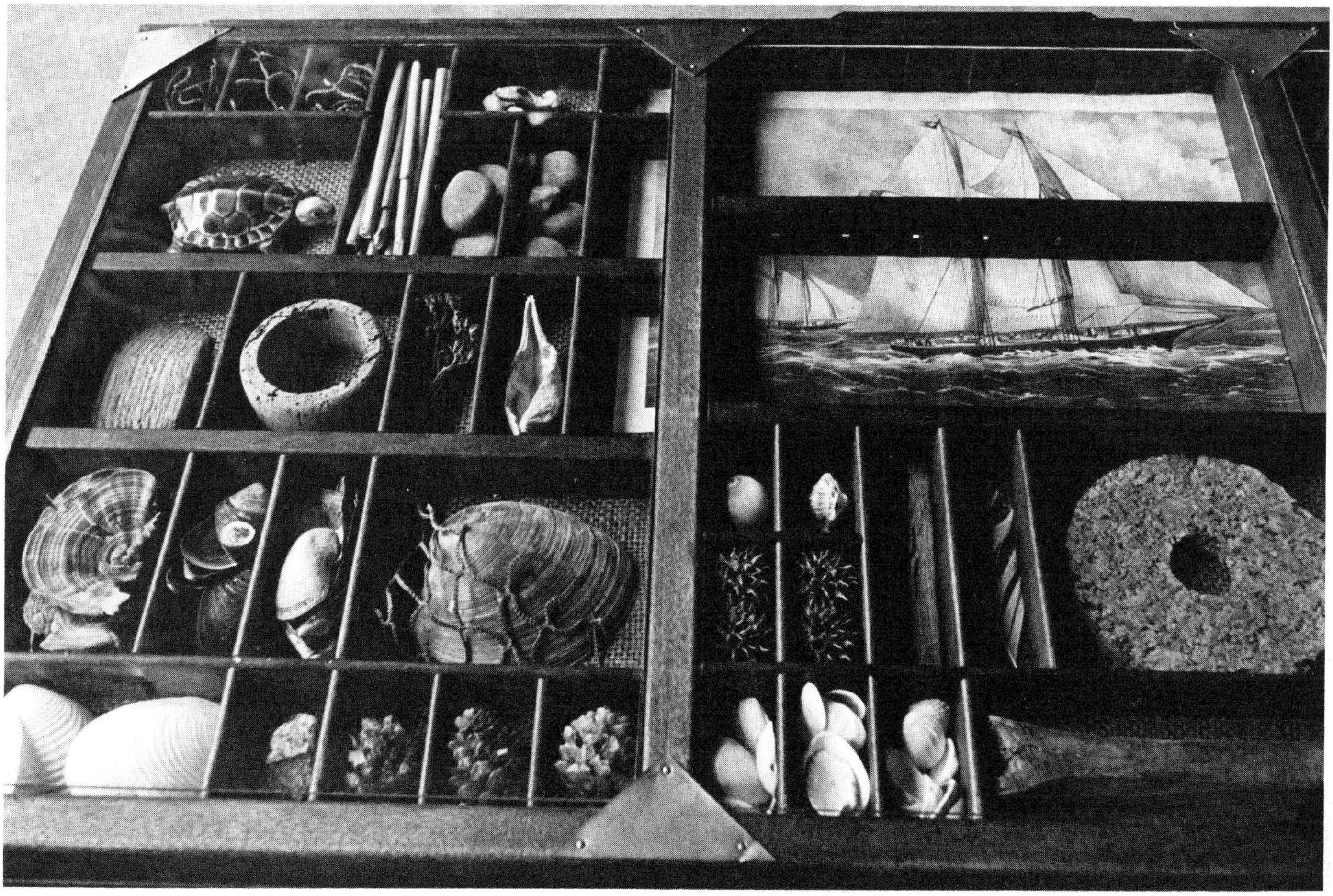

This handsome type table was made by Phyllis Lodato, who filled the compartments with seashells and other seashore memorabilia. The top is fitted with three pieces of glass since the type drawer has three main sections. The wooden separators divide the glass, and the base and legs are made of wrought iron to create an unusual and personal piece of furniture. If you can't have an iron base made, a wooden frame and legs would look as good.

The type trays are usually quite worn and have a soft patina finish. Clean the drawer and then, if desired, a wood stain can be used on the entire tray. When dry, coat with a polyurethane varnish in the finish of your choice. Some people choose to paint the type drawer, depending on the condition of the wood. Once filled, have a glass top cut to size. Small brass-coated corners can be nailed to the wood in order to hold the glass in place. These are available in hardware and craft stores.

Designed by Phyllis Lodato.

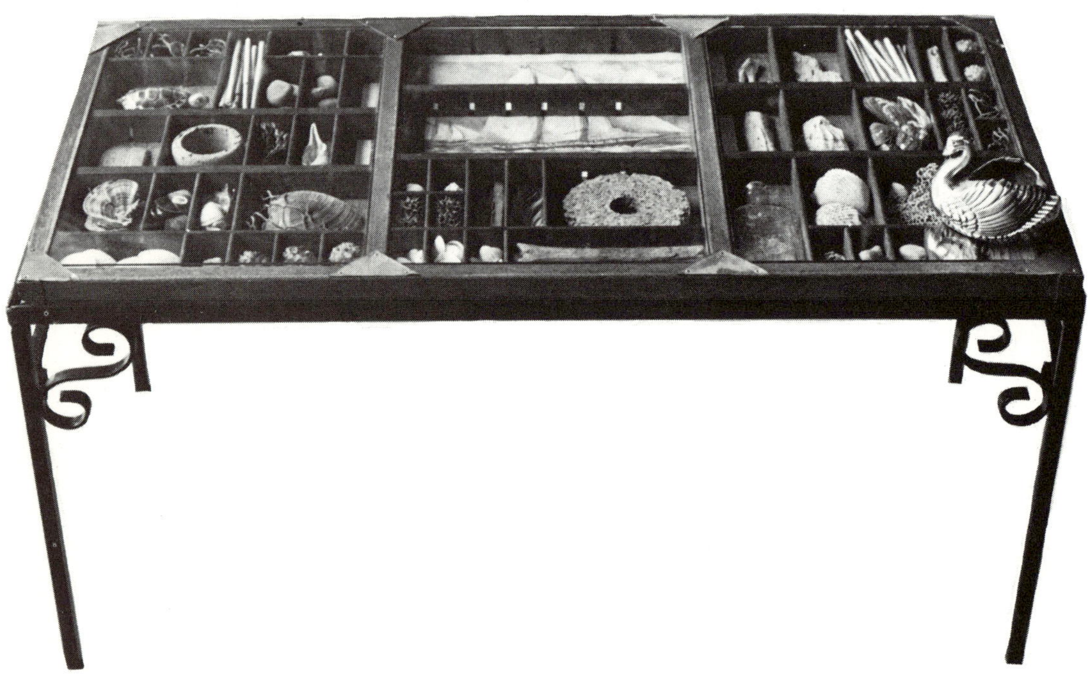

SEAWORTHY

Electrical cable spools come in tiny, medium, and giant sizes. There is a use for all of them. Not too long ago it was easy to stop a repairperson who was working on the telephone lines and ask for the spool holding the cable. Now they are so popular, nobody wants to part with them, and it seems that one must find a rotting or beaten-up spool wherever possible. However, because of their desirability as tables, the spools are being collected in junkyards and sold at reasonable prices. In some parts of the country where no one has yet made a business of it, spools can be found more easily.

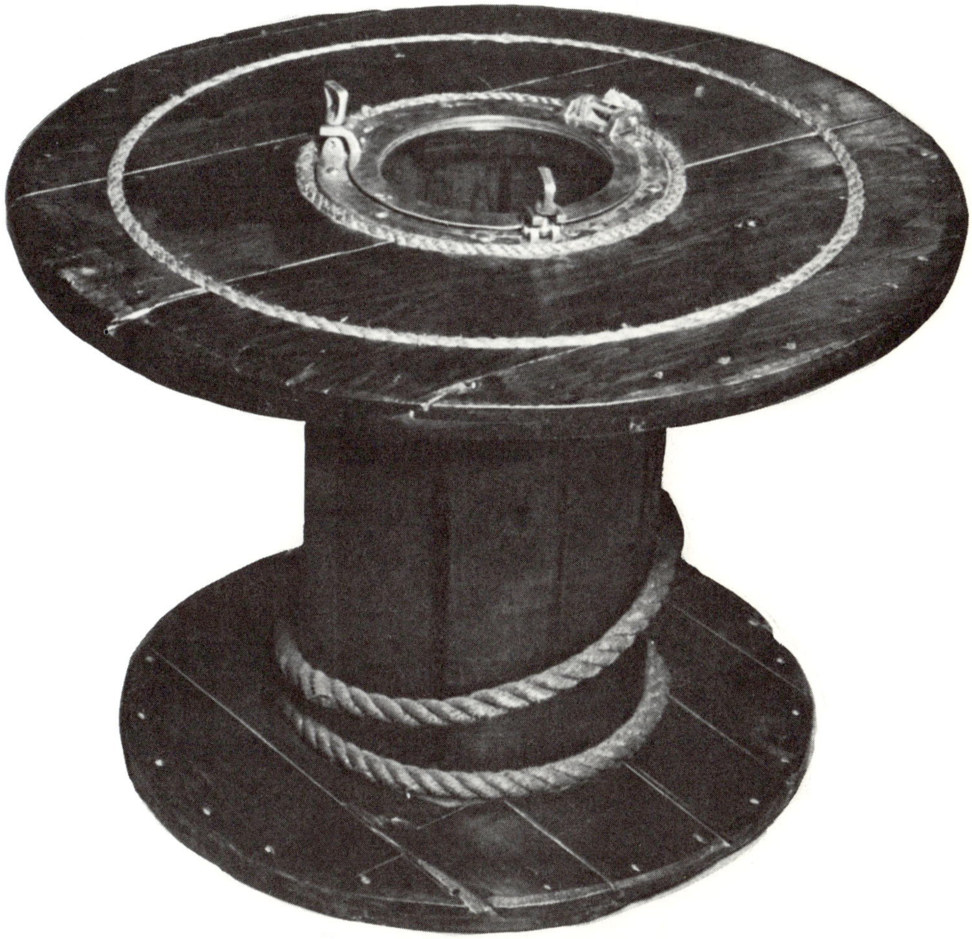

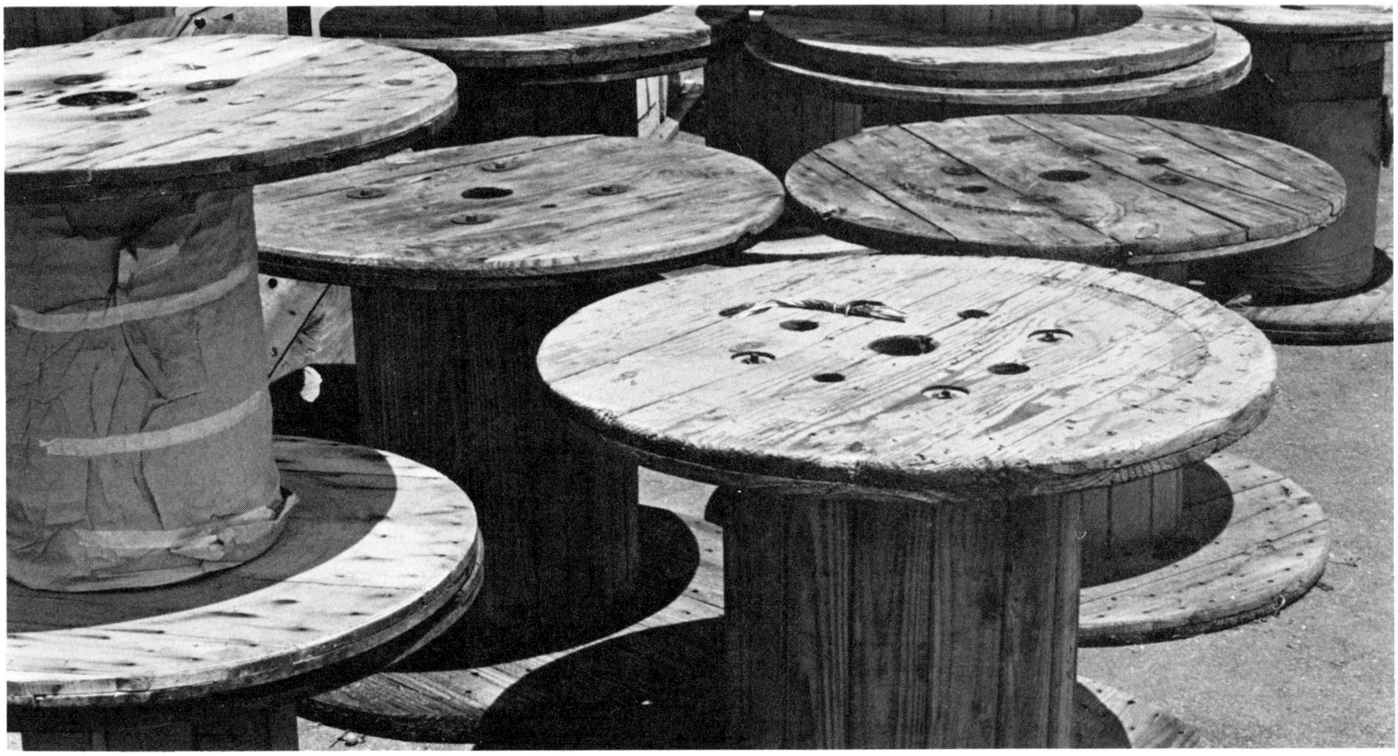

Spools can be painted, stained, decoupaged, covered with fabric or paper, and crafted in a hundred more ways. At one craft fair I attended two people had cut and reconstructed them into delightful children's rockers painted with whimsical designs.

This one utilizes a nautical theme accented by heavy rope. The spool was first sanded, stained, and varnished. The hole in the center was enlarged with a saber saw and a ship's porthole was dropped into place. For added decoration two circular grooves into which the rope is set were routed out. If you don't have a router, you can glue the rope around the edge of the rim. For another spectacular effect, a light can be set down in the center hole to shine up through the porthole. The inside of the spool is hollow, but there is a solid bottom on which to place the light fixture.

Porthole used in center of spool table.

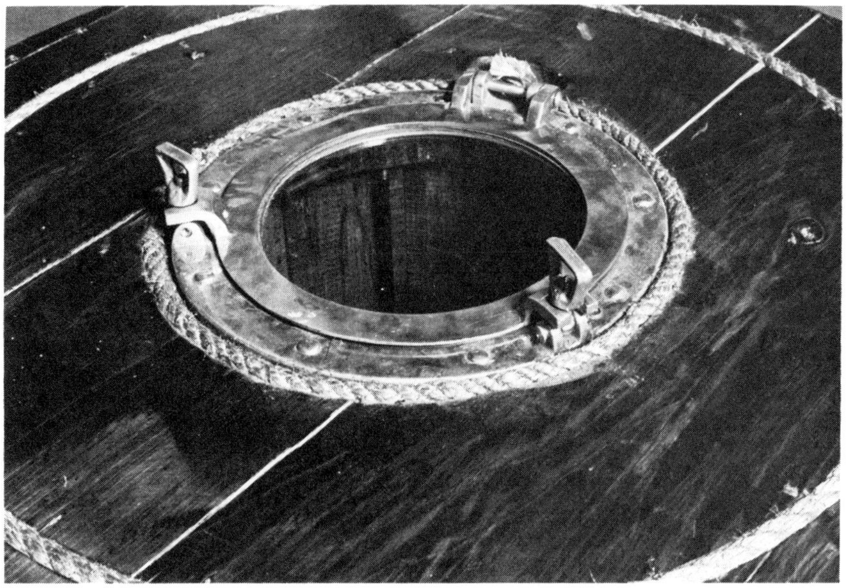

Ship's wheel mounted on ship's lantern is a base for glass-top table.

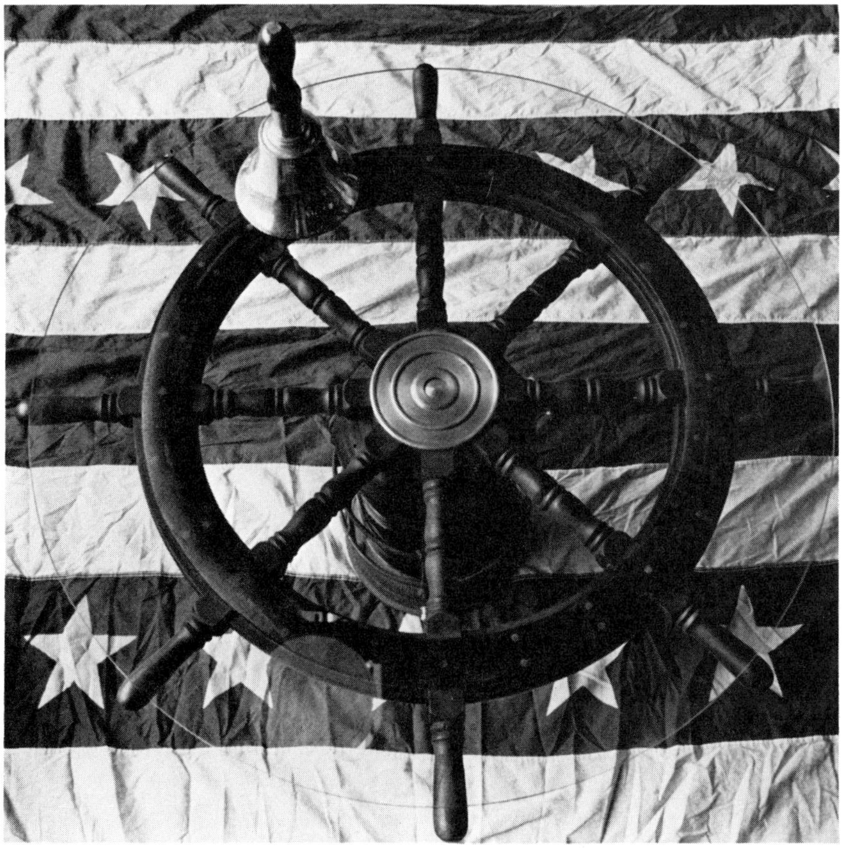

DOWN THE HATCH

A hatch is the opening in the deck of a ship, leading to the hold, and the hatchcover is the closing or the small door to the ship's compartment. These small, wooden-paneled doors have become sought-after nautical items along with ships' wheels, buoys, signs, flags, rope, and many more. Hatchcovers have been turned into coffee tables that are quite unusual. They can be attached to any kind of legs; even a barrel can be used as a base. Some have been assembled on top of ornate wrought-iron legs.

The hatchcover must be sanded carefully on both sides. For this you will need a finishing sander. Then give the cover a coat of oil stain in a dark, rich color like walnut. Let this dry for fifteen minutes before wiping away the excess. Let the stain dry thoroughly overnight. Next brush a coat of satin-finish polyurethane varnish over the top, sides, and underneath. Let this dry overnight. Two or three more coats will give it a satiny patina. Rub overall with fine steel wool and then coat with a clear furniture paste wax.

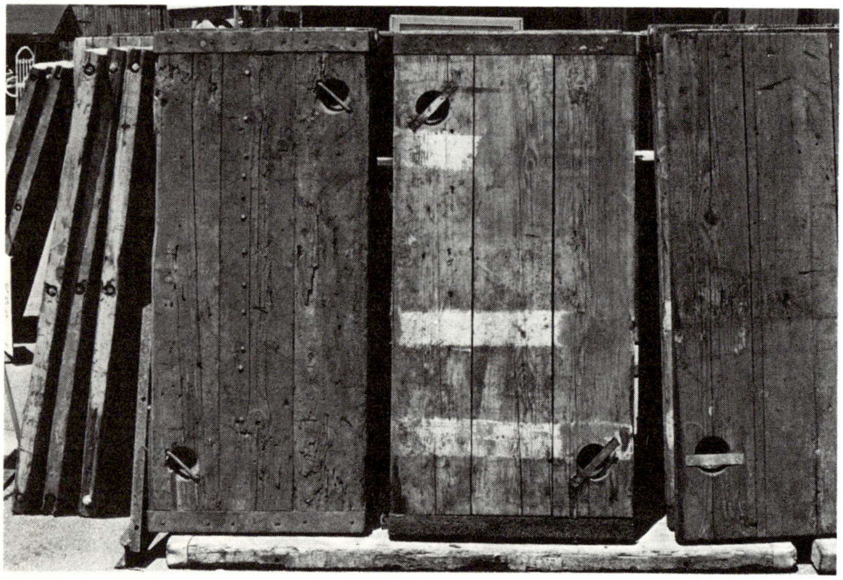

Hatchcovers in the raw.

A GRATE IDEA

A substitute for the hatchcover might be an air grate from a ship. It is harder to find than a cover, but if you come across one, it can be treated the same way.

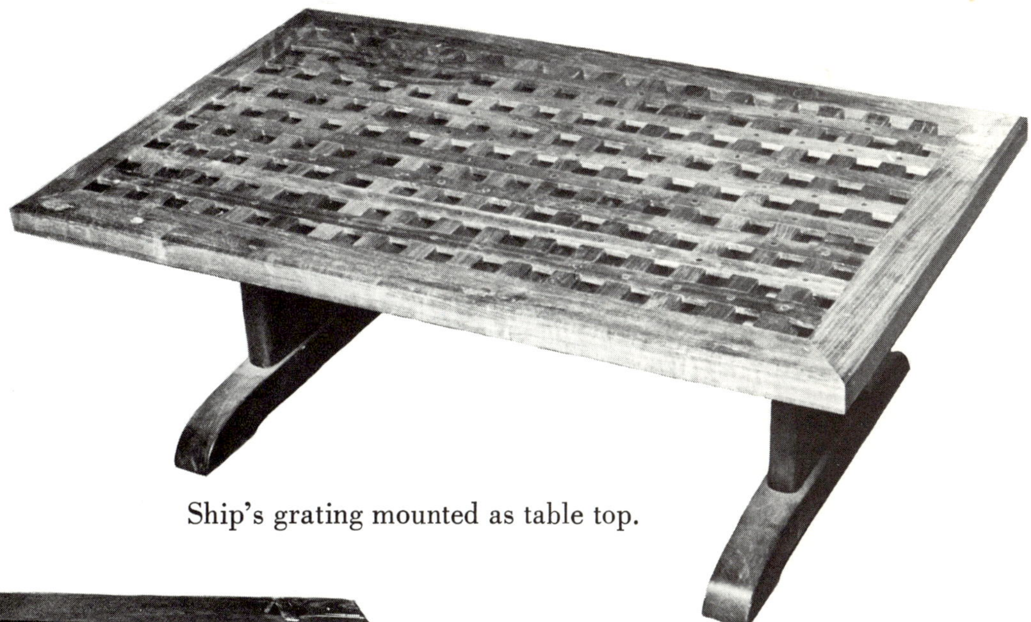

Ship's grating mounted as table top.

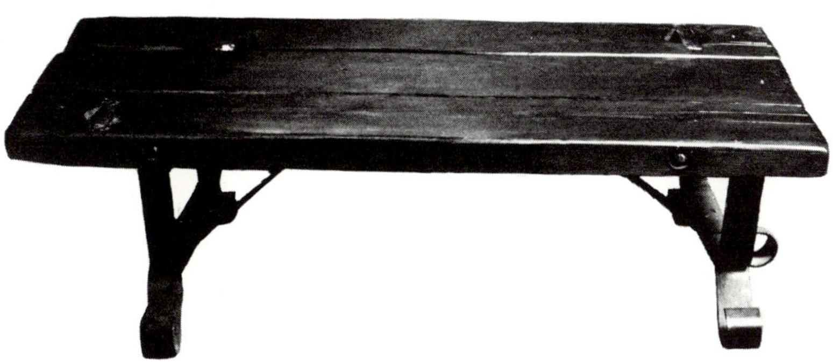

Hatchcover table.

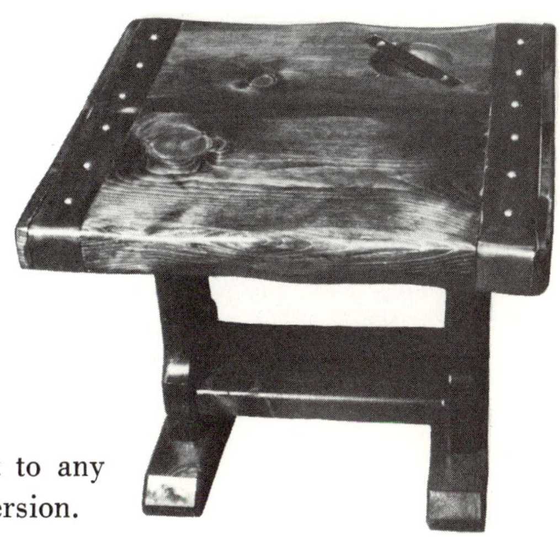

Hatchcover can be cut to any size for table top conversion.

ALL BOXED IN

Nothing could be more direct, basic, plain, conventional, or useful than a simple pine box. I paid two dollars for one and found several ways to utilize it other than as a storage bin for odds and ends in the garage.

The first thing I did was give it an overall sanding with an electric sander. This could easily have been done by hand, but the finishing sander made the job go faster. Next, the wood was brushed with an oil stain in dark walnut, inside and out. The interior can also be lined with a vinyl wall-covering. Then a coating of polyurethane is applied.

A box such as this is terrific for holding large potted plants. Line the bottom with a moisture-proof material such as rubber boat-decking, which can be bought by the yard in marine supply and camping stores, to keep it from rotting when the plants are watered. It comes in black-and-white stripes or earth tones. Heavy vinyl wallpaper could also be used, or you might want to try lining the inside with metal sheeting.

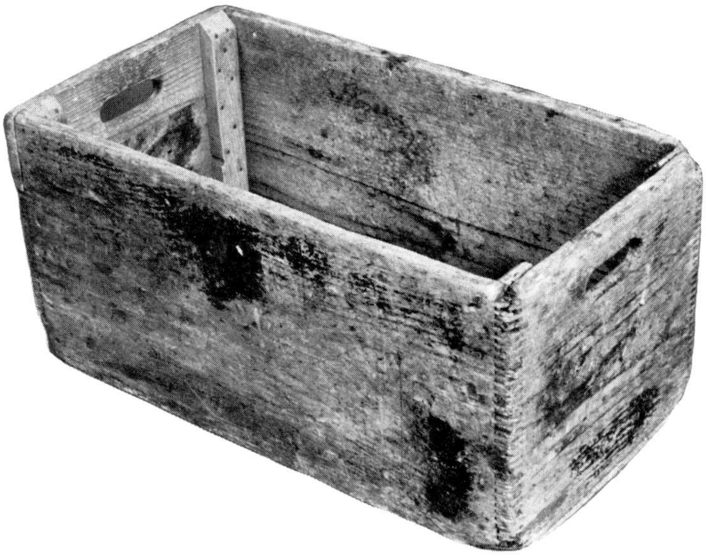

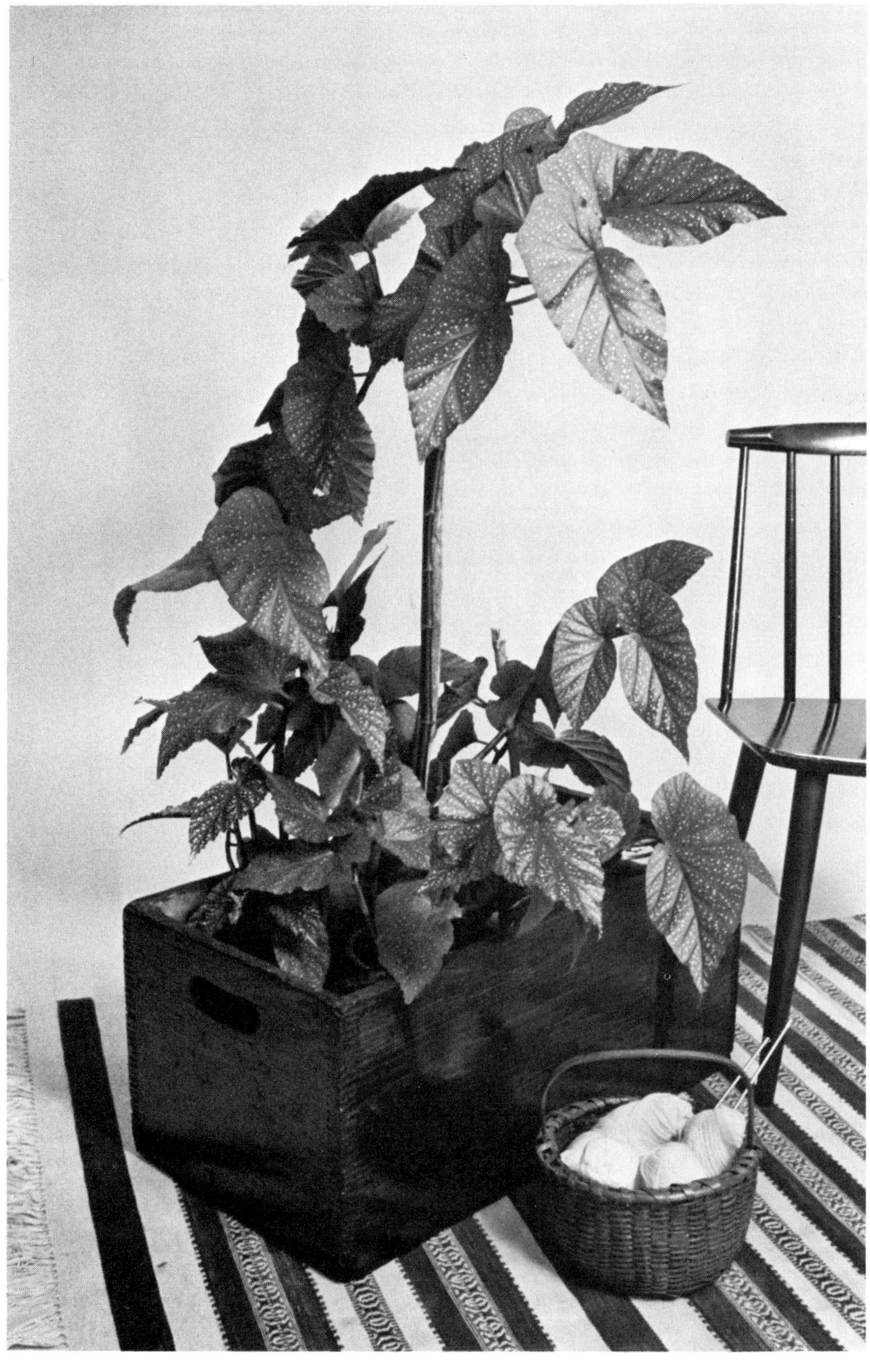

A TABLE FOR ONE

The same pine box is used here as a table. Too low to be used for eating unless everyone sits on the floor, it is perfect as a coffee table or next to a chair. Standing in a hallway under a mirror or framed picture, it might hold a pitcher or vase of long-stemmed flowers. The dark, rich background of the table is an interesting setting for a piece of clay pottery, both being of earth tones. For an occasional table you will find that the finish on the box will be smoother and have more luster if you use several coats of polyurethane. Each coat should be thoroughly dry, then sanded before reapplying. After the last coat rub it down with a fine #0000 steel wool. Wipe away the particles and sand with slightly wet finishing paper. 3M WetorDry #220 or #400 will give you an especially fine finish if it is first dipped into a cup of soapy water. Go over the surface, wetting the sandpaper as needed. Wipe the box with a clean cloth and then apply a thin coat of clear furniture paste wax. Let this dry for ten minutes and buff with a cloth. The table will glow.

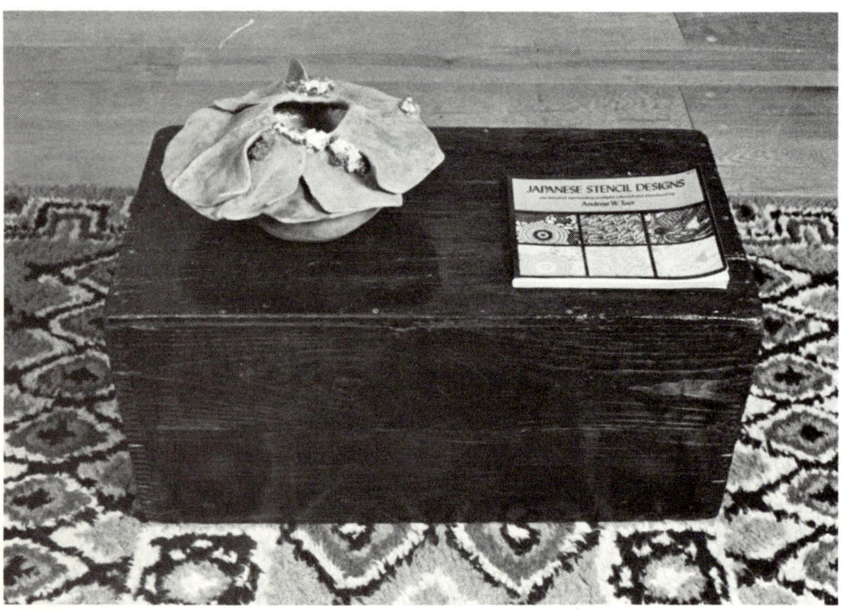

TICKED OFF

Another variation on a good theme is to turn the box into a window seat. The cushion is a regulation Army barracks pillow covered in mattress ticking. Determine the depth that's right for the cushion. Nail 1 x 2-inch wooden strips to the inside. Cut a ⅜-inch plywood platform to set into the box so that it rests on the strips. Use the area under the platform for storage. If you make rather than buy a cushion to fit the box, the ticking fabric can be purchased by the yard. Almost all fabric stores carry it in navy blue, black, and red with white. Of course, there is so much to choose from in the way of fabric design that you can create your own look. Perhaps you have curtains that you want to match, or couch pillows or upholstery. Try different ideas until one seems right to you.

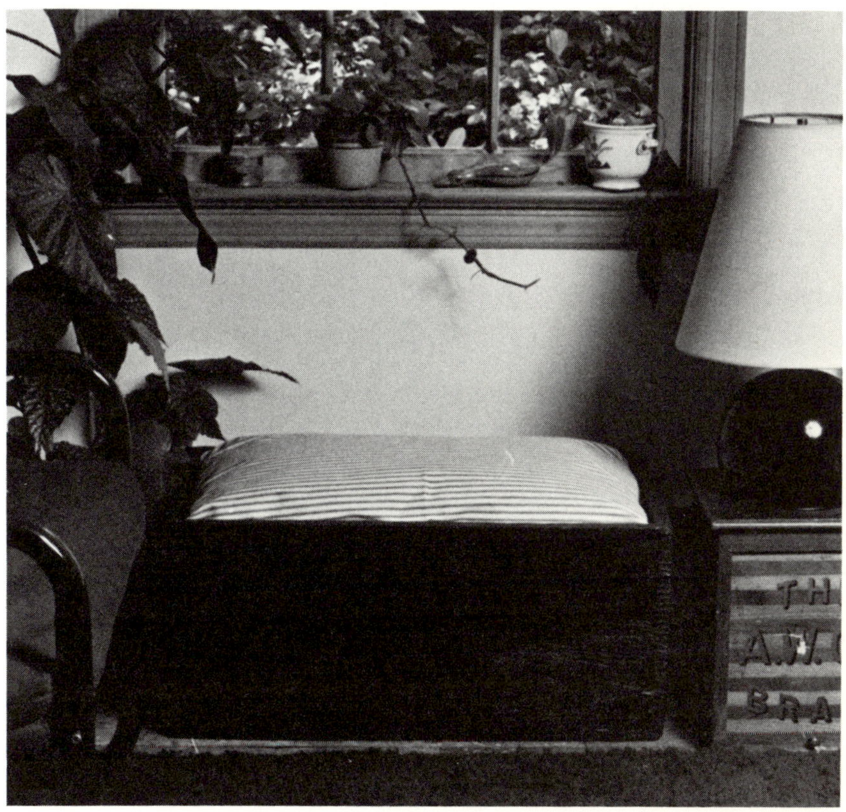

DEALER'S CHOICE

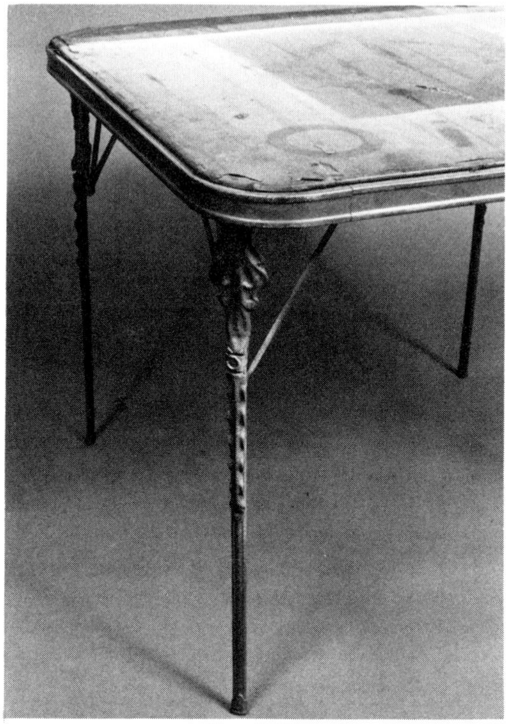

An old bridge table was retrieved from a tag sale for 50 cents and while the owner felt it was unusable because of the poor condition of the surface, it has much to recommend it. The steel frame and legs are in perfect condition, and the spring that operates the opening and closing of the legs works fine. Throwing a piece of fabric over a worn-out card table is one way to deal with the surface if you can't think of anything else, but there are many alternatives. This good-looking, newer version of a game table might give you some ideas.

The objective here is to make a false or removable top to go over the old. This table is thirty inches square. Cut a piece of ½-inch plywood a quarter of an inch larger than the table top measurement on all sides. This will guarantee a fit. Glue a piece of spongy weather stripping around the frame of the table. When the new top is placed over the table it will then fit snugly.

Look for molding at your lumberyard. The molding should have two prerequisites. First, it must be at least 3 inches wide in order to cover the depth of the sides as well as the plywood top. And second, it must have one square edge in order to nail it flush with the plywood. Cut the molding with mitered corners to fit the plywood. Apply white glue wherever the surfaces touch and nail the molding to the plywood with 2-inch brads. If there are any cracks or areas that need touching up, you can fill them in with wood filler. Put this aside to dry.

Next, sand any rust off the legs or clean up the exposed areas and spray paint with Krylon enamel. You can decorate the top any number of ways and then paint the molding with a complementary color.

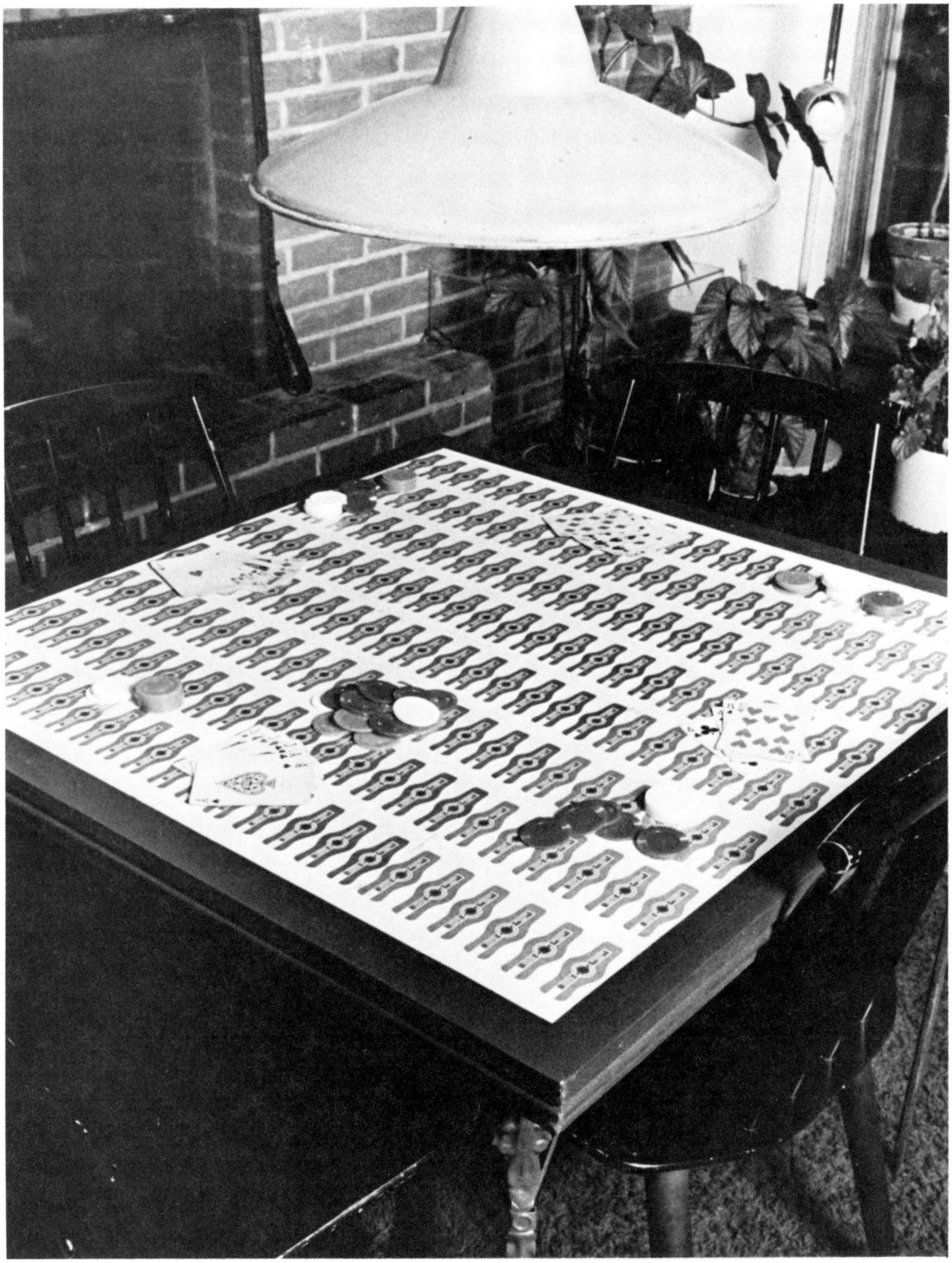

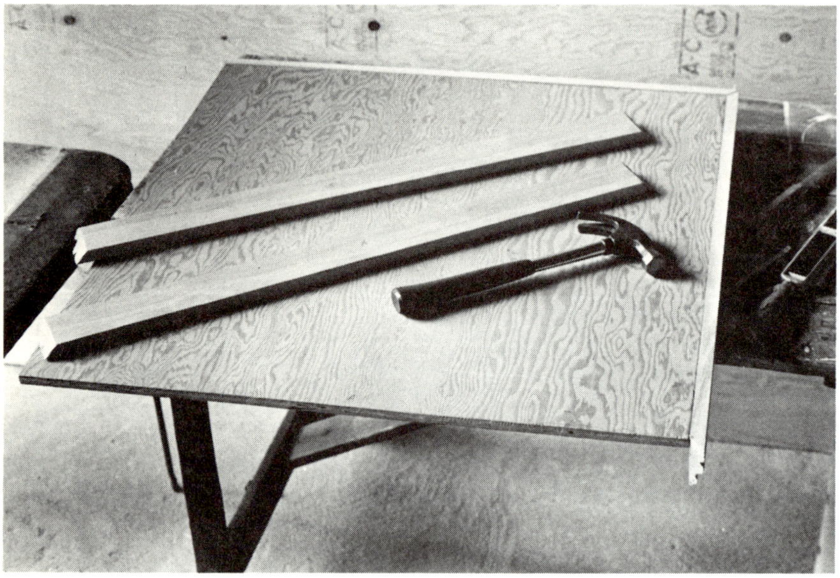

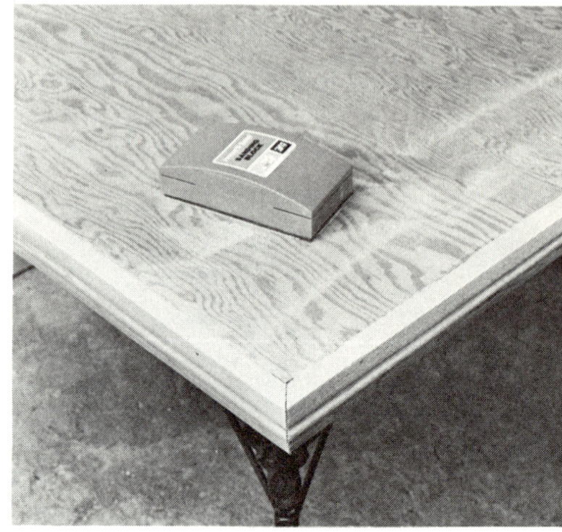

Plywood and molding used to create new table top.

The table top here is decorated with press sheets for cigar bands, obtained from the printer who prints the bands for Top Stone cigars. They are decorative because of the many colors and the gold ink that is used. Press sheets will give you many creative possibilities. There are printing establishments in every city in the country. Visit a good-sized one, as the small printers usually don't do large four-color jobs. To get the presses ready for a four-color printing job, printers run one stack of paper through over and over to check each color. The abstract designs that are created are fabulous. Many people use this art for posters or to cover entire rooms. Ask for "make-ready sheets"; the printer will know what you are talking about. Look through what he has. If he doesn't have any that interest you at the time of your visit, ask that he save others when a job is run.

Get a few press sheets. They will not be the exact size you need. In this case the cigar-band sheets were cut up and

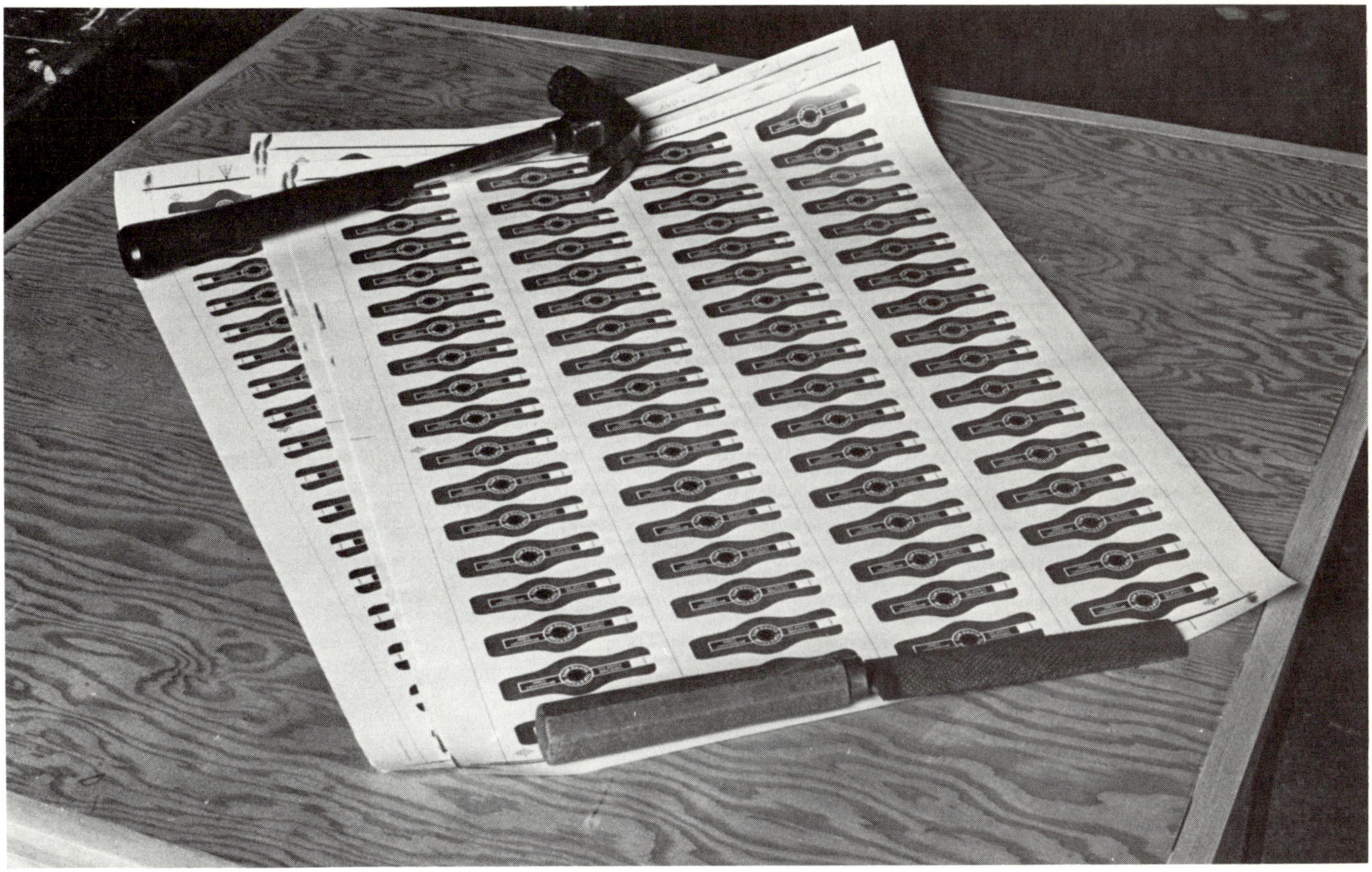

Press sheets are pieced together to create larger size.

patched together to make one big square. They were first taped on the back before being mounted as one piece onto the table top. The larger composite sheet is then dry-mounted with rubber cement. A slip sheet of tracing paper is necessary to insure perfection. Coat the plywood surface with rubber cement, which is available in art-supply stores. Coat the back of the press sheet as well. Let these dry. Place a piece of clean tracing paper under the press sheet, between it and the table top. Line the edges of the press sheet up so that it is parallel to the edge of the table. Press it down along one edge so that it is smooth and free of air bubbles. Keep sliding the slip sheet down as you apply a little more of the press sheet to the table. If you don't use the slip sheet to separate the two, you cannot be sure that you will do an accurate job. Once the cement on the press sheet touches the cement on the table top surface, it is difficult to remove the press sheet for replacement if there is an error. Since there is no rubber cement on the slip sheet, it will not stick to either surface. For perfect contact run a rubber brayer, or similar type of roller, over the paper to smooth it down everywhere.

Once all is mounted in place, coat the surface with a high-gloss polyurethane varnish. This should be done with a 2-inch flat varnish brush. Do not overload the brush with varnish. Start at the center of the table and draw your brush to the outer edges, always just in one direction. In this way there will be a thinning as you get to the outside, thus eliminating drip marks that may run down the sides while the varnish is drying. Coat the molding and legs as well for an overall shiny finish. Let this dry overnight and reapply. When thoroughly dry rub the top with a very fine steel wool and polish with clear furniture paste wax.

Other ideas for a new top are a painted surface that can be used as a game table, with a backgammon board, checker board, or so on, done with decorator tapes and paint, mounting an oversized map of your city or state (check source list for obtaining maps), a printed graphic photostated to the exact size of the table and mounted as described, or a collage of wine labels, postcards, photographs—whatever is appealing to you.

NO-NONSENSE DESIGNS

SERVICE FOR ONE

Restaurant supplies are becoming recognized as good buys. The chinaware, glasses, and cooking utensils aren't fancy, but they are sturdy and direct and there is something appealing about them. Perhaps it is their familiarity that has suddenly spurred everyone into furnishing their kitchens with cafeteria staples. For everyday use they are practically nonbreakable so you certainly get your money's worth, although to really get a bargain you have to buy in quantity.

The tray is made of red plastic and is the kind found in fast-food chains, cafeterias, and other institutional places where food is served. To give it a bit of character a placemat from a coffee shop, your favorite diner, or a breakfast menu can be glued to the tray top, then varnished for permanency. (You might try this also on an old table. Glue a placemat at each setting and coat with several layers of high-gloss polyurethane varnish for a smooth, hard finish.) The sugar and creamer, napkin holder, relish containers, and salt and pepper shakers are other supplies that can lend a jaunty air to your morning setting.

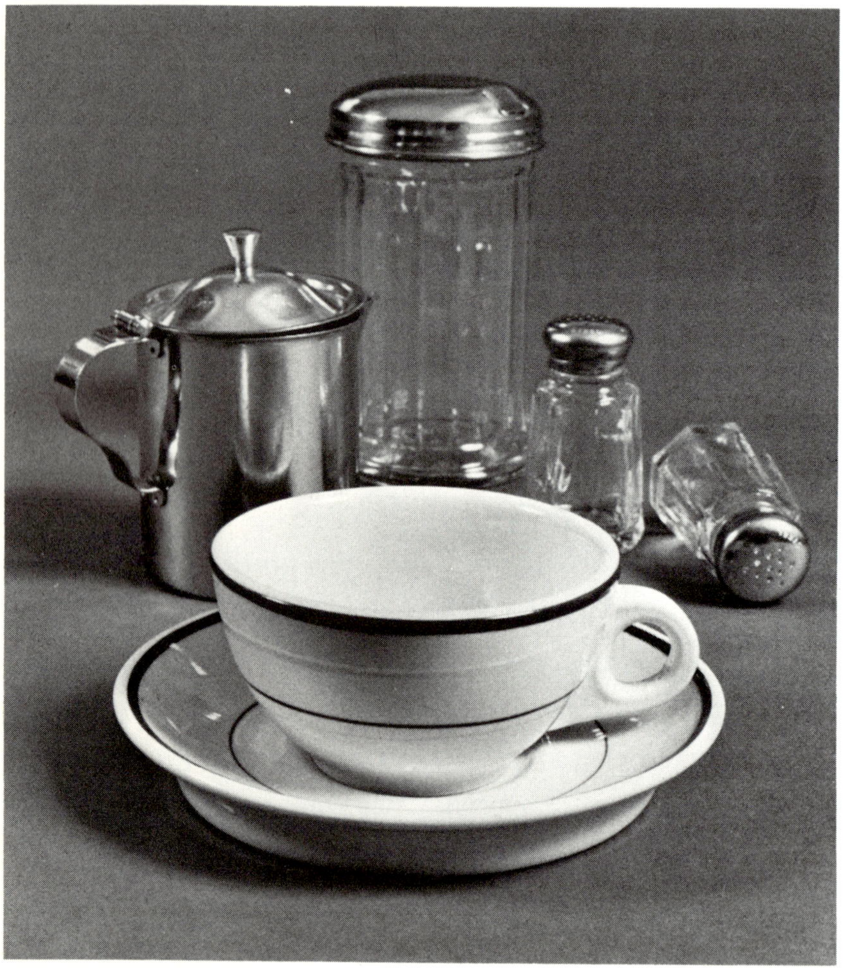

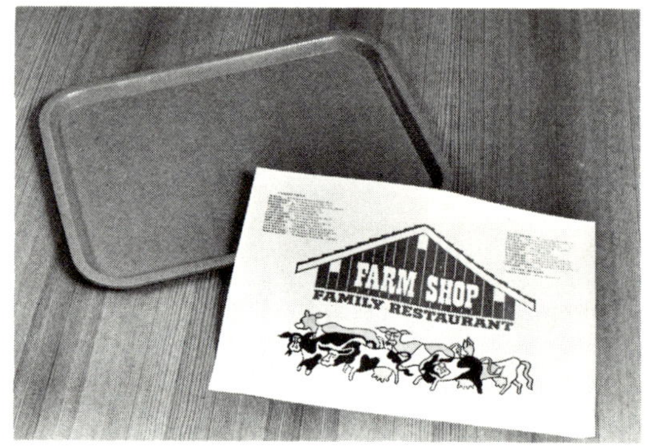

Fast-food tray, placemat, and restaurant fare; a good combination for home service.

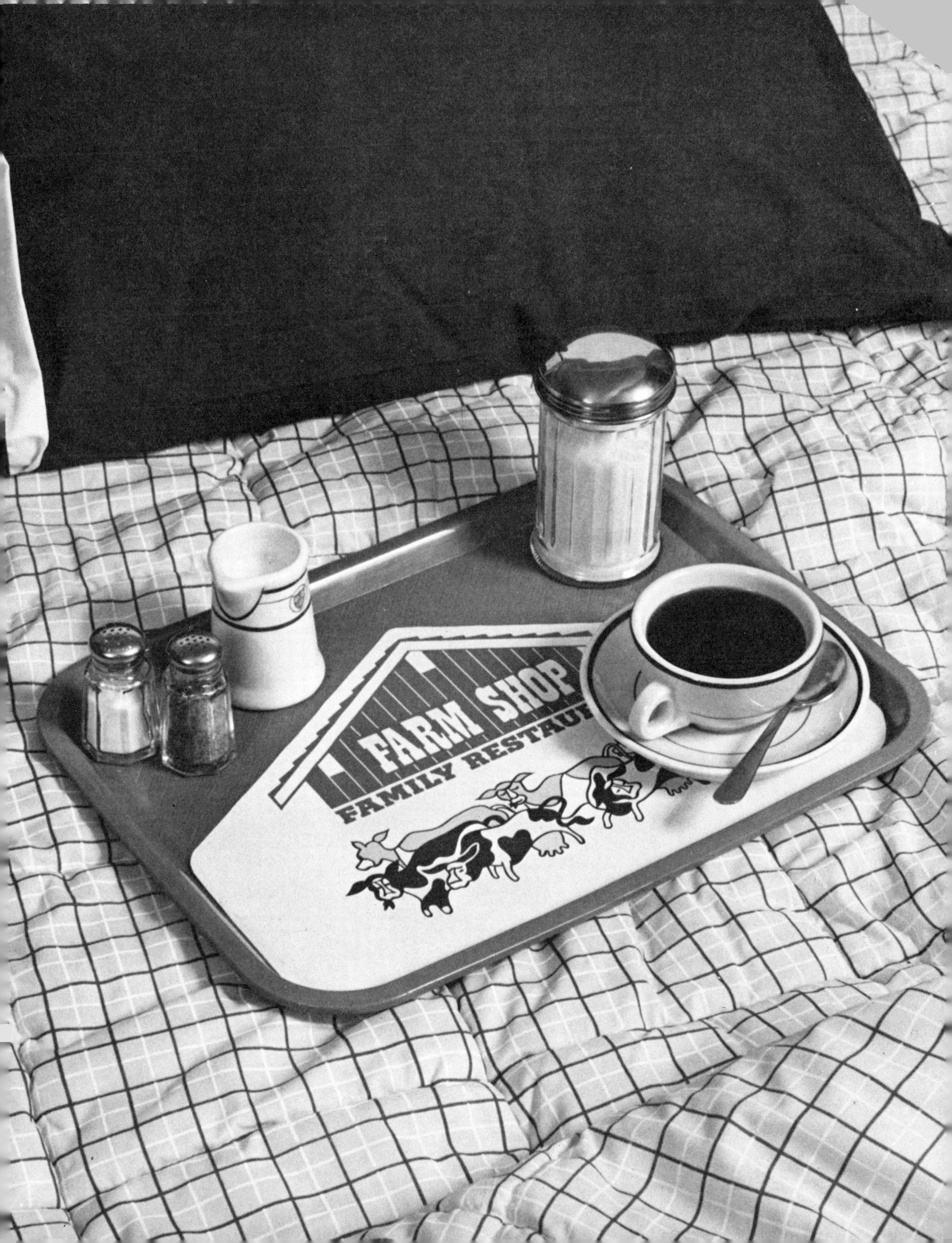
FARM SHOP
FAMILY

NAVAL STRATEGY

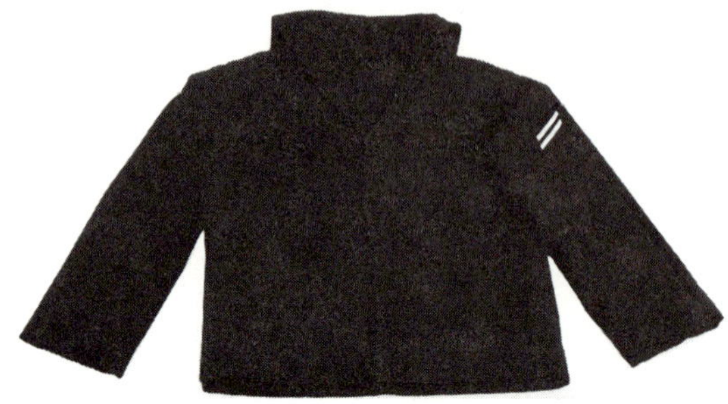

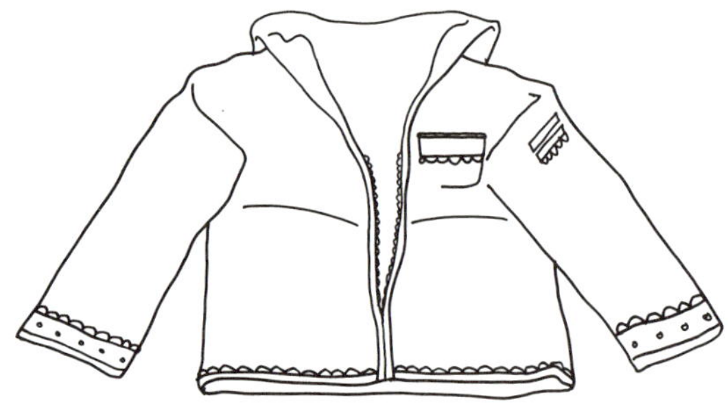

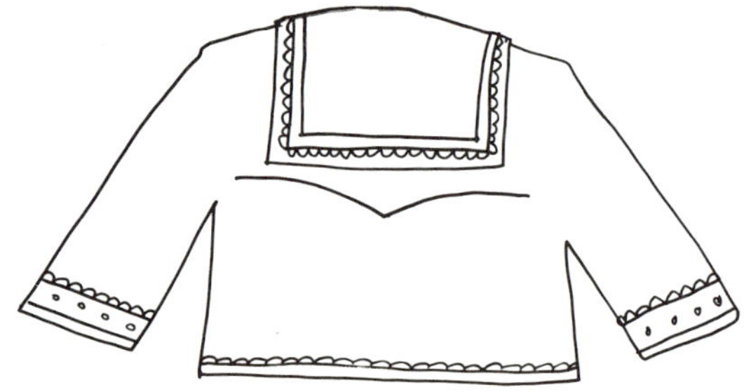

The Navy middy blouses are made of wool for cold weather and white cotton duck for summertime. The dark navy-blue blouses are lightweight and make excellent jackets for cool weather. They are found everywhere in surplus and Army & Navy stores. Some have insignias on the sleeve. However, they do present one problem. Since they were made for men, the shape does not fit well on a woman's body. The bottom edge is very narrow and makes it difficult to pull the garment over the head and down over the hips. Once on, however, these blouses make almost anyone look trim and sporty.

In order to alleviate the problem, we made our middy into a jacket. Simply cut down the middle of the blouse and machine stitch a jacket zipper to the front. With the addition of decorative blue-and-white striped ribbon, this becomes a contemporary-looking jacket to wear over a sweater and jeans. If you want to make it more feminine looking, add some embroidery down the front, on the sleeves, or around the large back collar.

For jogging, the lighter weight summer Navy blouses are inexpensive, cool, and loose fitting. Try on several before buying one. The sizes don't tell you much.

BOWL THEM OVER

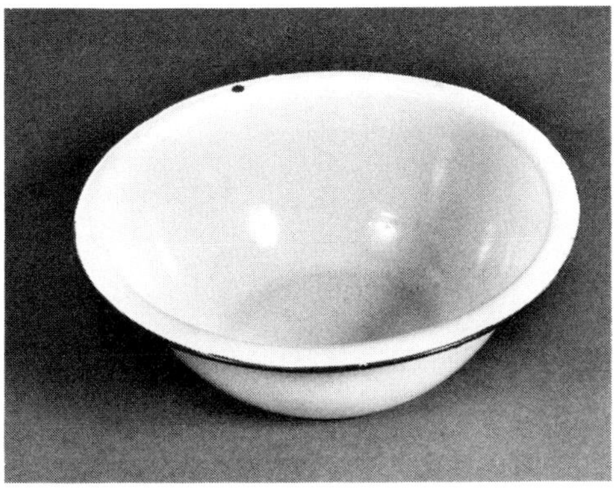

Use acrylic paint for trim.

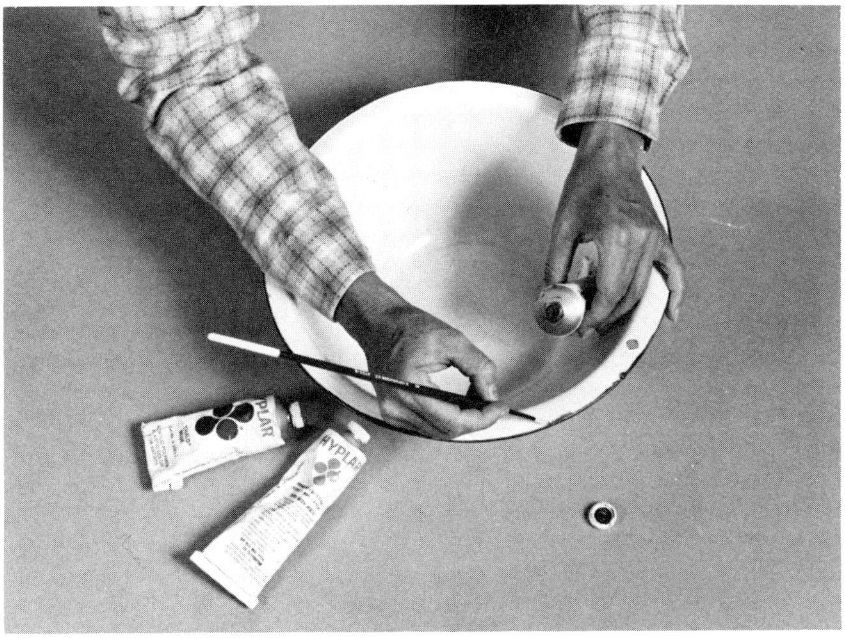

Found at a flea market, an enamel dishpan or washbasin was retrieved and painted to be used as a salad bowl. It is deep, round, and excellent for serving a salad large enough for four. When not in use, the hole in the top is convenient for hanging the pan on a decorative wall hook.

Acrylic paint, which is permanent and waterproof, is used to create the trim. Use a stiff-bristle paint brush or a pointed artist's brush, both available in art-supply stores. I chose a theme of red and royal blue and painted a trim of each color, one inside the other, around the rim of the pan. You will need a steady hand to do this, but it needn't be perfectly neat. A freehand look is rather attractive and casual, which is appropriate for this item. The bottom of the outside and underneath the rim can also be decorated so that, when hung on the wall, the basin will look pretty.

For a table setting, look for a piece of fabric that enhances the casualness of the pan, which has a French country feeling. A checkered or pinstriped design would be appropriate. However, I especially like to use as a table covering linen dishtowels sewn together. Some fabric shops, such as Fabrications in New York and Boston, carry French dishtowel fabric that can be purchased by the yard. Each section has a red or blue stripe running through it that reads "Glass" or "China." I found linen dishtowels in the five-and-ten. They come in a package of three for under a dollar and are large enough to use as lap napkins for a buffet. They might also serve as placemats or be sewn together for a card-table-sized cloth. White with a red stripe around the edges, they are here folded into a triangle and used as oversized napkins. They are good-looking and serviceable.

A glass quart-sized milk bottle found in a junk shop has red lettering on it and is perfect for holding flowers, or as a wine decanter for a casual dinner. The smaller, pint-sized milk bottles are used here as individual wine decanters and hold enough for two glasses of wine. Red and purple plastic plates are used to repeat the color scheme, but you might like to use the stainless-steel camping plates. They are good-looking, sturdy, and cost under a dollar apiece. Further, the aluminum mugs, washbasins, salt and pepper shakers, and billy pots found in camping stores, when used together, are ruggedly good-looking, inexpensive, and quite unique for home use. Another suggestion for serving pieces is the clay plates used under plant pots.

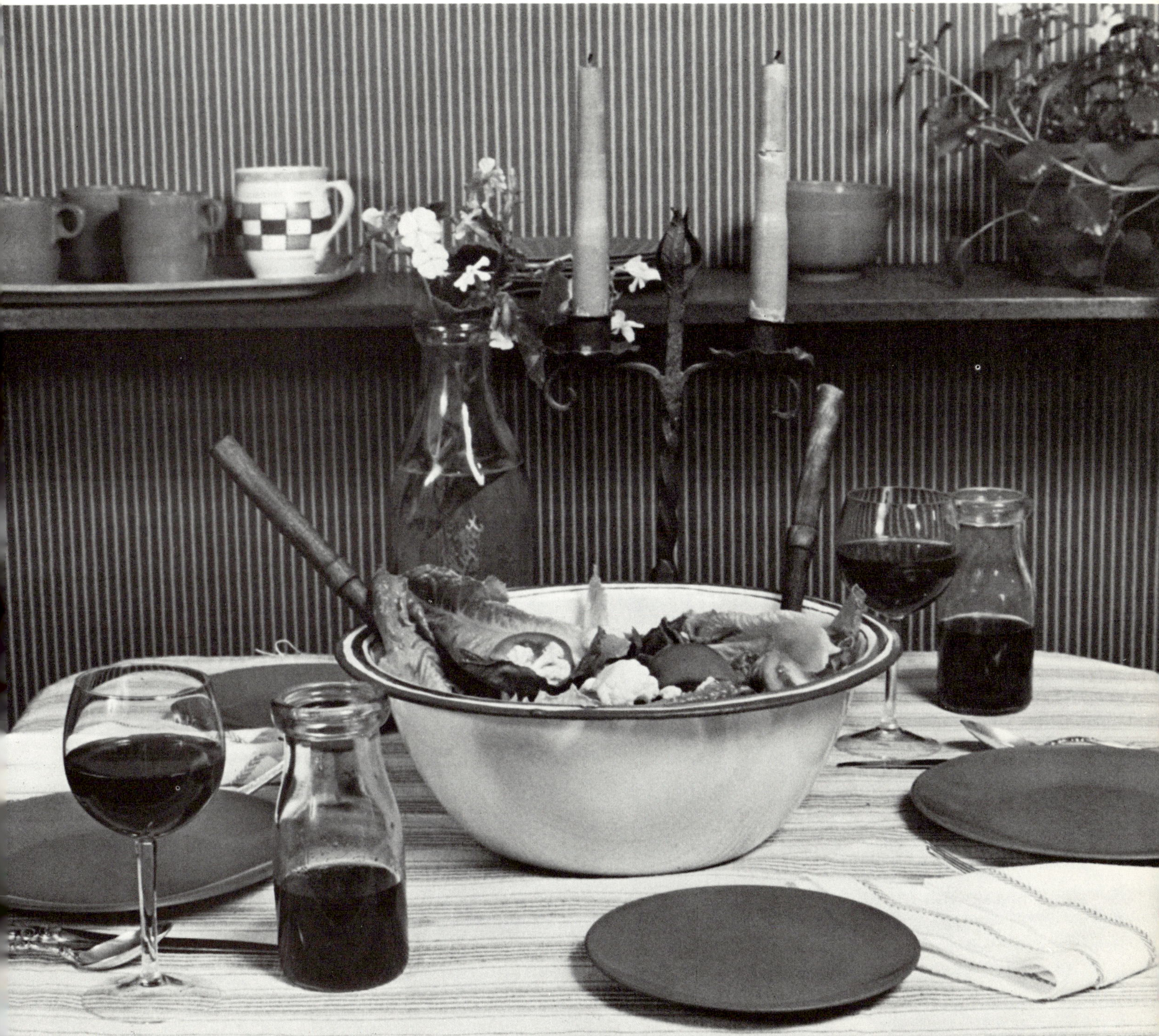

BLANKET POLICY

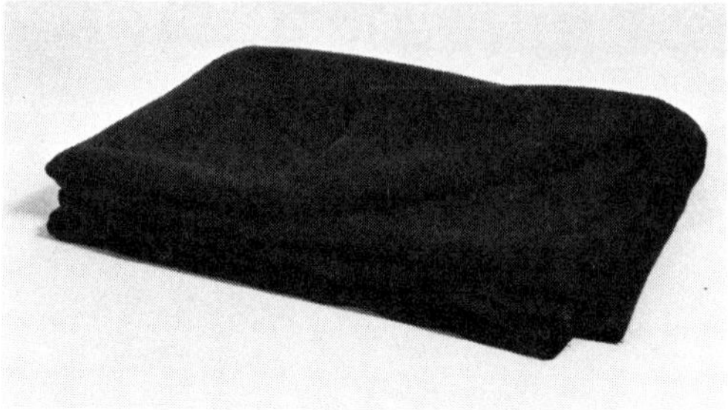

Army blankets are made of wool and have to be one of the greatest buys at seven to nine dollars apiece. They are lightweight but warm and last forever, and they come in navy, gray, and maroon. The edges are whipstitched and the overall size is 60″ × 80″. They will fit on a single bed and when doubled can be used as a heavy crib or carriage blanket for a baby. For very little extra money and a bit of imagination these basically sturdy blankets can be made to look like a boutique specialty item.

Fabric and notions shops carry decorative trims that range from exquisitely elaborate antique lace to ribbons trimmed with sequins and beads. There are reams of flowered, striped, embroidered, and appliquéd ribbons in every conceivable width. Lace, eyelet, and satin binding can also be found. The variety of trims to choose from is as varied as most people's tastes. You will need two yards of each trim in order to decorate the top edge with a little leftover. You might consider adding a matching trim to the hem of a pillow case.

Pin the trimming to the blanket and machine stitch them together. This blanket is navy and decorated with pink flannel that has an embroidered repeating rosebud and green leaf design. The top edge is overlayered with white eyelet that has been interwoven with ½-inch pink satin ribbon. White eyelet lace trim is added to the bottom edge of the flannel. In this way it appears as though a delicately edged sheet has been folded down over the blanket. For a personalized baby gift, the child's initials could be embroidered in the center of the trim or in the middle of the blanket and surrounded with a decorative design.

Since these blankets are lightweight, they fold up easily and can be stored in very little space. This makes them good

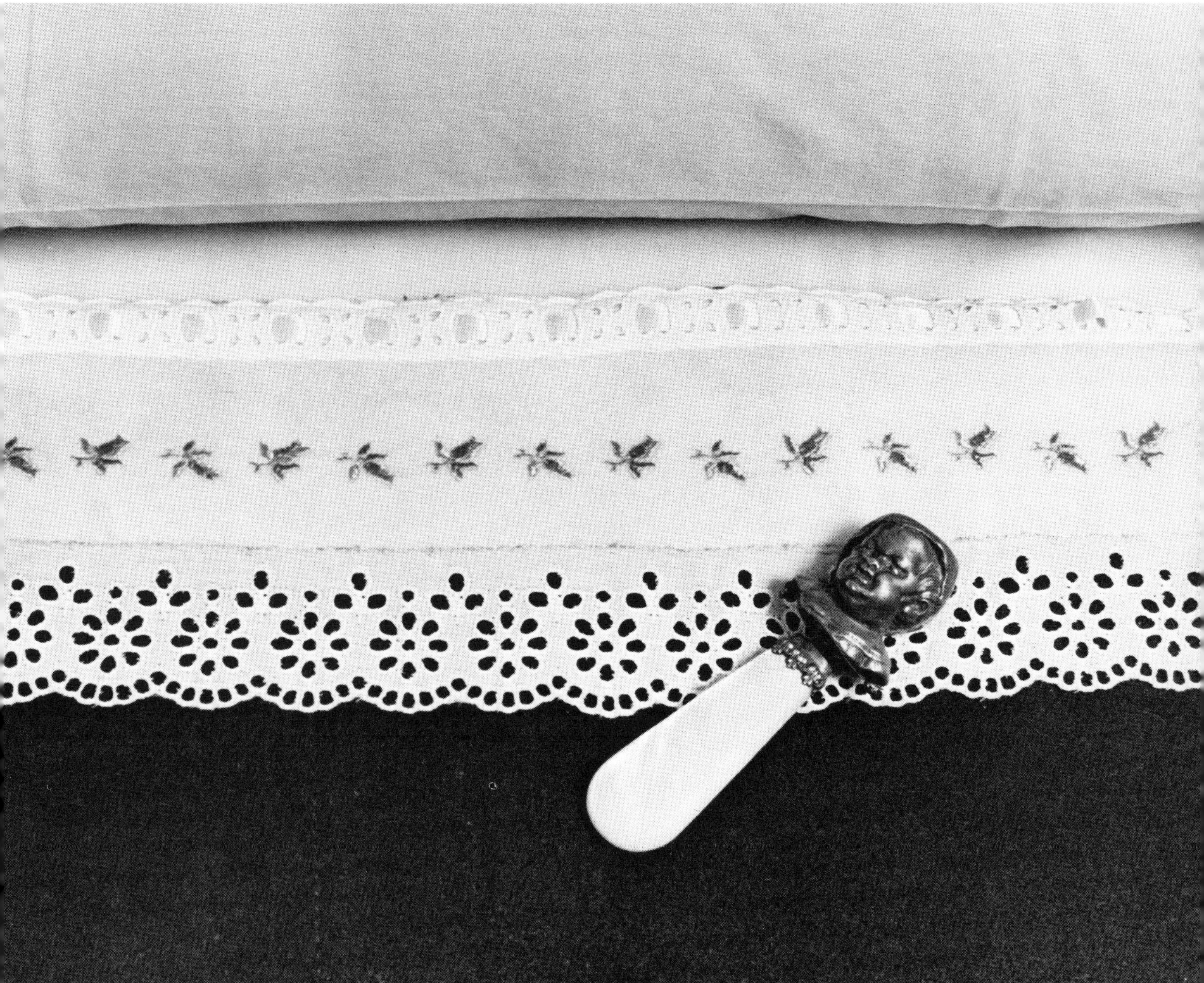

extra blankets for company, and they can be decorated in an appropriate way. For a larger bed size, sew two blankets together with a decorative trim over the seam.

ACCESSORIES AFTER THE FACT

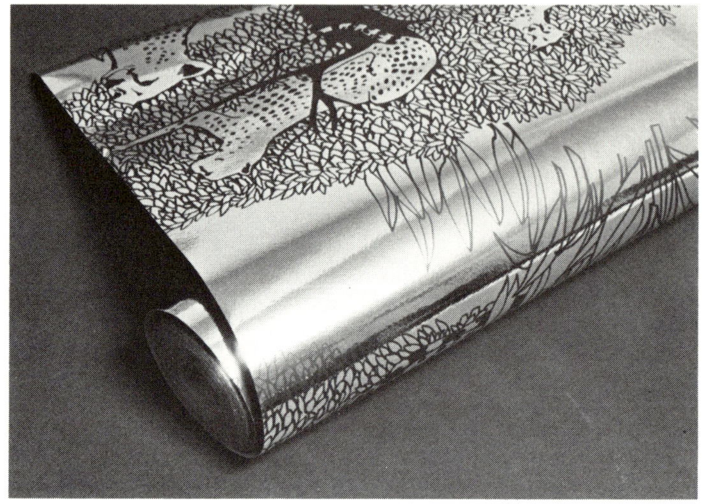

An unfinished wooden cube is the perfect size and shape for an occasional table. This one was given a shiny, contemporary streamlined look by covering the raw wood with brushed aluminum stove tiles. Lightweight and inexpensive, they come in a package and are self-adhesive for easy mounting. Here only the top is covered with the $4\frac{1}{4}$-inch tiles. The four exposed sides are covered with vinyl wallpaper. The silvery background reflects the floor covering and the brown animals in the print are a striking contrast. The accessories used on the table look like expensive silver items, but in fact they are all basic camping supplies and their total cost is under five dollars. A Thermos liner, lunch box, camper's plate, and metal matchbox make up the group. Other items to consider might be a billy pot to hold a floral arrangement, aluminum drinking cup for cigarettes or flowers, and aluminum bowls. All the aluminum pieces are reflected in the stove tiles. A mirrored surface could be used in place of the tiles, or aluminum tape can be applied to the cube top. Another suggestion for this project is silver Mylar for an overall space-age effect.

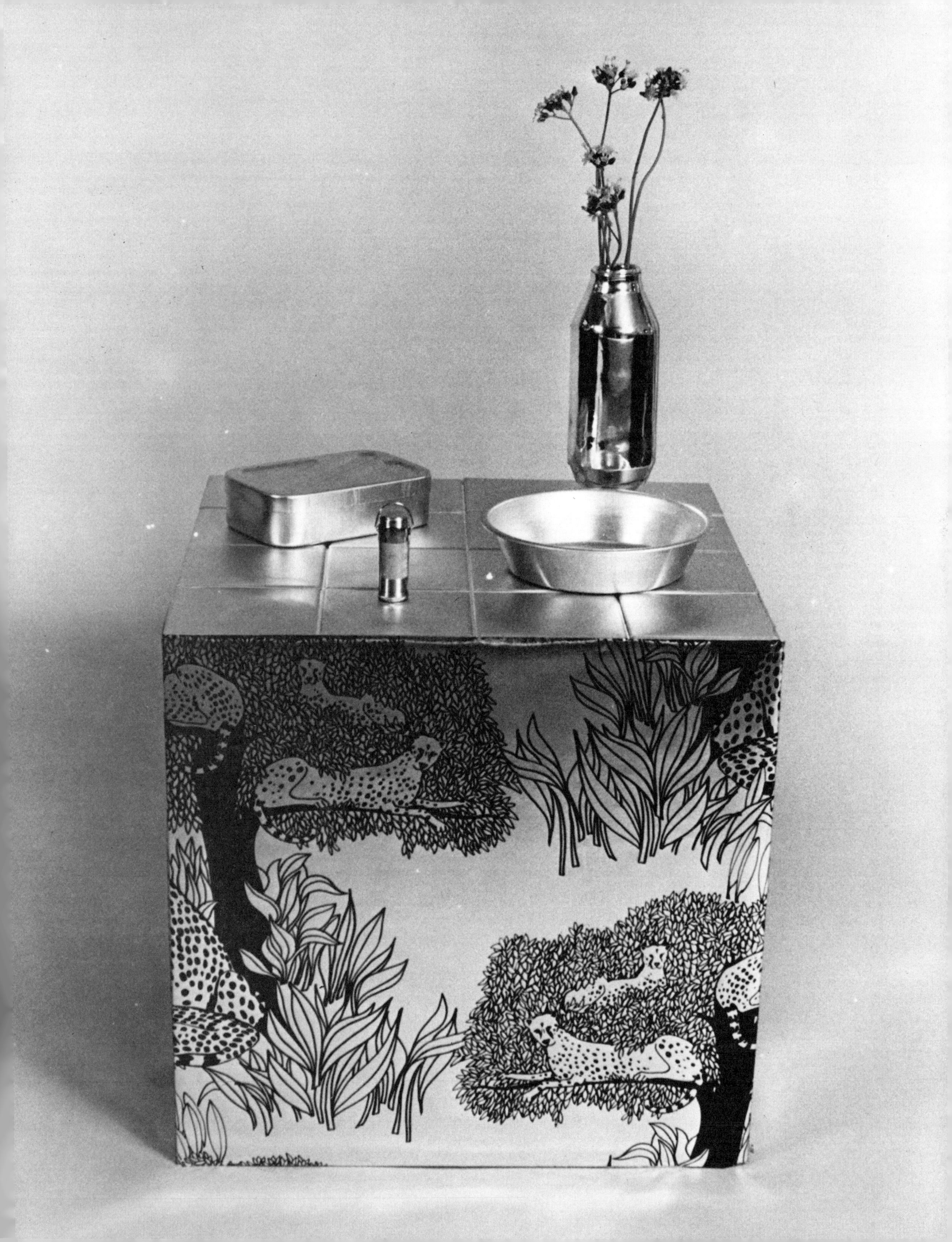

Thermos Liner Vase A Thermos bottle lining is made of shiny aluminum and is often sold separately in hardware or housewares stores. If you have an old Thermos, don't discard it without checking to see if the lining can be recycled as a vase.

Conversation Match Holder For an unusual match holder that's a good basic idea, fill a waterproof metal matchbox with safety matches. Made of seamless nickel-plated brass, the box measures just 2½ inches long and ¾-inch in diameter. This is a perfect little item to complement the others on the table.

Campers' Plate Made of strong, durable aluminum to withstand years of rugged camping use, these plates are rustproof, cost under a dollar, and come in two or three sizes. They are simple and functional as ashtrays or candy dishes.

Occasional Box An aluminum lunch box or soap dish is useful for holding small objects on a table or for desk items such as paper clips, rubber bands, and so on. It is airtight, has decorative indentations on the top, and both halves can be used separately if desired.

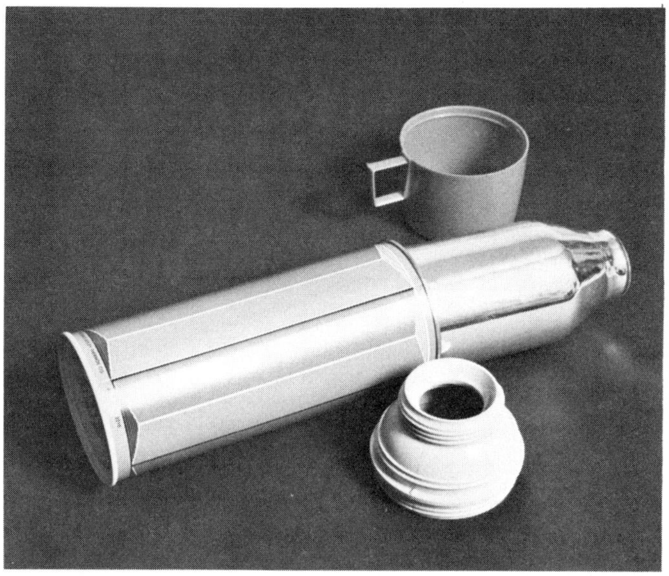

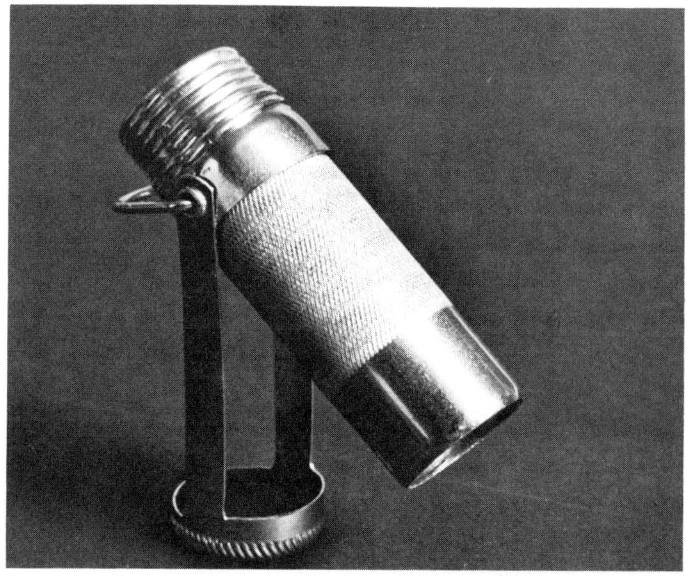

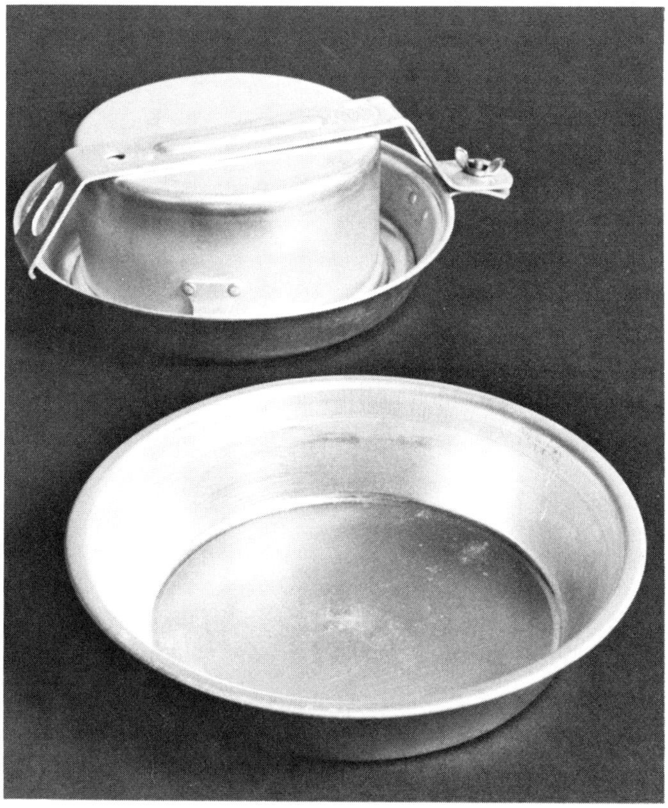

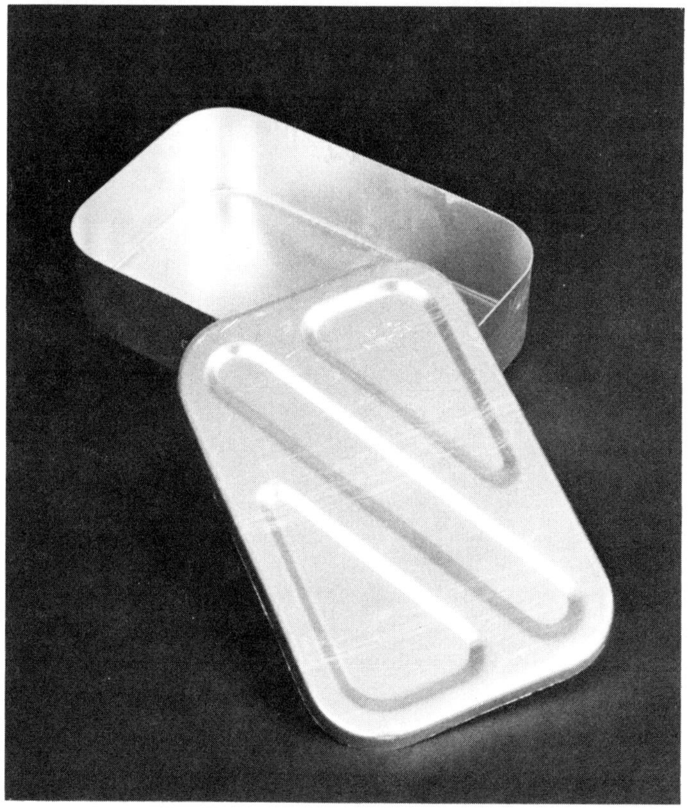

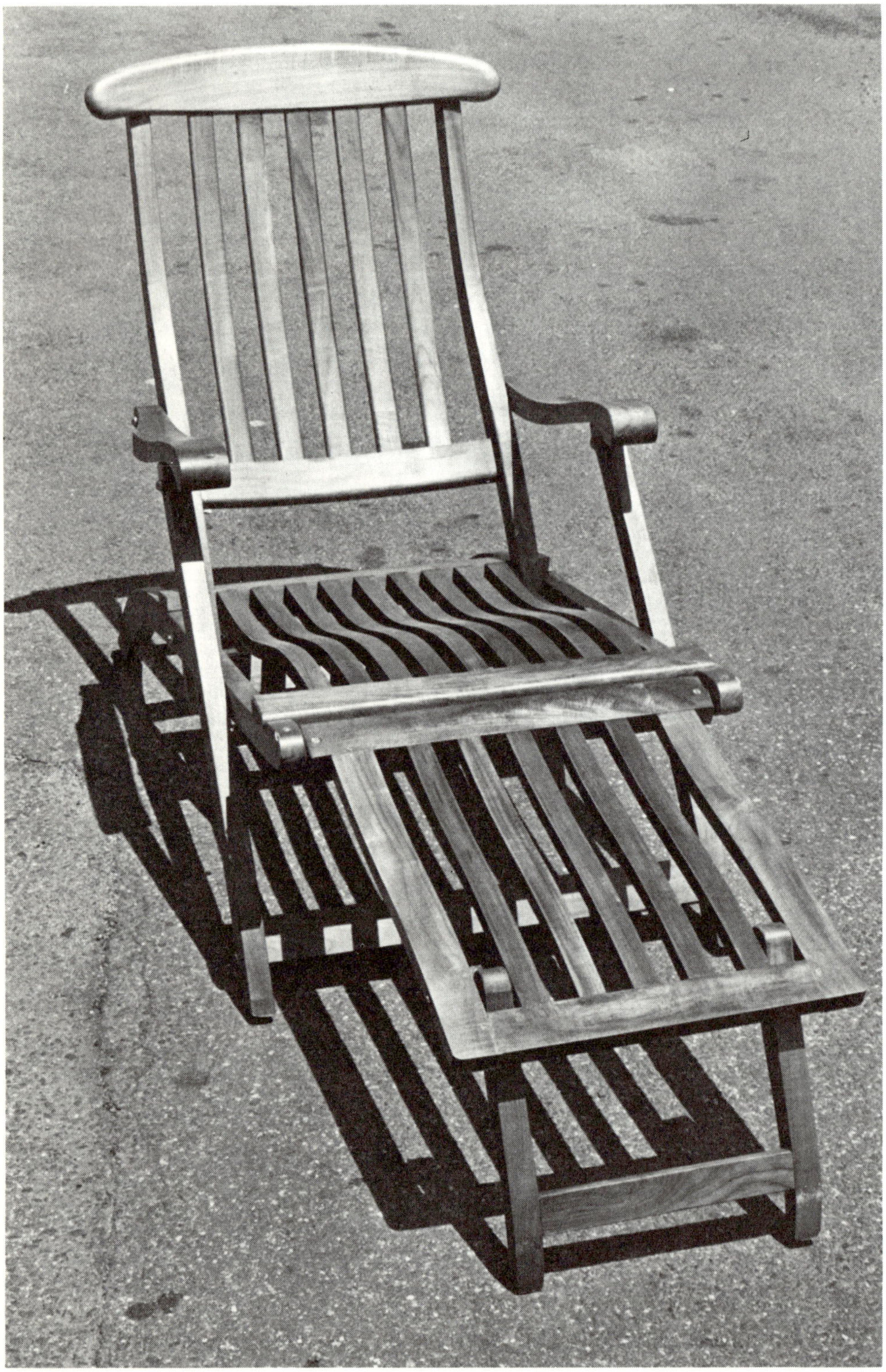

FABULOUS FI

There are some products that we don't think about although we may see them all the time. We simply aren't used to buying them for home use. Some are used for industrial purposes; others are so commonplace that we tend to overlook them. For instance, fiber barrels used in all commercial and public areas for garbage disposal have unlimited potential. Grab bars found in public restrooms and on boats are made of stainless steel and are simple, good-looking, and serviceable. Hooks of every conceivable shape, size, price, and use—you'd be surprised how different a plain wire 15-cent hook from the five-and-ten can look when spray painted. Industrial gooseneck lamps are far less expensive than the ones sold in decorator shops and home furnishings departments. The following are a few of the goodies that I have found and use often. Perhaps they will spark your imagination. The five-and-ten, hardware stores, and industrial catalogs found in the library can be a real source of inspiration.

Would you believe? A solid teak deck chair from a cruise ship.

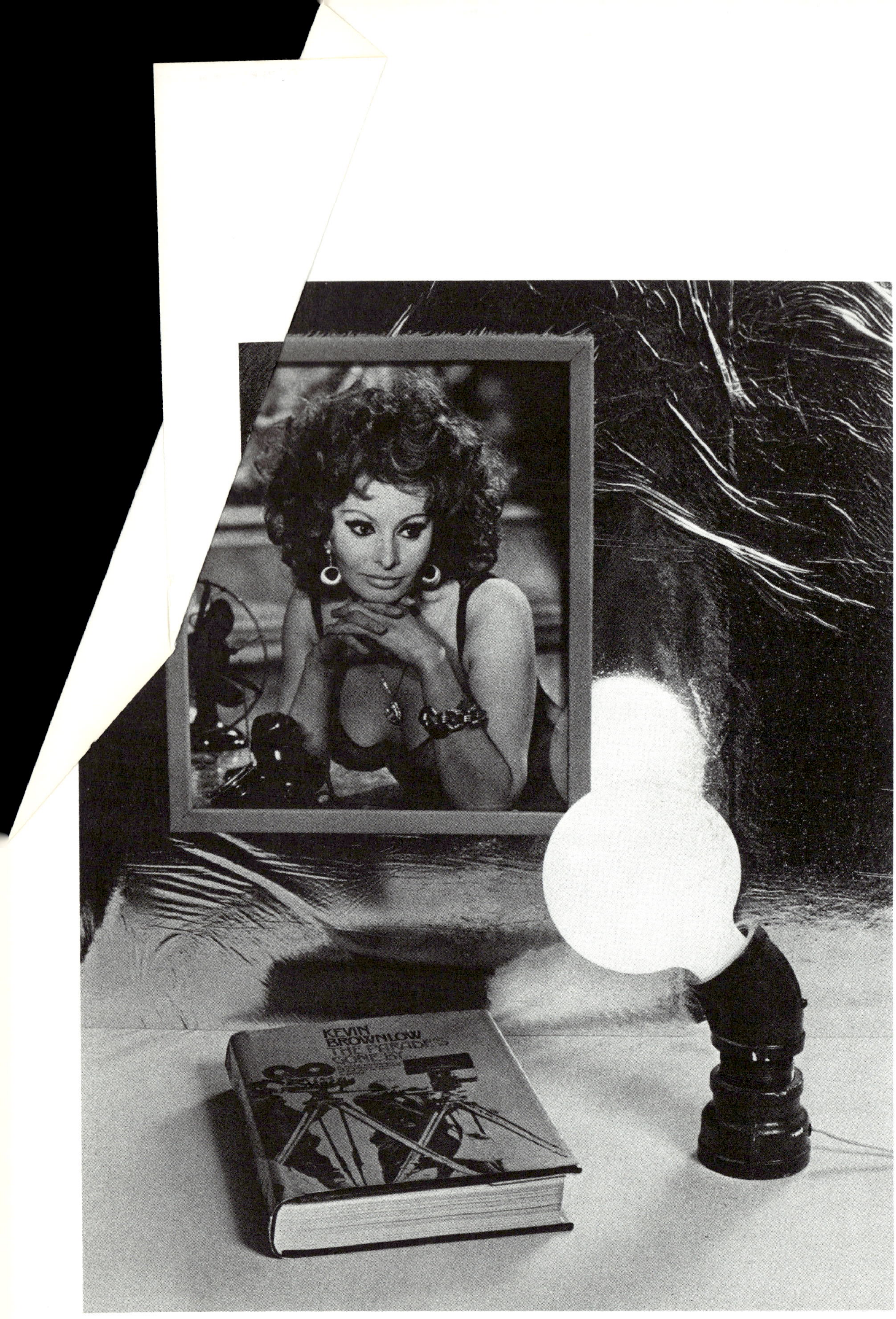
KEVIN
BROWNLOW
THE PARADE'S
GONE BY

PIPE LINE

Plumbing pipe joints are wired for lamp, and back band molding (see page 77 for instructions) frames Sophia. Mylar on wall can be applied so that it is smooth or crinkly.

Shelving units, display groupings, and trade-show exhibits have long utilized plumber's pipe and plastic PVC joints for their practicality. They are cheap, easy to get at a hardware or building supply outlet, and a cinch to assemble to fit any space. Now there is even furniture being made of the lightweight plastic pipes and joints, and it is excellent for outdoor use. Design the frame on paper, then take your sketch to the supplier and pick up the materials needed. For a low coffee table you will only need to have a glass top cut to the size of your frame. Experiment with the different sizes. You'll be able to create some pretty sophisticated shapes for seating units as well.

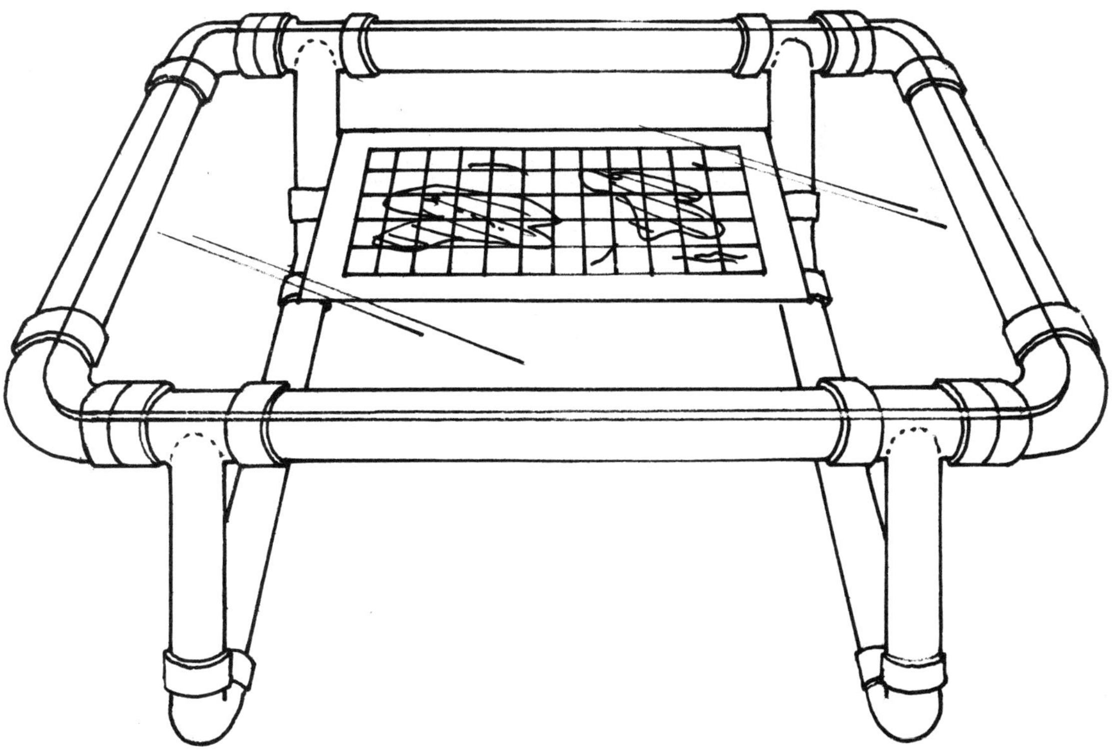

MOVER'S BLANKETS

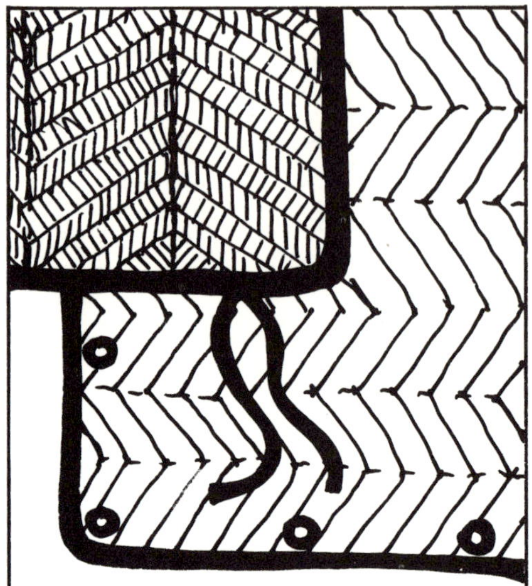

Wherever there's a moving company you'll find moving blankets, and they are becoming very desirable for upholstery material, to hang on the wall, and for rugs and bedspreads. They are quilted and even come in bright colors. Some that I've found are made of beautiful patchwork. Inexpensive, they are great for taking to the beach. As with most surplus clothing, these padded, cotton blankets should be cleaned before using and if you want, can be dyed in the washing machine with fabric dye. Some have grommets for hanging in elevators, others have tie strings, making them all the more handy for rolling up neatly or hanging on the wall. Try using them for tie-dye, batik, or as a background for appliqué.

CASTERS

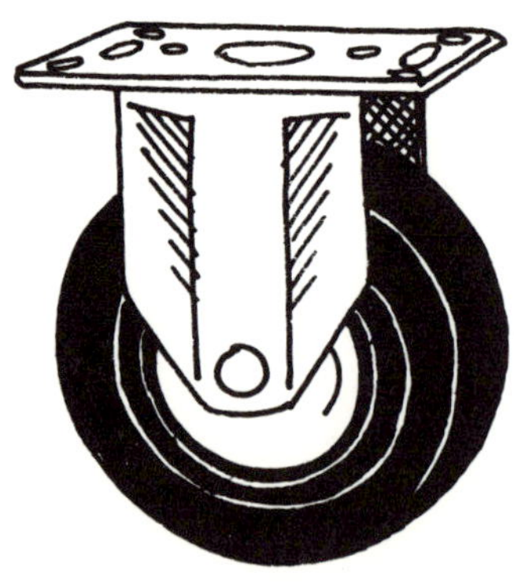

The large industrial casters that are used to push barrels and large cartons around in factories are excellent to hold large planters. If the redwood tubs and oversized barrels that hold heavy plants could be moved easily, they would be more desirable for home use. The heavy-duty rubber casters have a metal attachment that makes them easy to screw into the underside of any large object. If you use the fiber drums to hold heavy objects, attach three casters to the underside before filling. In this way you will have more flexibility in using them.

INDUSTRIAL LAMPS

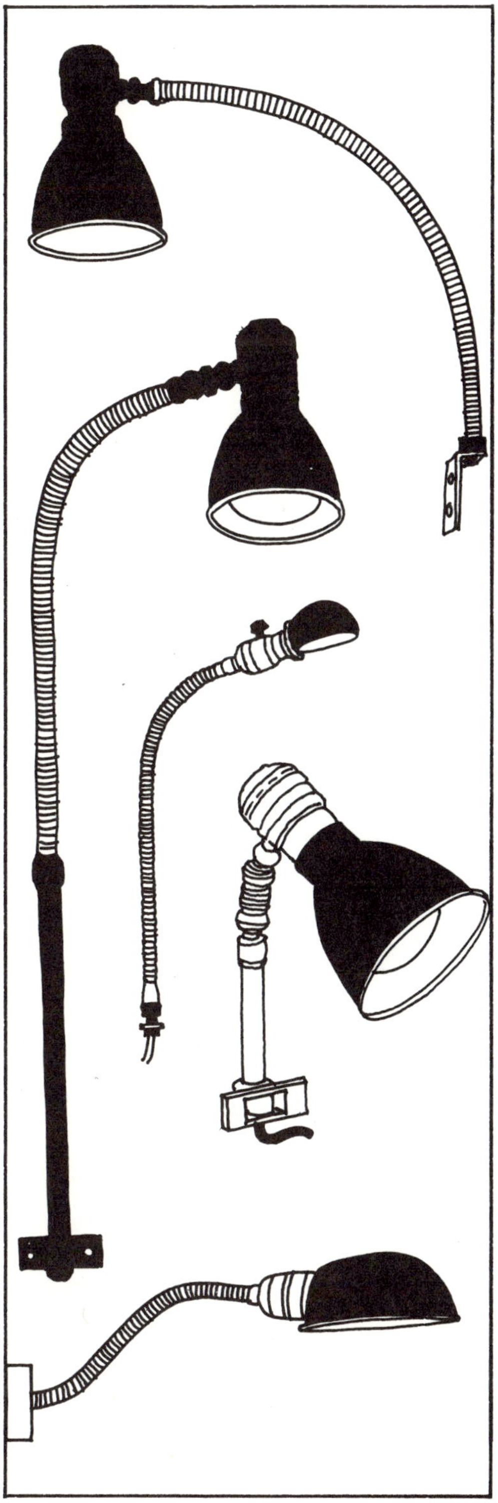

Why spend a lot of money for an expensive desk lamp when you can buy one that will fit absolutely any use for half the price? These industrial gooseneck lamps are often seen in factories where precision work is done. Some clamp onto a desk, others attach to the wall or electrical outlet, and some are made to be freestanding on the floor or desk top. They are not beautiful. However, many designer outlets are carrying adaptations of these standard lamps because they were industrially designed to serve a purpose, and that is to light a specified area in the best possible way. Because the exterior is not contemporary looking, they have been redesigned in shiny chrome and bright enamel finishes. However, we pay dearly for this. You can update an industrial lamp yourself, and you may find that some, when grouped together, are quite impressive as is. One such idea comes from your local garage. The lights that have a heavy rubber housing and metal cage covering the bulb hang under the car when the mechanic is working. Hang several upside down and you'll have an interesting, brightly lit work area. Industrial glass lamps are another popular lighting solution that has been brought into the living room. A fluorescent fixture can be covered with fabric and no one will realize that it isn't a contemporary light.

Since most of the industrial lamps are made of heavy-duty metal, they will take a bright spray-paint enamel beautifully. In minutes you can turn a dull gray, swivel-top, precision-work plant light into one that looks as if it were purchased at Bloomingdale's. Some even have special features, such as screw-in bases and extension arms.

HANGING LAMPS

Aluminum work lights can be found in all sizes and are often used over work areas or plant corners in homes and offices. Photographic reflectors and clip-on reflector shades are readily available, inexpensive, and easily converted where lighting is needed. Wire the socket into the reflectors with the appropriate washer and screw unit to hold the elements together. These are available in lamp stores and hard-goods stores; you can even find wiring kits to do the job. The cords can then be strung through eye bolts that have been screwed into the ceiling. Put another eye bolt in the corner where the wall and ceiling meet and run the cord down the wall to the outlet. Add a line switch for turning on and off.

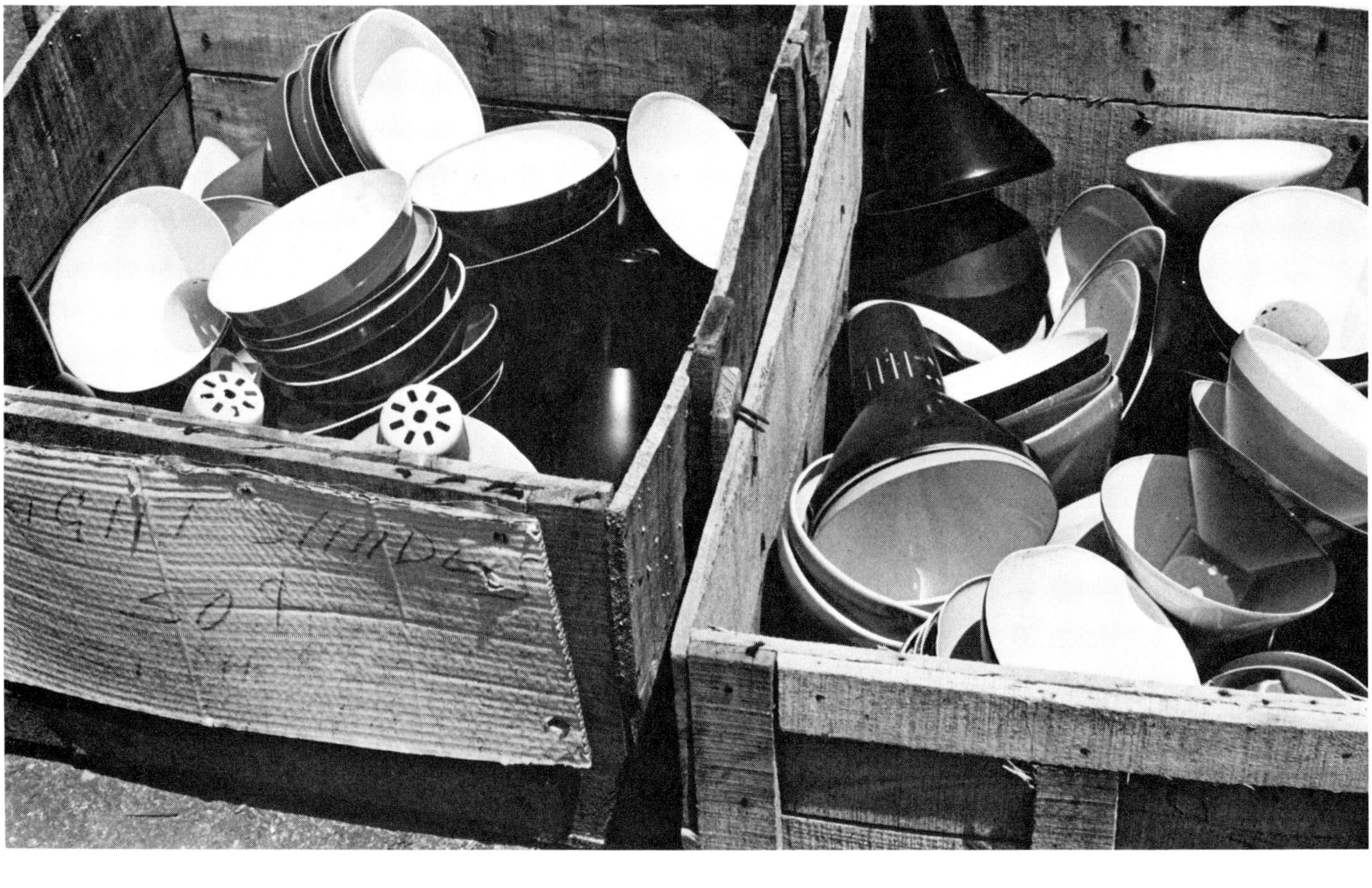

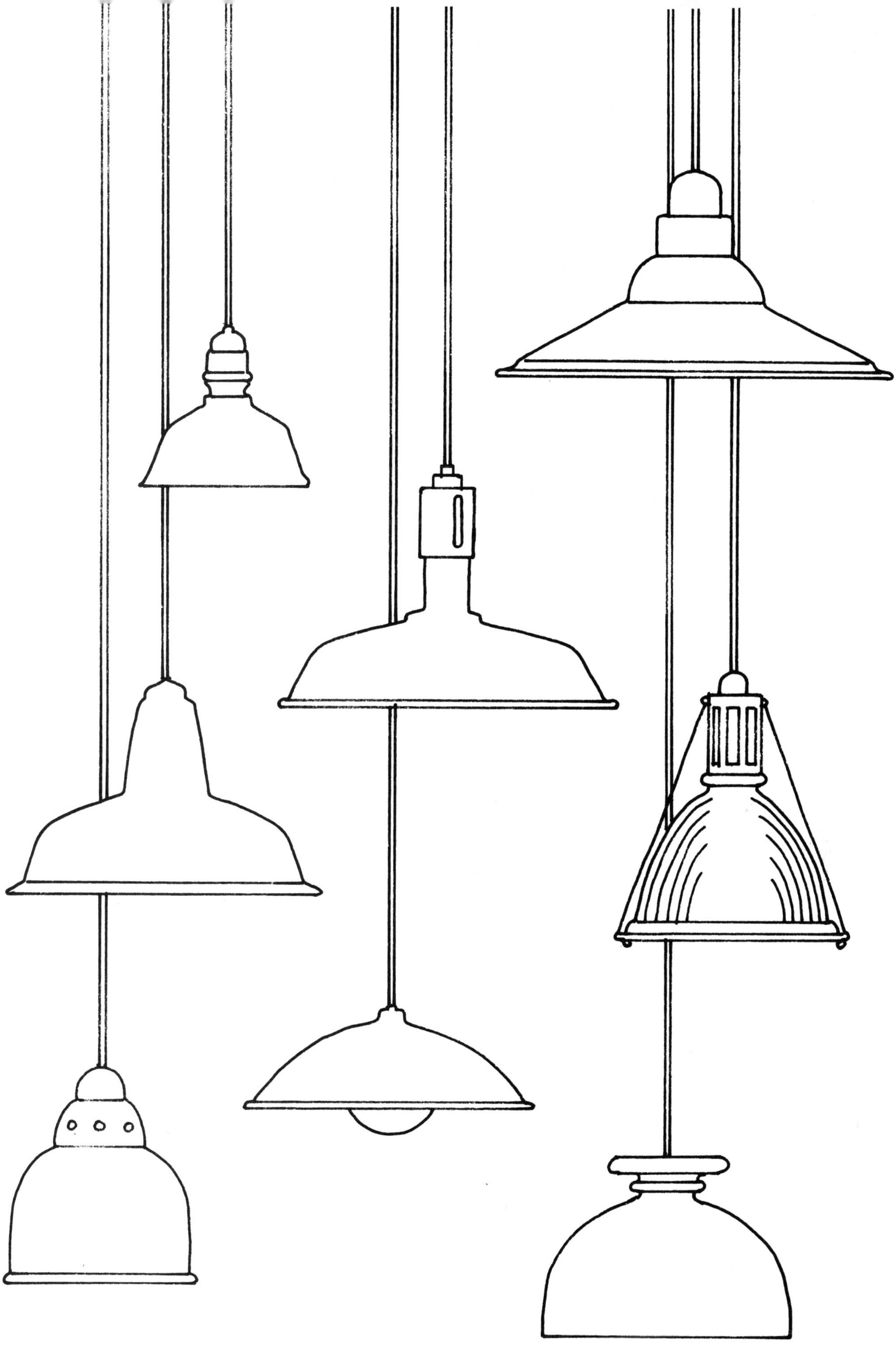

HOOKS

Hooks seem to have come into their own. You can spend any amount of money on decorator hooks, but there's no need to. Actually, I have found that the very decorative, expensive hooks don't always do the job. The worst hook I've used is the colorful china screw-in type. It looks sensational, but if you don't secure it to a wall stud it will not hold up for long. Almost all doors are hollow and there is no way that this hook will work on the back of such a door. However, for areas where it can grip to something solid, it is pretty and a bargain for 79 cents.

Heavy-duty hooks found in houseware departments are terrific, and they are finally coming out in bright colors rather than the standard metallic color. The huge hooks for holding bicycles off the floor in the garage have a plastic coating, usually orange, and are strong. A heavy outdoor plant could easily hang safely from this hook. Use them also for stacking chairs that can be folded away when not in use.

A meat hook is made of chrome and is beautifully functional. It sells for between three and four dollars and can be found in well-equipped stores that sell kitchen implements. Use it in the kitchen for holding cooking utensils. It is strong enough to hold a heavy skillet or a good-sized planter.

The old-fashioned coat hook can be found in silver, gold, or black metal and is exceptionally versatile. Two or three screws hold it in place and it will stay up forever. While it isn't a much sought-after decorator item, if you line several in a row and hang tote bags on each you can store anything.

The 15-cent wire hook has usually gotten short shrift, but with a coating of bright red spray enamel it doesn't look so ordinary. It is unbeatable for price, function, and durability and is available everywhere.

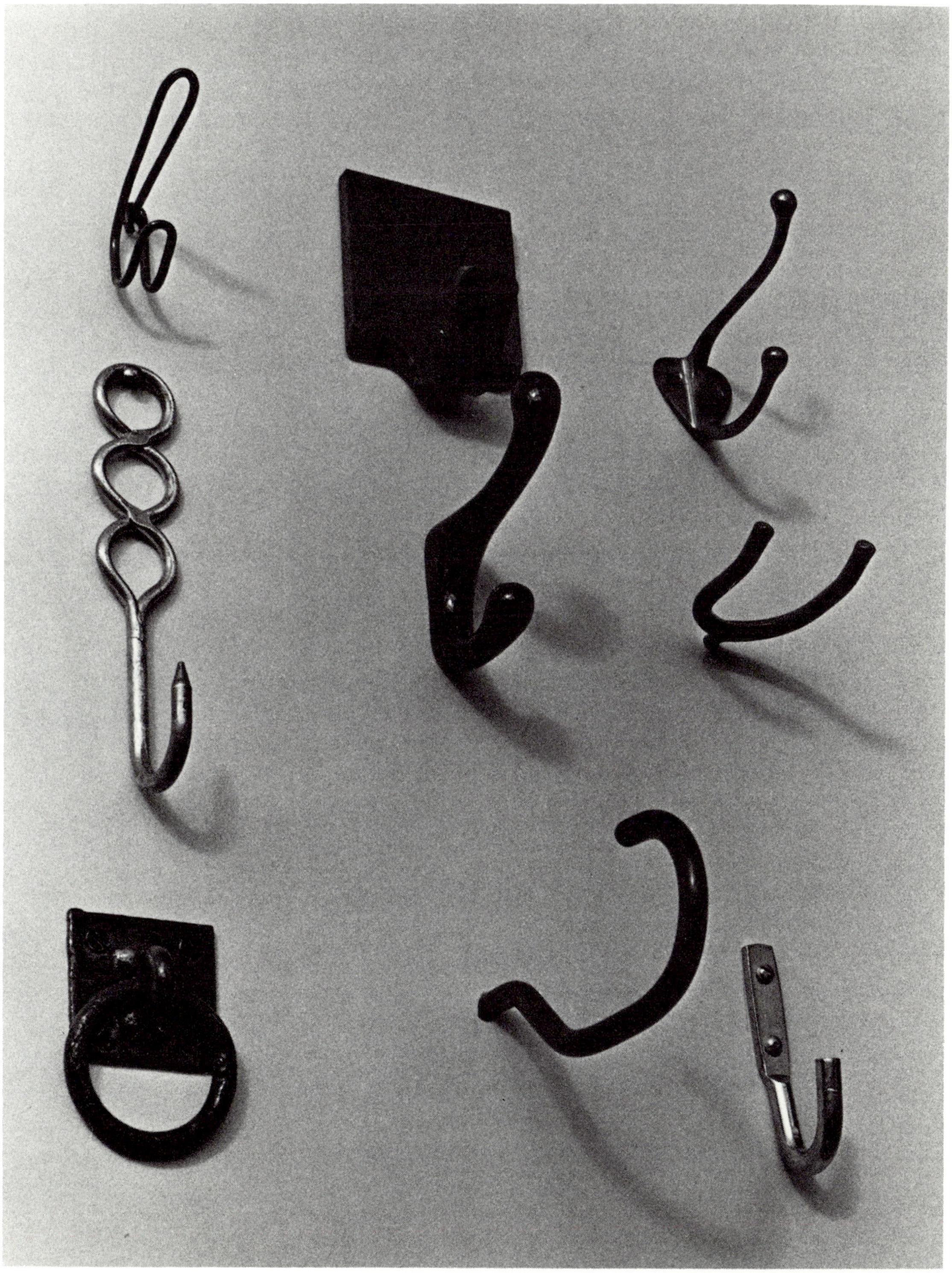

RUNNING HOT AND COLD

An old-fashioned brass faucet handle which reads "hot" and "cold" on either side of the porcelain is a nostalgic item. As with many such finds you will have to use your imagination to come up with a creative use. This one is hung on a chain and used as a light pull. It might be unique as a window shade pull or simply hanging around your neck for a bit of humor.

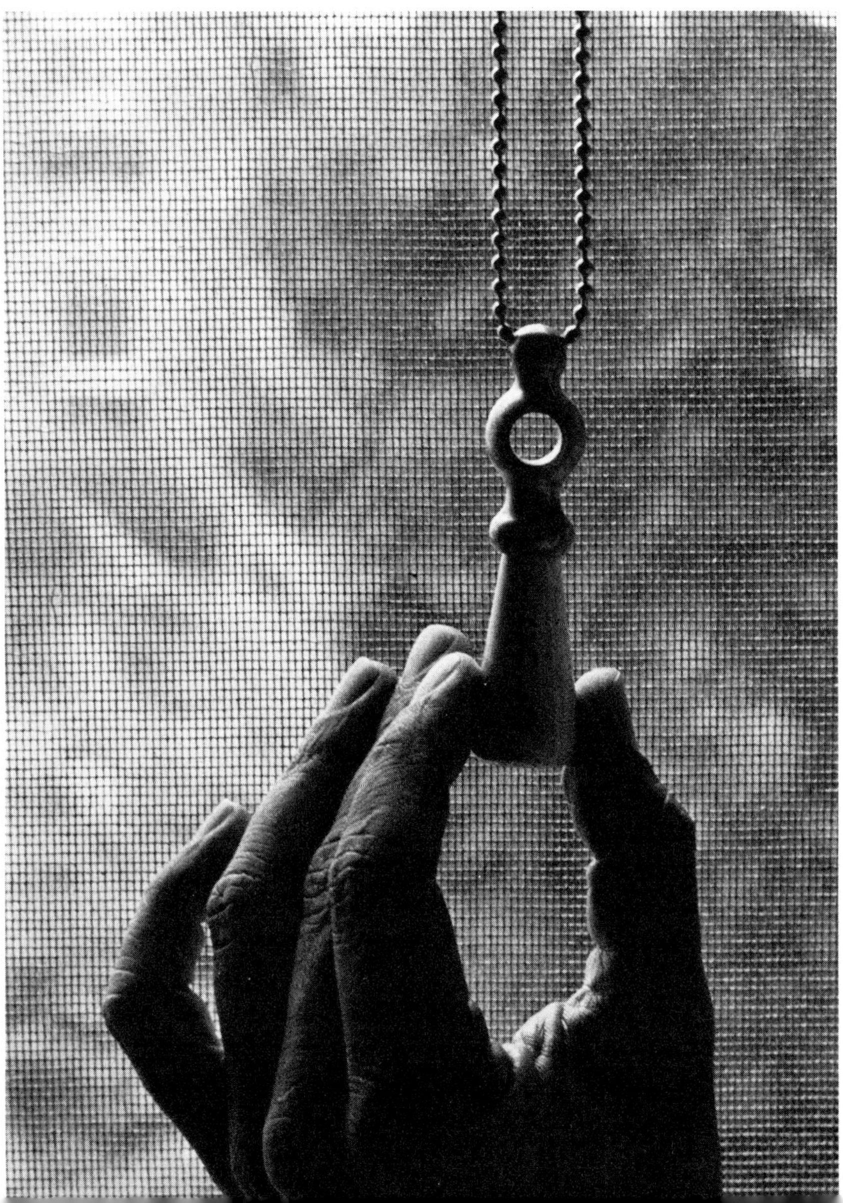

There are many such offbeat ideas that simply require rummaging around for the products. Stores that sell hardware or plumbing materials will yield many such items. Finding and using old-fashioned fixtures as such to use in home decorating for the original purpose is also a popular decorating idea. For instance, in a very contemporary bathroom you might consider the use of these lovely old finds. And, if they seem to elude you in terms of home decor, turn something unusual into a gifty key-ring holder.

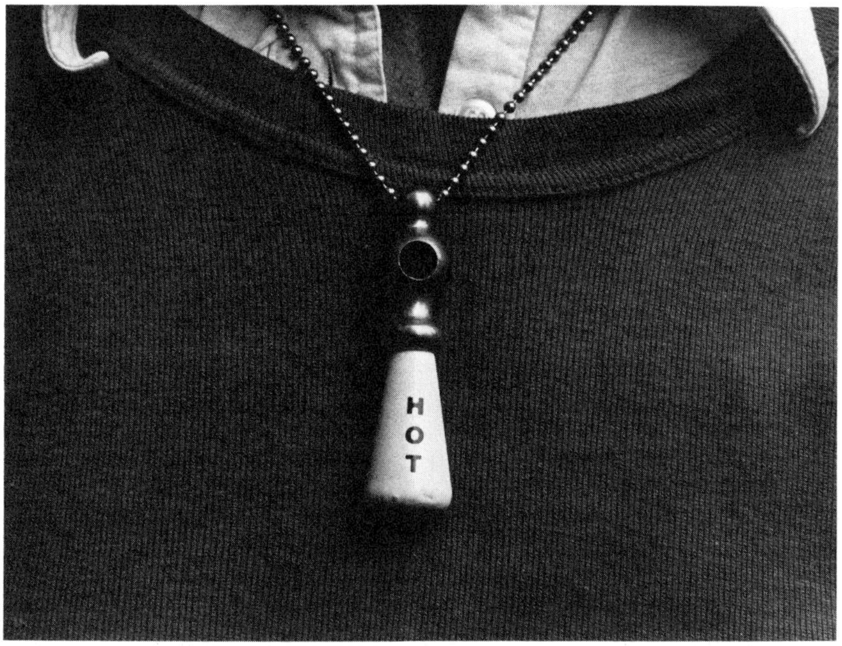

SHIP SHAPE

Marine hardware has always been designed and made with special care. Before plastics and special metal alloys, boat fittings were made of either heavy metal, like bronze, or of wood. The metal items were made to last indefinitely. In order to reduce weight and cost, many old hardware items are not used today. However, many interesting items are still available and sought after by collectors. Once the old metal blocks and snap locks are polished they are often displayed as nostalgic memories of a simpler life. But marine hardware has a great many practical uses as well.

Mast hoop Small Cat boats were prevalent before 1900. The sails were equipped with little wooden hoops, enabling them to slide up and down the mast easily. These mast hoops varied in size and have been made into bracelets by removing the metal fittings and finishing the wood with clear lacquer. They are also used as coasters by cutting and fitting a piece of cork into the opening. Mast hoops have little nautical use today and may be found in marine antique stores. See source list for a mail-order source for novel marine hardware and fittings.

Shackle and Snap Hook These common items are available in many sizes, designs, and metals. The older types shown here are examples of bronze metalwork. They are heavy and durable. When restored with metal polish they look like sculptured jewelry. The shackle and snap hook have become popular for use as a belt buckle. The shackle has a removable pin which is put through one end of the belt to secure it. The snap hook has a ring through which the other end of the belt is fed and folded over for permanent fastening.

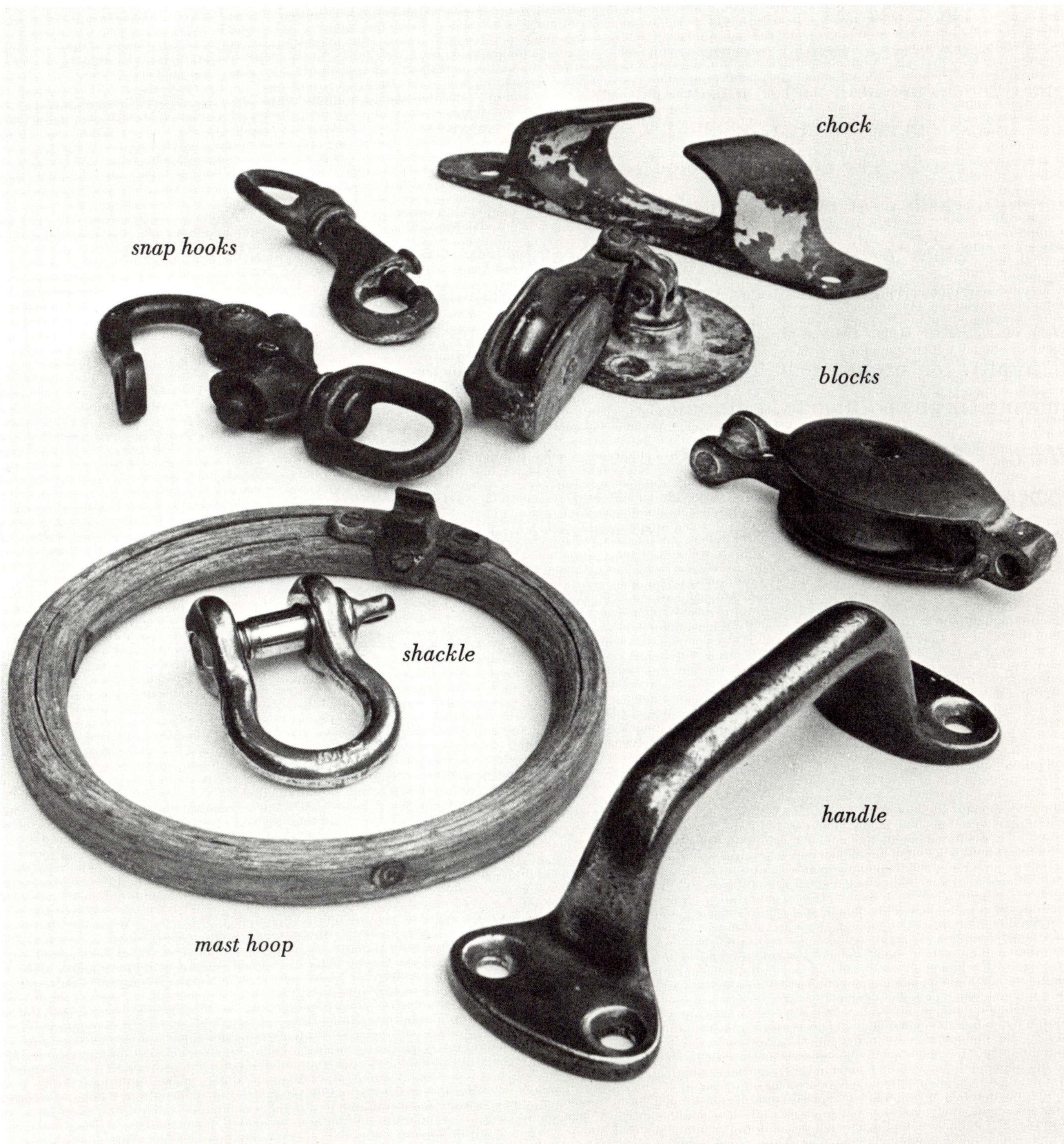
chock
snap hooks
blocks
shackle
handle
mast hoop

Block The types of blocks or pulleys used at sea are endless. They are designed to accommodate lines of every size. Small blocks are both useful and decorative for landlubbers. The blocks can be used to raise and lower a hanging planter with great style. The deck snatch block can be fastened to a ceiling as easily as screwed into the deck of a wooden sailboat.

Chock Lines are held in position on the boat by chocks. These jaunty little metal pieces might seem devoid of potential for home use. However, they are excellent for hanging decorative or useful items on a wall. The chock can be mounted in any position to fit the object.

Handle Handles, like all old ship's fittings, are heavy and generously designed. When polished and mounted on a wooden door or drawer it becomes a very attractive accent.

FRAME UP!

THE BACK BAND FRAME

If you want to make your own picture frames, you might be stymied before you start. Picture-frame molding is not always easy to get. Most framers do not sell the frame molding by the foot. Further, to frame a picture nicely, especially a large one, can be very costly. One good solution is to use something other than picture-frame molding. Every lumberyard carries a selection of moldings for windows, baseboards, and so on. Back band is a common molding which is extremely inexpensive and is sold by the foot. It is also easy to work with and makes excellent frames. Back band is only good for prints or artwork on illustration board. Thicker material such as a stretched canvas would protrude in the back so that the picture would not hang flush against the wall.

Begin by cropping the picture to the size you want. The picture and the glass must be ½-inch larger than the area that will be seen. The frame hides ¼-inch on each side.

You will need two items for frame-making: a miter box for cutting the corners on a 45-degree angle and two corner clamps for holding the glued pieces together at right angles. Both the miter box and corner clamps are readily available in hardware stores.

When you cut each section of frame, match it to the glass to make sure it fits. The frame should be a little larger than the glass, so that when the frame is all glued, the glass will drop in easily. The glass to be used is regular window glass and can be cut by a glass cutter unless you are good at this yourself.

Apply white glue to one end of a short and a long section. Clamp these together and set aside to dry. Repeat this process with the other two pieces. Next, tap ¾-inch brads into the joints to secure them. You will need four per corner. When these sections are completely dry, unclamp them. Repeat this process with the corner clamps, making the finished frame.

Fome-Cor, a styrofoam board that is ¼-inch thick, is a good backing material. This is available in art-supply stores. If you have a thin picture, such as a poster, you may want to mount it on the Fome-Cor with rubber cement to insure flatness. This is done by coating the back of the poster and the front of the Fome-Cor and letting each dry. Carefully place the poster on the Fome-Cor and smooth down. Trim the Fome-Cor if necessary with a razor blade or X-acto knife.

Once you have the knack, you will be able to make frames extremely quickly with no trouble at all. They can be stained,

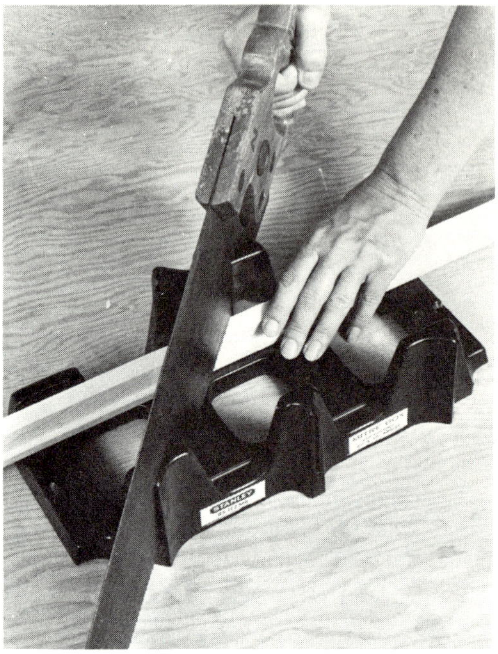

Molding is cut in miter box at a 45-degree angle.

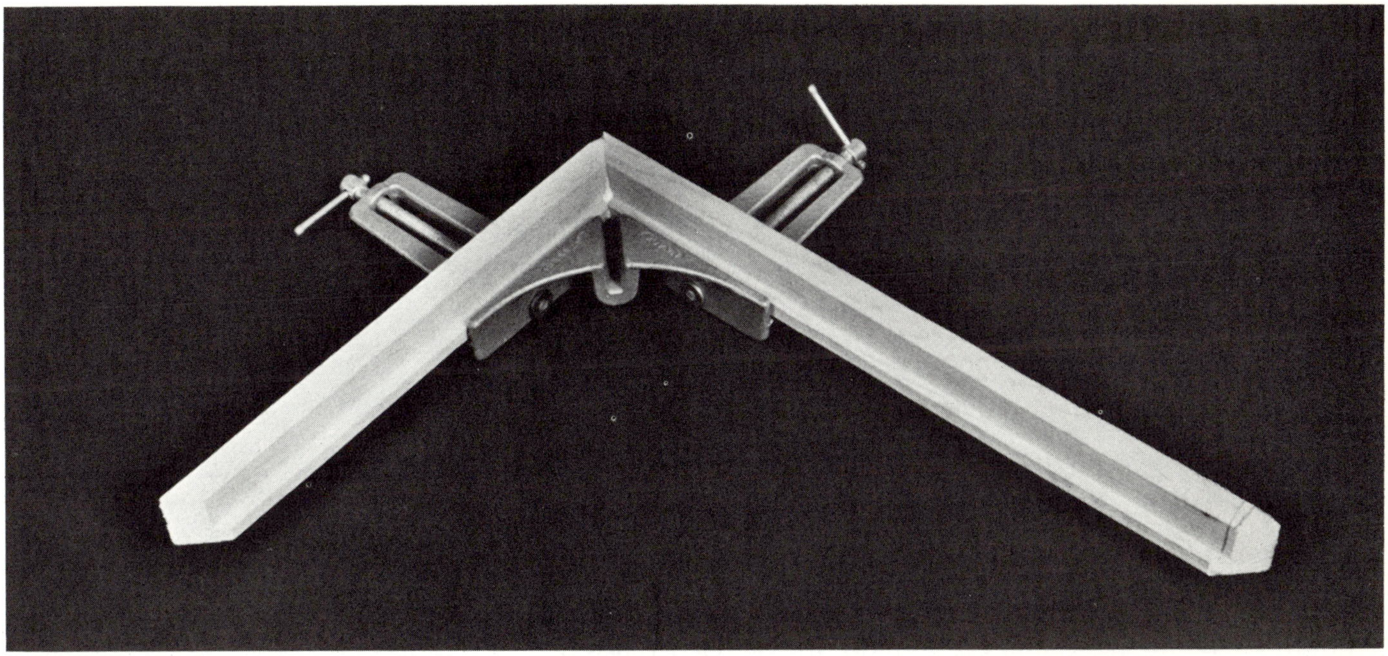

Glued corners held while drying.

painted decoratively, or spray painted with enamel in a color that matches the artwork.

When using the back band to frame a large poster, the placement of the picture wire is important. Attach screw eyes to the back sides of the frame. To these tie picture wire so that it is taut. When hanging the framed picture, the sides will be drawn in tightly, preventing bowing in a lightweight frame.

We used this method for almost all the framing projects in the book because it is good-looking, simple to make, and looks well with all the graphics. Also, many of the framed objects were quite inexpensive. It would seem foolish to then spend a great deal on expensive framing. With this method none of the wall art cost over five dollars, in some cases much less. However, none of it looks less impressive than if it had cost quite a bit more.

UP AGAINST THE WALL

It is not easy to find prints or posters for framing that are both inexpensive and unusual. The larger the graphic, certainly the more expensive to frame. This idea came from a natural food store in my area called The Organic Market, and they were happy to contribute it for this project. The design that is matted and framed here is actually the front of a fifty-pound brown rice bag. The background is natural wheat color and the type and rice color is mustard. Once emptied of its contents, the front of the bag is cut in a rectangle and mounted on poster board. Choose a board color that complements the colors in the design. Mount the bag (or whatever you are using) with rubber cement and trim it so that there is an even border all around. You will need a straight edge and an X-acto knife to do this. Have a piece of window glass cut to size and the "poster" is ready for framing. (See back band framing instructions, page 77.)

This is an example of how attractive a throwaway commercial packaging item can be made. Look for similar ideas in places where you shop. You will be surprised at how much you overlook and take for granted.

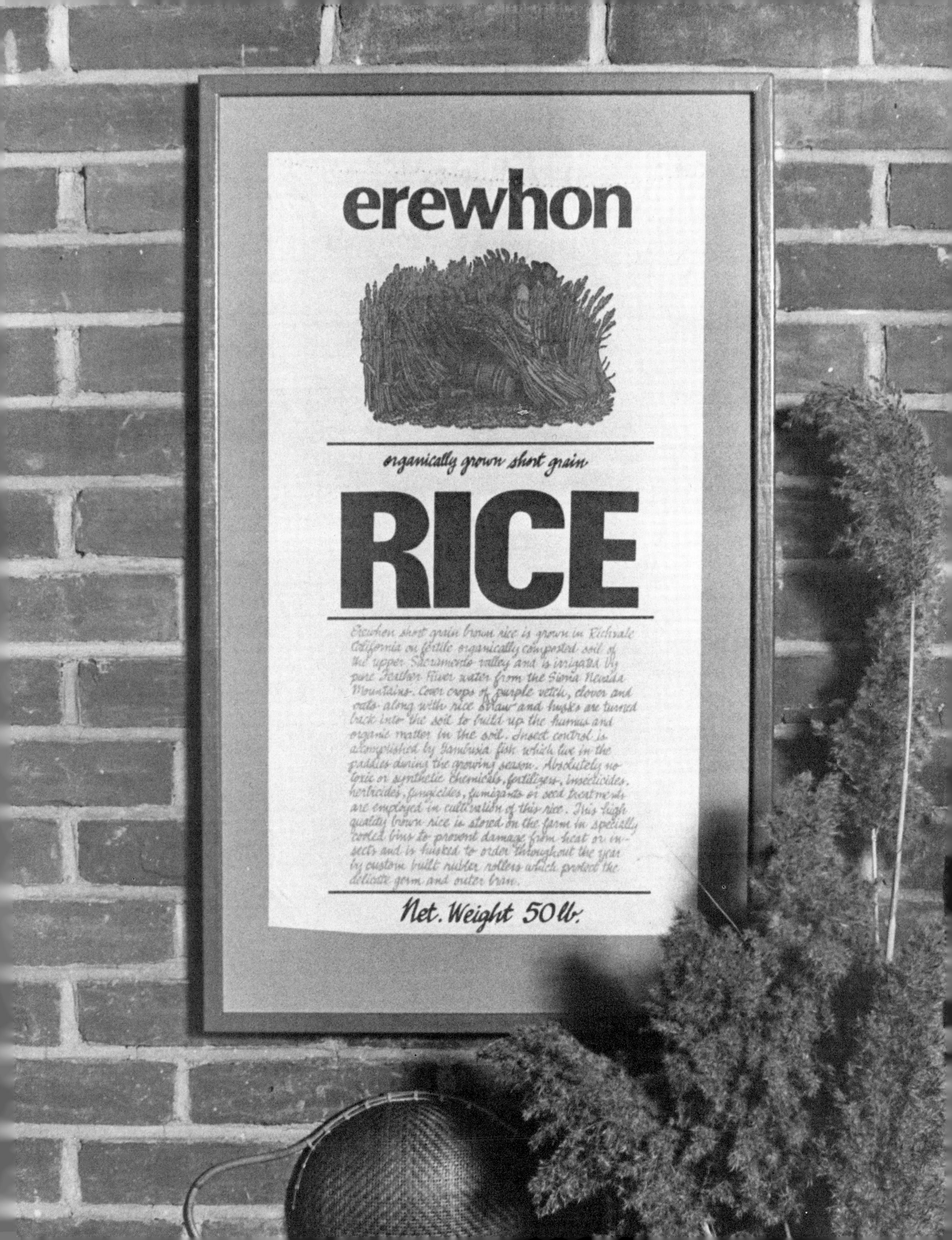
erewhon
organically grown short grain
RICE
Erewhon short grain brown rice is grown in Richvale
California on fertile organically composted soil of
the upper Sacramento valley and is irrigated by
pure Feather River water from the Sierra Nevada
Mountains. Cover crops of purple vetch, clover and
oats along with rice straw and husks are turned
back into the soil to build up the humus and
organic matter in the soil. Insect control is
accomplished by Gambusia fish which live in the
paddies during the growing season. Absolutely no
toxic or synthetic chemicals, fertilizers, insecticides,
herbicides, fungicides, fumigants or seed treatments
are employed in cultivation of this rice. This high
quality brown rice is stored on the farm in specially
cooled bins to prevent damage from heat or in-
sects and is husked to order throughout the year
by custom built rubber rollers which protect the
delicate germ and outer bran.
Net. Weight 50 lb.

FRAMELESS!

While the back band frames are a good solution for many framing projects, they aren't for items that require something more simple. Sometimes we want to hang a print, poster, or photograph but would rather that the frame be unobtrusive. Many galleries hang paintings so that the frame doesn't distract the viewer. There are variations on the sandwich framing technique. Some that you may be familiar with are Braquettes, Kulicke, acrylic, and those with metal corners. None of these is quite as effective as the Gallery Clip system. This is a new framing technique designed by a photographer for hanging flat artwork with glass. The clips are used to hold anything as thin as a piece of paper, a piece of glass, and the backing, which is usually ¼-inch-thick Fome-Cor. You can frame almost any size artwork with these. The tension is on the nylon cord that pulls the clips together, making the whole thing tighter as it hangs. These Gallery Clips are the least expensive and certainly the least obtrusive of framing methods. They are simple to assemble and reusable. Gallery Clips are a beautiful frameless method for displaying a large poster. (See source list at end for where to find them.)

Inexpensive museum poster in frameless frame.

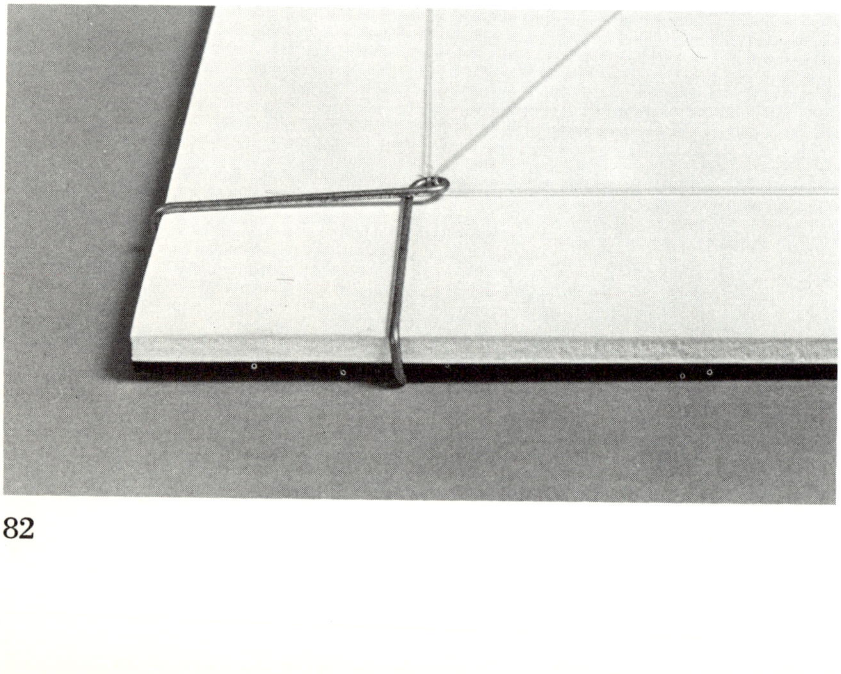

Materials for mounting and framing.

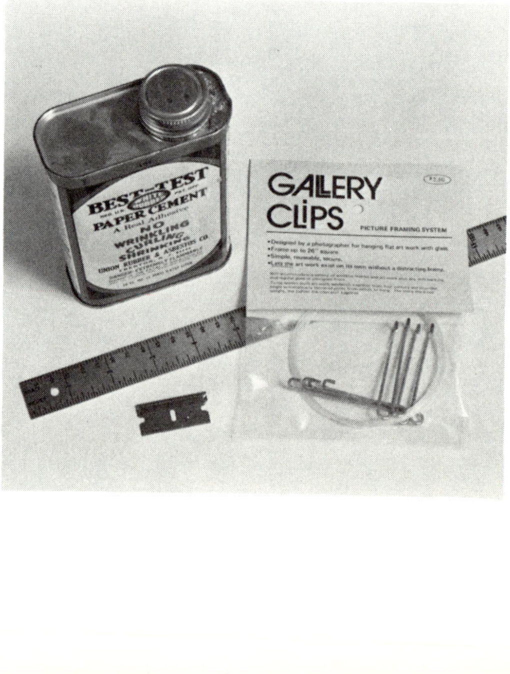

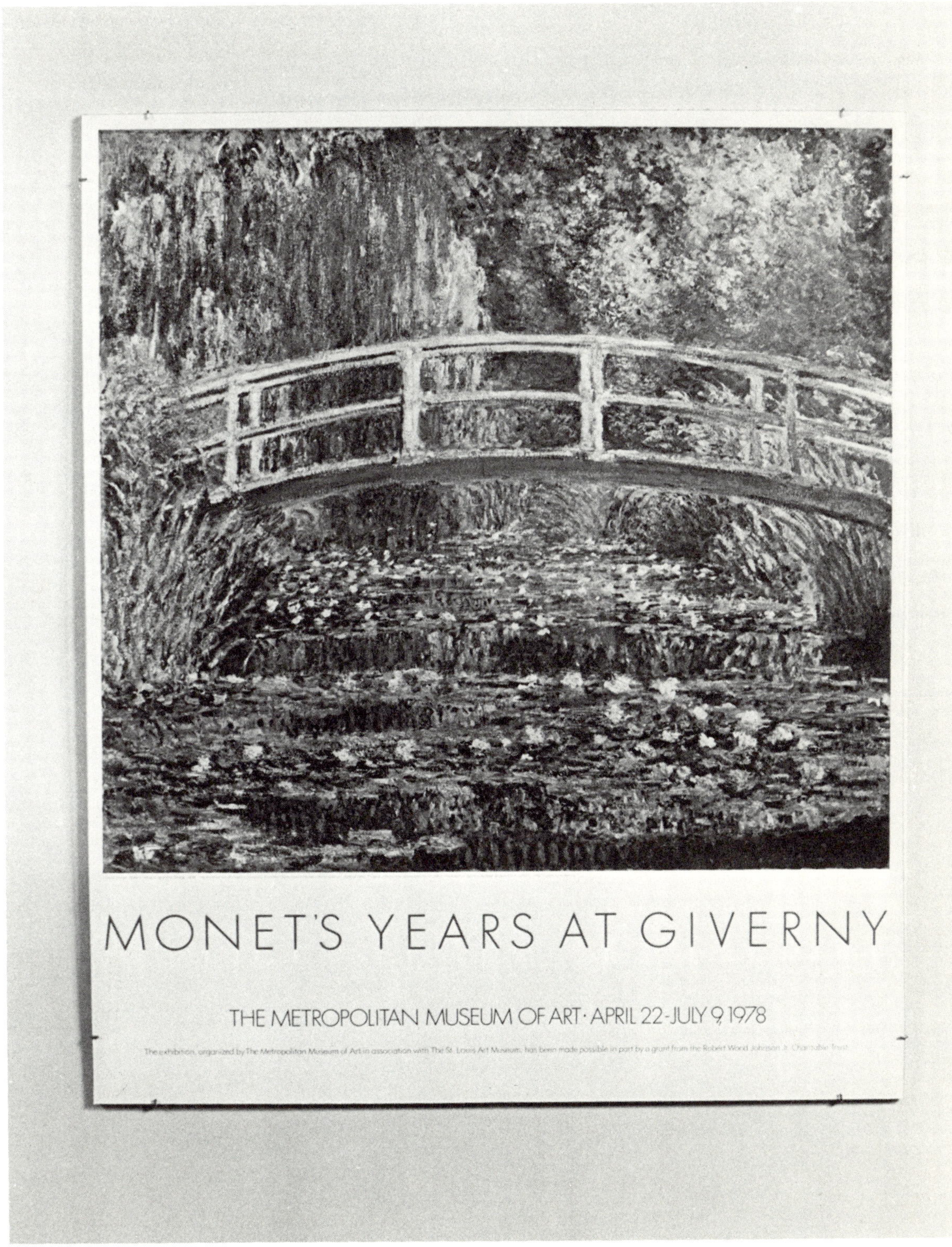
MONET'S YEARS AT GIVERNY
THE METROPOLITAN MUSEUM OF ART · APRIL 22-JULY 9, 1978

ALL MAPPED OUT

There are some subjects that can be framed in a variety of ways, and each method will change the appearance greatly. The U.S. Geological Survey maps are excellent for framing. The entire United States has been marked off into a grid of rectangles, each rectangle being a map measuring 22″ × 27″. You can design your own mural on the wall depending on how much of an area you want to exhibit. It could be part of your state, your town, a place you'd like to visit, or an area where you have enjoyed a vacation. Nantucket Island, which has an odd shape, takes four separate maps to construct. The back band frame is used here for two Nantucket maps showing the center of the island. Each map sells for $1.75, a terrific bargain.

The Gallery Clips are especially good for this project. Because there is no frame to divide the mounted maps, they can be hung so that they are flush against one another. In this way the map flows continuously from one panel to the other. (See source list for maps.)

Survey maps framed first with Gallery Clips, again with back band frames.

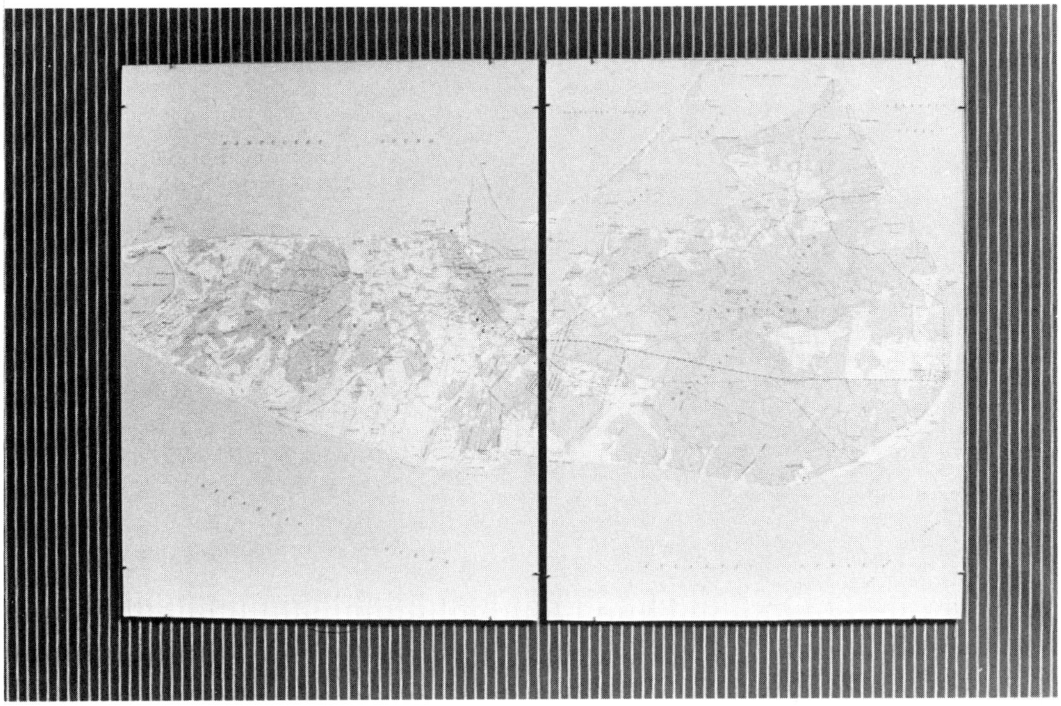

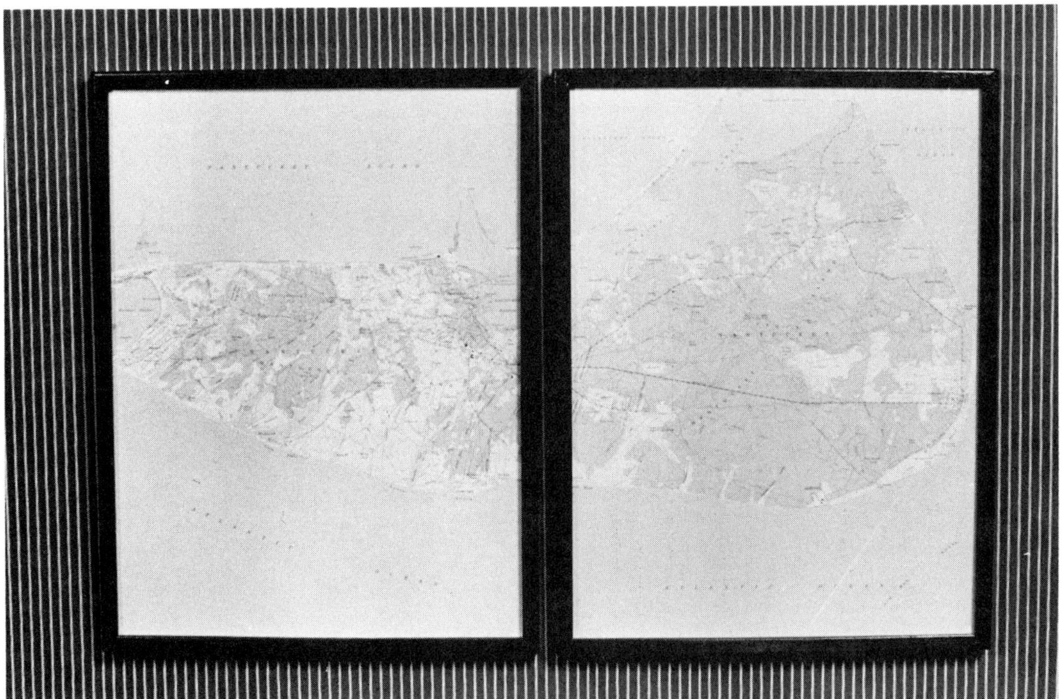

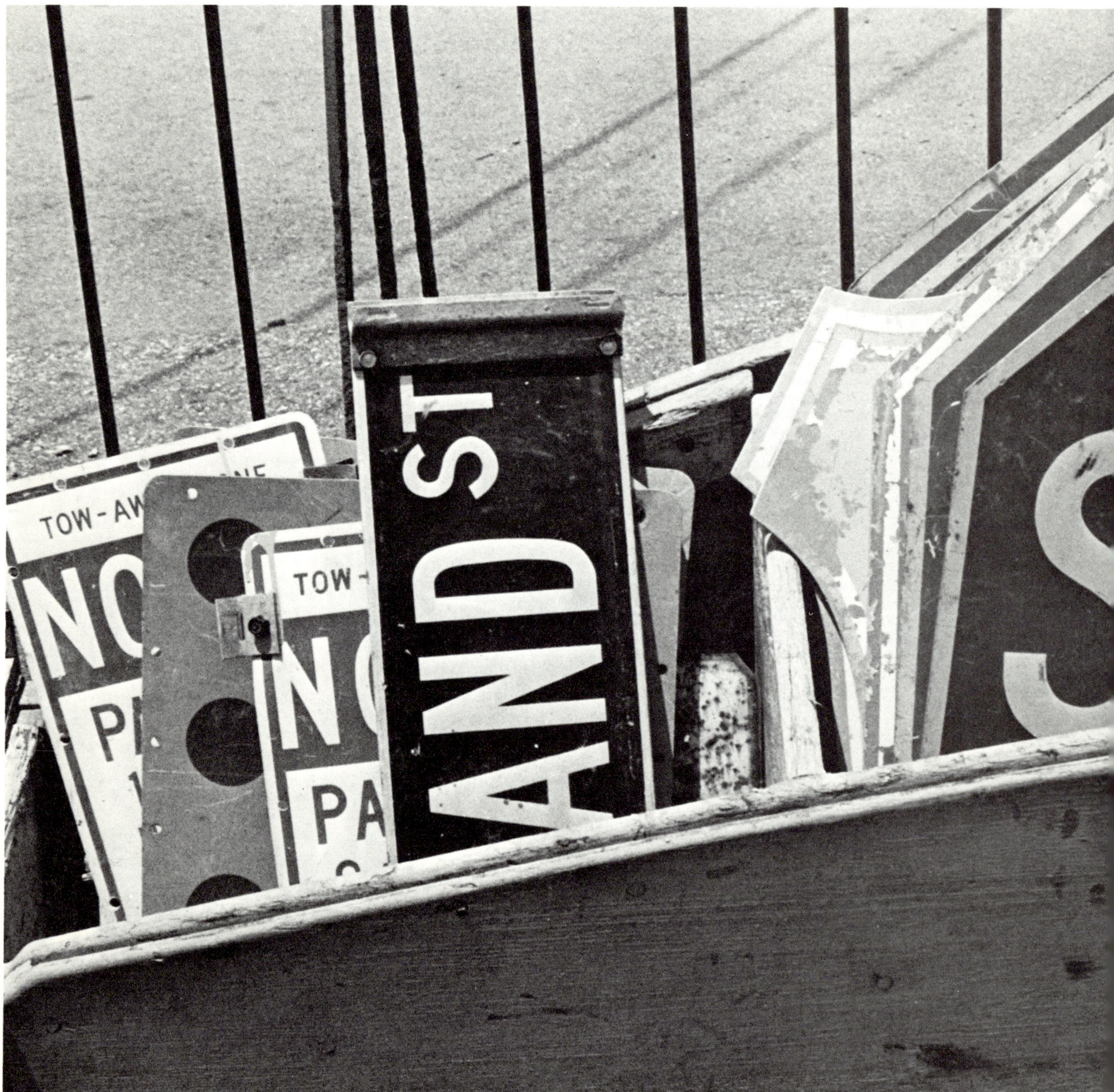
TOW-AW
NO
PA
TOW-
NO
PA
AND ST

SIGN UP HERE

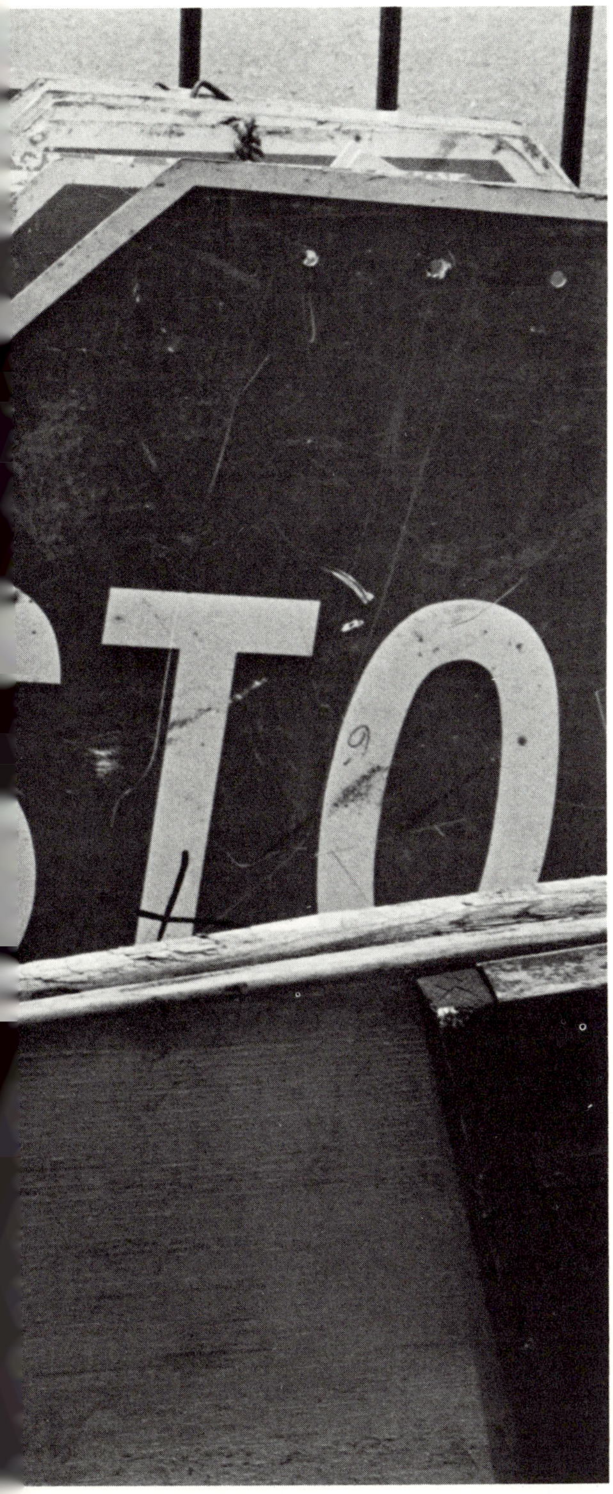

Commercial signs, letters, and numbers can be found in all sizes and typefaces. If you buy them new the cost is greater than if you come across used ones. Aside from neon signs, you can easily get large plastic, metal, or wooden letters in junkyards and manufacturers' outlets. And there are mail-order sources for signs and letters of every style. Architectural graphics used for commercial buildings are worth finding as they are good for strong, bold decoration in a home. The plastic and wooden letters are interesting wall decorations and have been used by interior designers for years. When grouped with other unusual items such as posters or prints, the space becomes more personalized. The plastic lowercase "a" hung on the wall with the field cup planter is an example of this.

Junkyards always have decaying signs turning to rust on the ground. It has been my experience from years of "junking" that the minute you show some interest in a particular one, it becomes a "rare sign that is very hard to come by." However, signs are an excellent way to provide individuality to an area, usually for very little expense. As with bumper stickers, your philosophical preferences can be displayed for all to see. Sometimes they simply lend a note of humor or have some nostalgic value.

TEED OFF

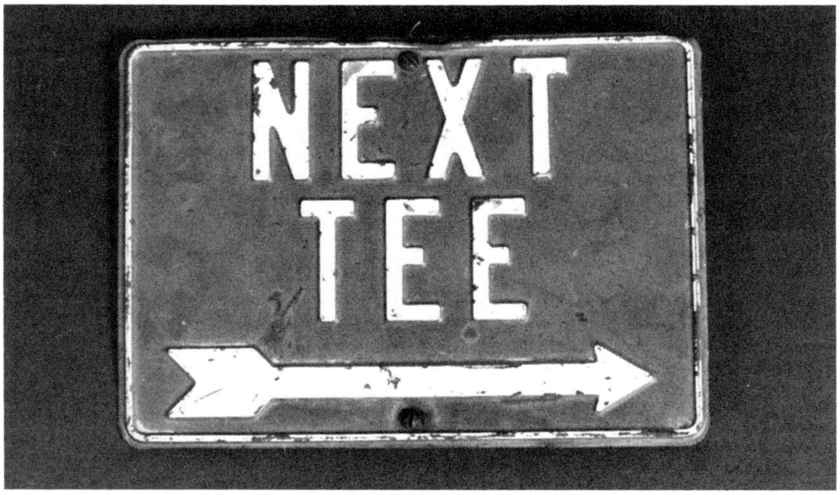

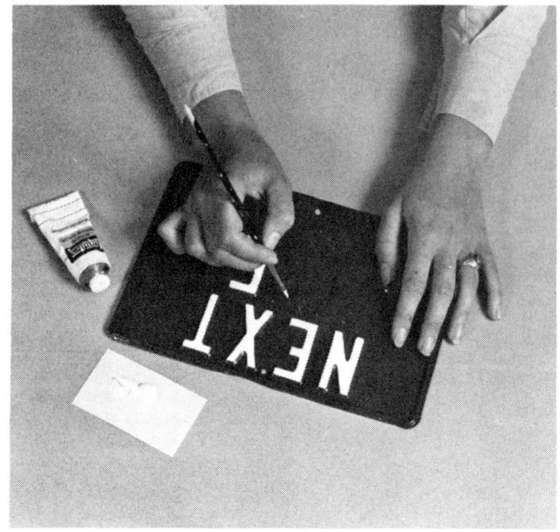

Retouching sign is done with acrylic paint.

A metal sign from a golf course that had obviously fallen on hard times was picked up at a local junkyard. There were hundreds just like it. It was rusty and bent and wasn't worth the dollar I paid for it, but I saw potential. The first thing to do with such an item is to clean it up the best you can. Sand off the rust and bang it back into shape. The background color was originally green, but brown seemed more appealing. The entire sign was spray painted with a leather-brown color and allowed to dry. A commercial sign-painting company would ordinarily paint the letters with a roller at this point. However, unless you are very confident, I recommend doing the letters by hand. The letters were refurbished to look like new with white acrylic paint. Since they are raised it is not difficult to paint each one so that it looks as though it were done professionally.

When the paint dries give the sign several coats of spray varnish to protect it. Each coat should be dry before reapplying. The background for mounting is a piece of plywood that is larger all around than the sign. The plywood is covered with burlap to give the sign a border.

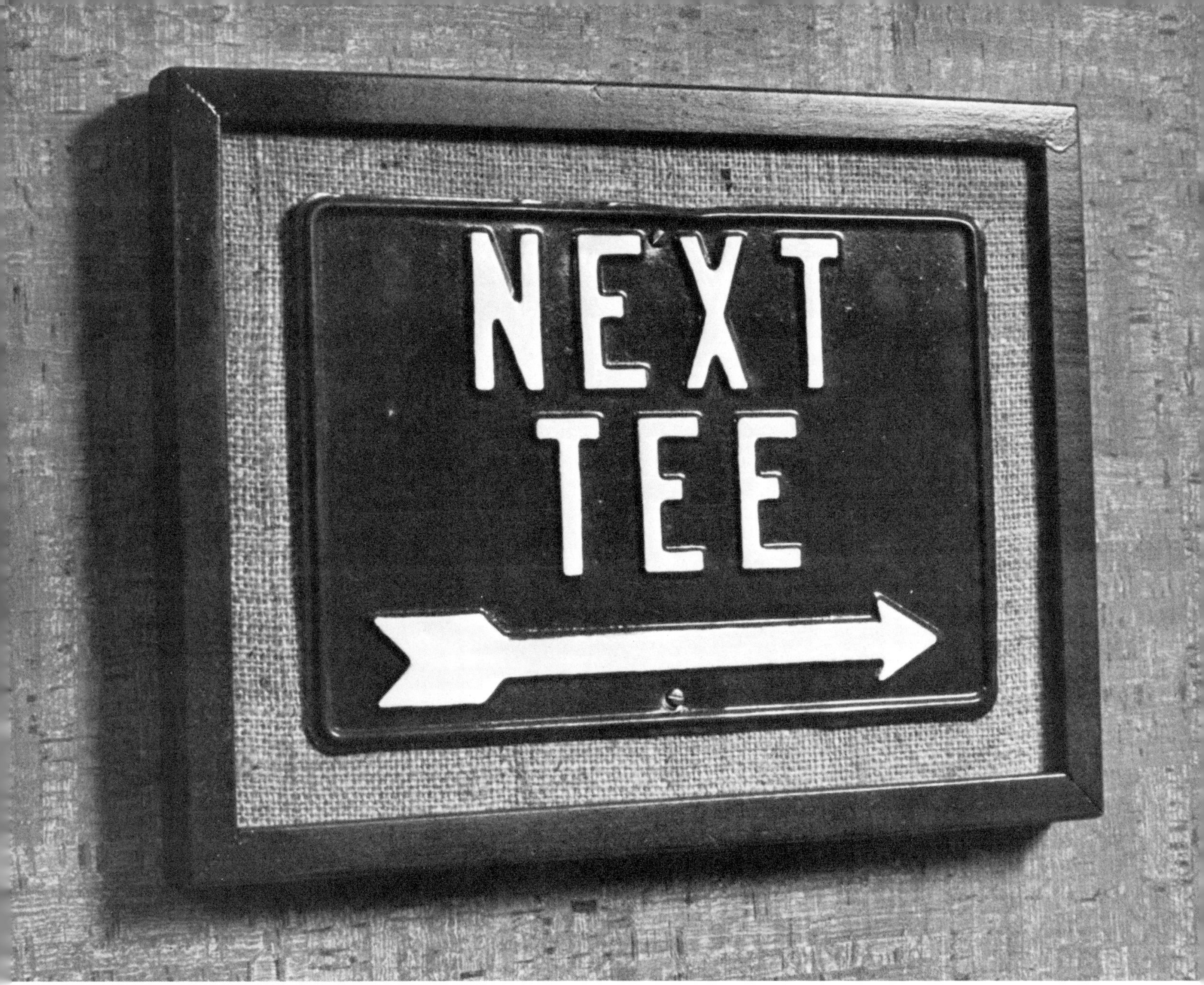

Cut the burlap so that it is large enough to wrap around the plywood. Spray the entire piece of fabric with spray adhesive and lay it onto the board. Be sure that it fits tightly. Pull the edges around to the back and press down. The burlap will adhere without any tacks or stapling.

Next, center the sign on the burlap and screw it into the board. Following the directions on page 77, make a back band frame and spray paint it the same color as the sign. Fit the board into the frame and tack it at the back. Add screw eyes and picture wire to the back for easy hanging. I thought this would look well in the bathroom, over a bar, or in the den of a golfer.

OF GLOBAL MERIT

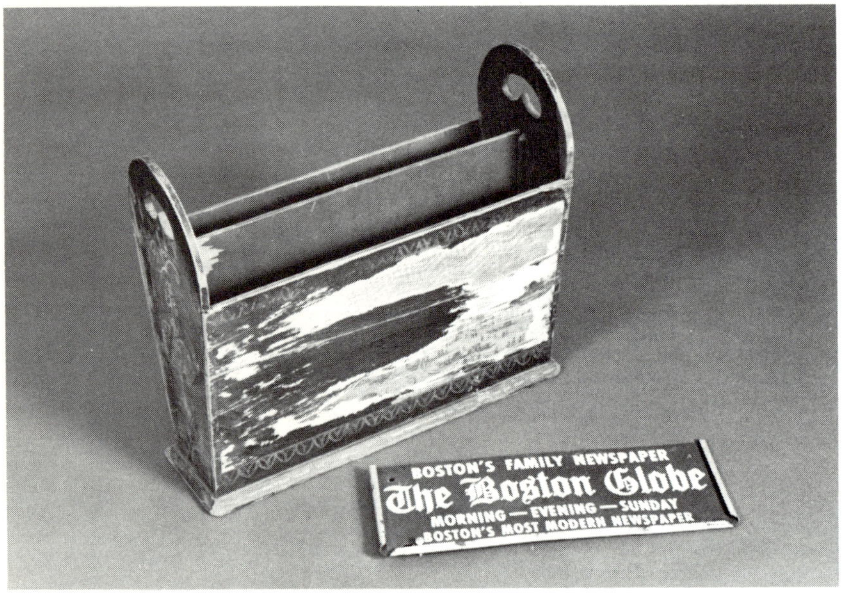

A battered object is never too far gone for refurbishment.

A *Boston Globe* newspaper dispenser has obviously lost a sign, but how it got from Boston to Al's junkyard in Connecticut only Al knows. However, teaming it up with an equally beaten-up magazine and newspaper holder gave it new life. This project is a good example of how you can create something from found objects that seem to complement each other. If you want to use an old piece of furniture, it must first be cleaned and sanded. It will probably have an old finish already on it, and sanding will enable you to successfully paint over it. If you have something that might look best with a wood stain, however, the old finish must first be removed. This can easily be done with an all-purpose finish remover and a scraper. Finally, smooth the surface once again with a medium-grit sandpaper.

If you are covering something with fabric or, as here, with wallpaper, simply clean and sand lightly. The vinyl wallpaper is very good to use for covering furniture or an accessory such as this. It is durable, thick, easy to apply, and

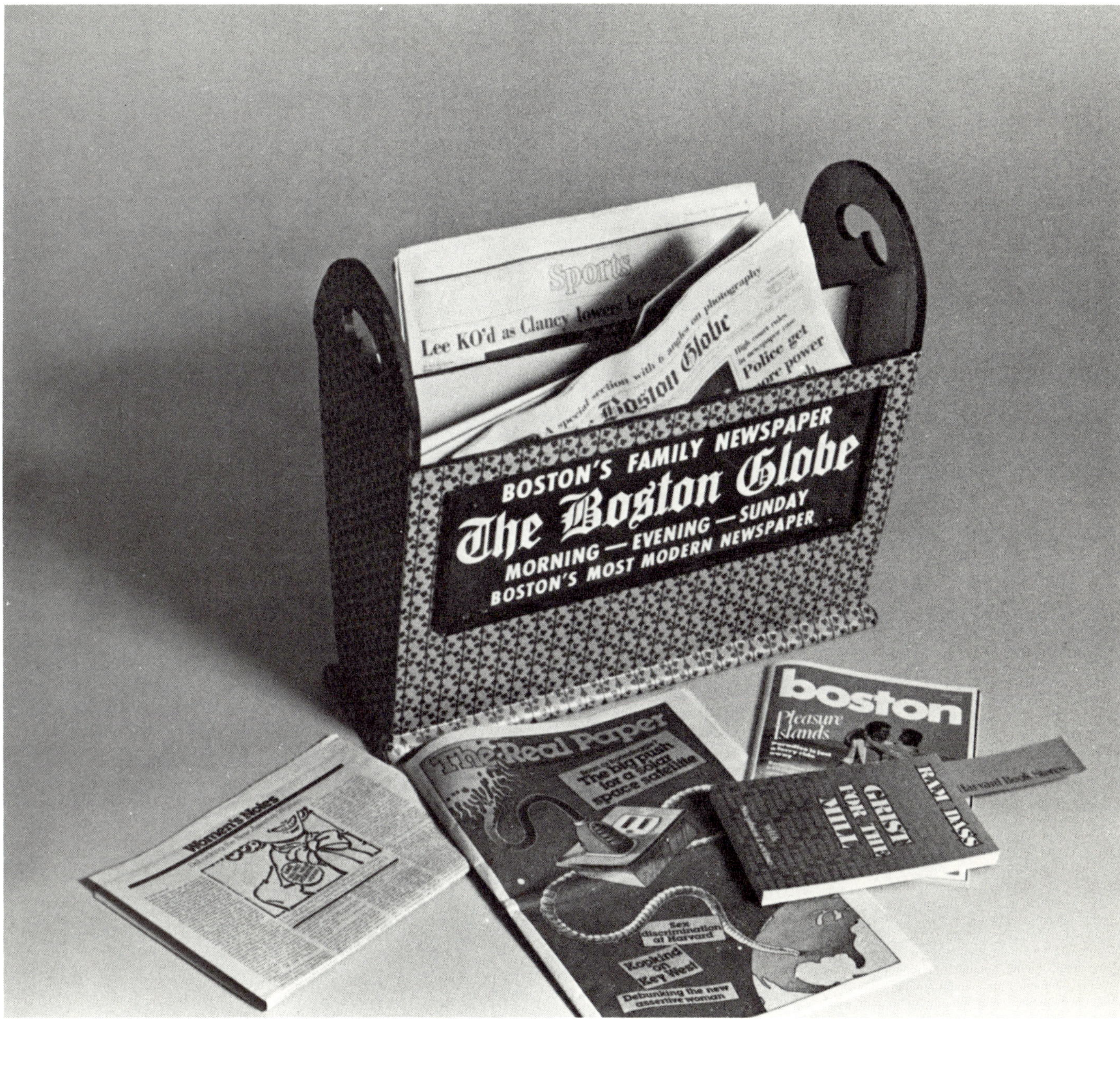
Sports
Lee KO'd as Clancy lowers
Boston Globe
BOSTON'S FAMILY NEWSPAPER
The Boston Globe
MORNING — EVENING — SUNDAY
BOSTON'S MOST MODERN NEWSPAPER
boston
Pleasure Islands
The Real Paper
The big push for a solar space satellite
Sex discrimination at Harvard
Kopkind on Key West
Debunking the new assertive woman
Women's Notes
GRIST FOR THE MILL
RAM DASS
Harvard Book Stores

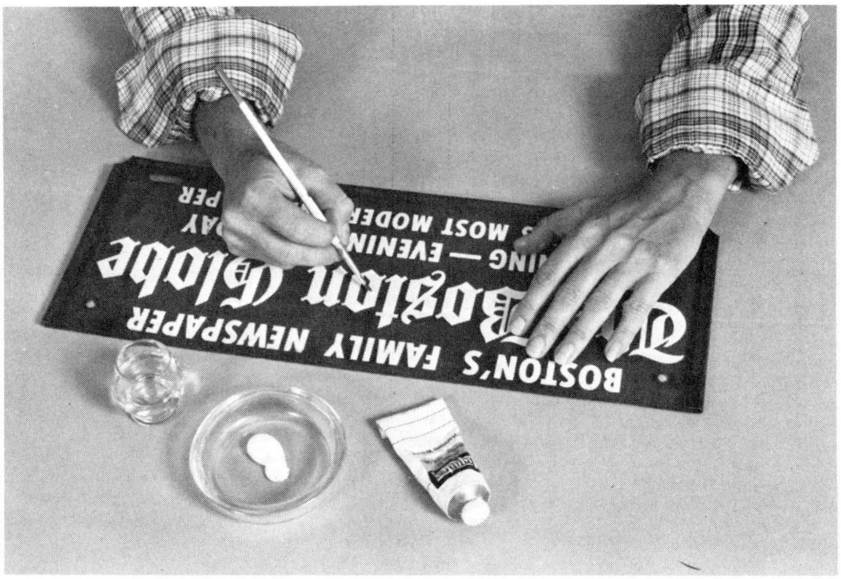

Retouching sign with matching paint color.

washable. The print used for this object was designed by Laura Ashley for the Raintree Collection.

The inside of this magazine stand is first spray painted with a contrasting color that goes with the wallpaper print. To do a similar project, measure all sides to be covered and cut out each piece of paper. The sides should be cut slightly wider than they actually are. In this way the paper can wrap around the edges. The other two pieces should be cut exactly to fit. Coat each section of paper with spray adhesive. This will make it easy to apply, enabling you to lift and reapply it if you don't do it correctly the first time. Trim any excess paper around the edges with a sharp razor blade.

The *Boston Globe* sign was badly scratched and needed a paint job. If this is the case with your project, mix the color you need with acrylic paint. Use a pointed artist's brush to touch up the paint where necessary. Next, center the sign on the side of the box and screw into the wood.

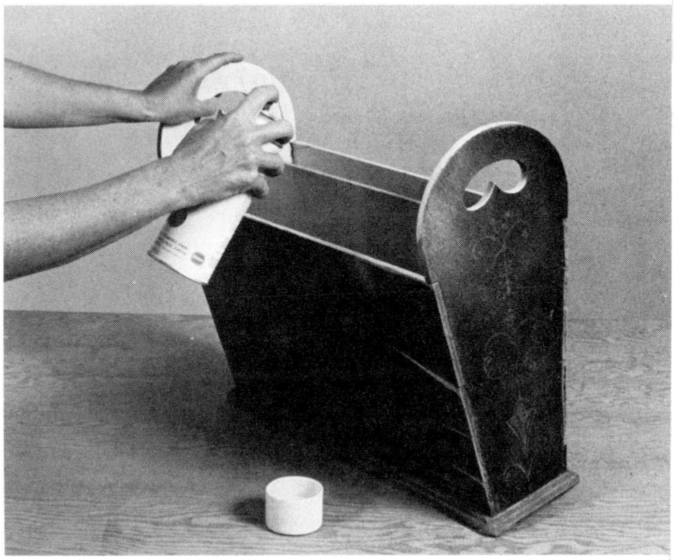

Sand and apply coat of spray paint.

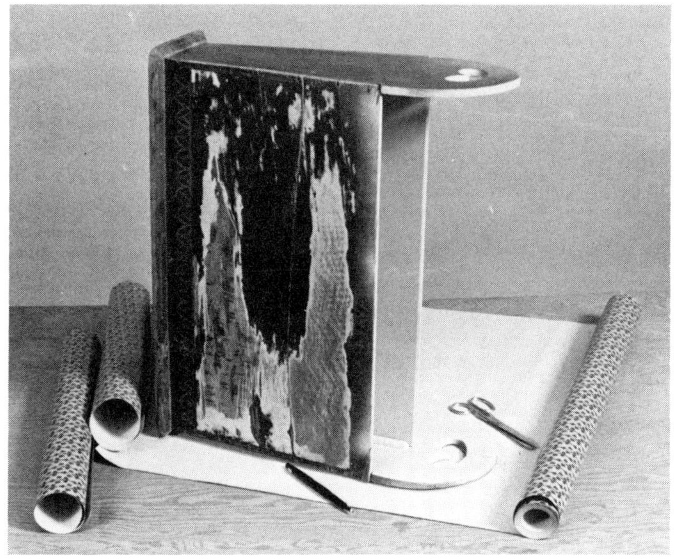

Measure and cut wallpaper pieces.

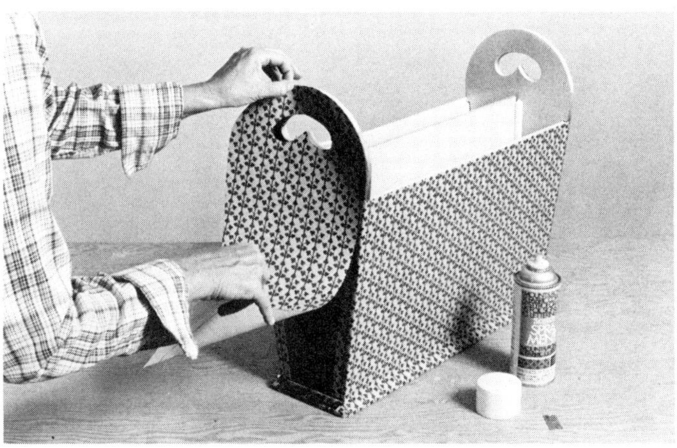

Spray adhesive aids in mounting paper.

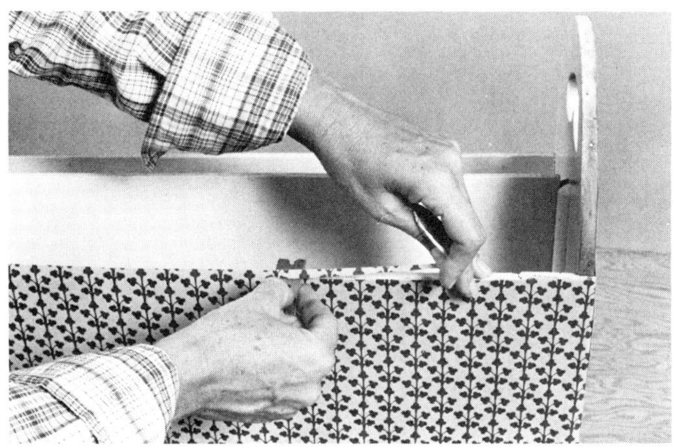

Trim excess with razor blade.

THE JIG IS UP

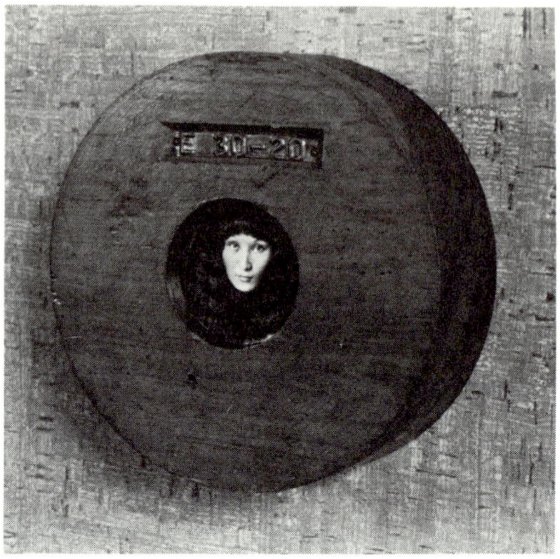

Foundry molds—hunks of wood in varying shapes and thicknesses—are always thrown away as scrap after a job is done. Lumberyards and dump yards frequently have piles of such scrap material, and with a little bit of creative thinking you can have a unique item for practically nothing. They are terrific for frames, planters, bookends, or whatever you can see in the pieces you find.

The first object I picked up was a round hunk of wood with a hole in the middle. It has a brass plate with numbers set into the front, which is interesting.

The dark brown round wood is unusual and makes a good picture frame for a small photograph that is set into the hole. Since it was very greasy, the piece was first washed and sanded, but the old shellac finish was left as is. If you find an old piece of wood you might prefer to sand the finish off so that the bare wood is exposed. The photograph was first mounted on a piece of cardboard and then inserted into the existing hole. In order to hang the frame flush against the wall, double-faced adhesive tabs were used.

IMAGE MAKER

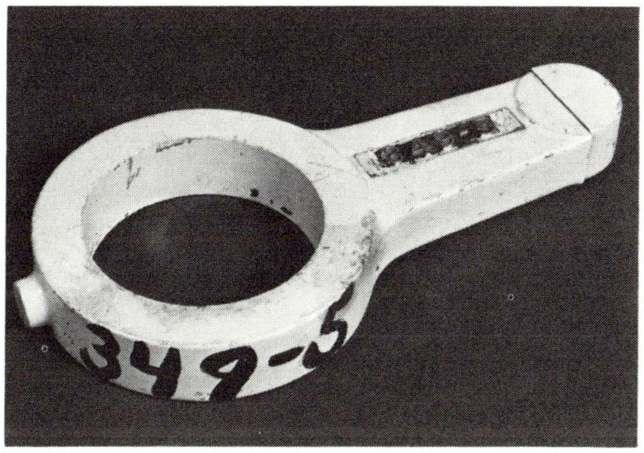

Unusual but nondescript pieces of wood are terrific to be used as frames. You are automatically starting with something that is different and commands attention. A mirror for the open space can be cut to any size by a glass cutter. This one is slightly larger than the opening. Having one cut to order is actually cheaper than finding one in a variety store. Place the mirror on the back of the frame and secure it with masking tape. Cut a piece of cardboard the size of the object and place it over the back of the mirror. With a staple gun staple the cardboard to the wood frame and it is ready to be hung. This can be done with picture wire or double-faced adhesive tabs. Any project like this is fun and easy to do and can become the focal point for other wall decorations. Design around your original creation.

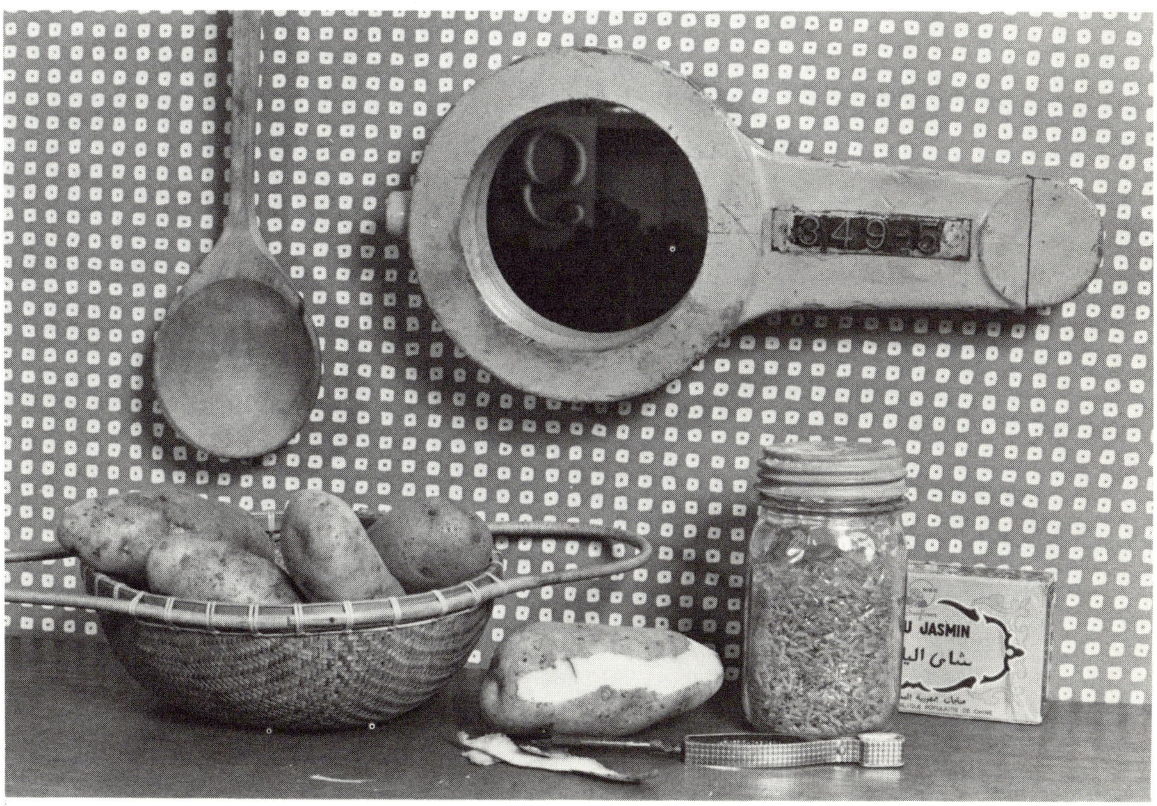

STORAGE & SPACE SAVERS

AT EASE

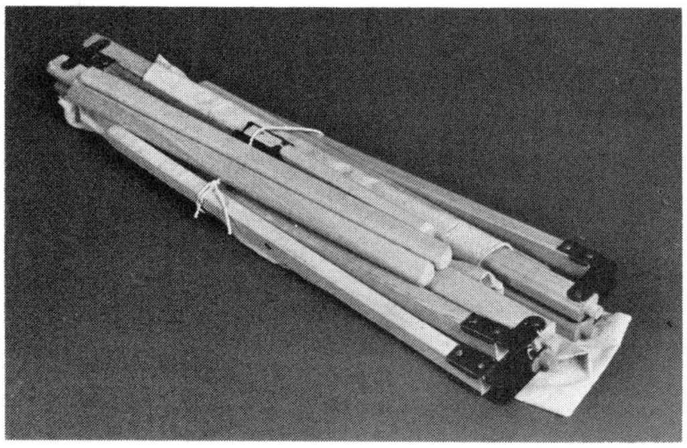

The ultimate space saver for a seating area, extra overnight guest, or relaxing on a porch or in the yard has got to be the fourteen-dollar fold-up cot. If you can find a used one, it should cost no more than a dollar. Available in Army & Navy stores, the folding cot has a slip-on cover made of duck. The overall size is 25″ × 76″ × 15½″, and it weighs 15 pounds. All three legs have metal reinforcements. The entire frame is made of high-grade, dry, Northern-grown hardwood. The legs and side rails are of substantial size to insure proper strength and rigidity. All metal fittings are baked green enamel, and the whole thing folds up very compactly for quick and easy storage. The duck covering is natural color and is specially woven for extra strength. There is also a smaller size available for a child; any child can erect and fold it up easily. When used as is, the cot is not very appeal-

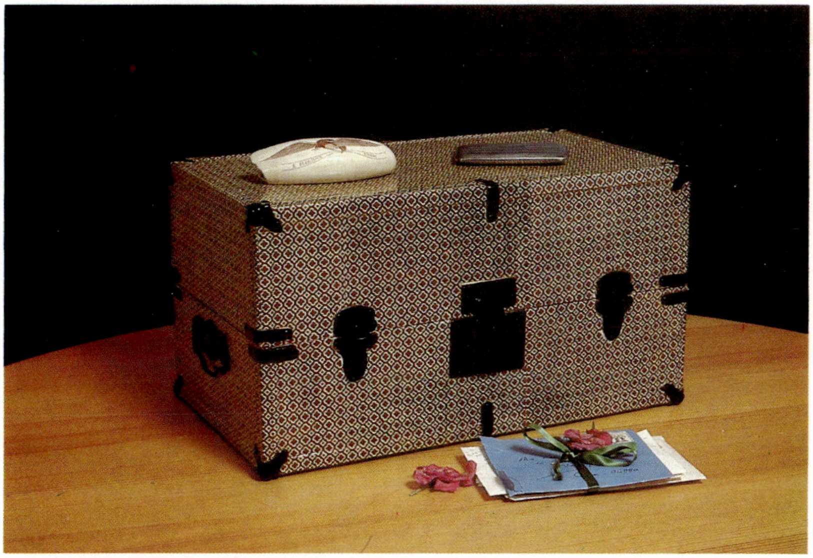

Wallpaper-covered trunk.

Fabric-covered apple barrel.

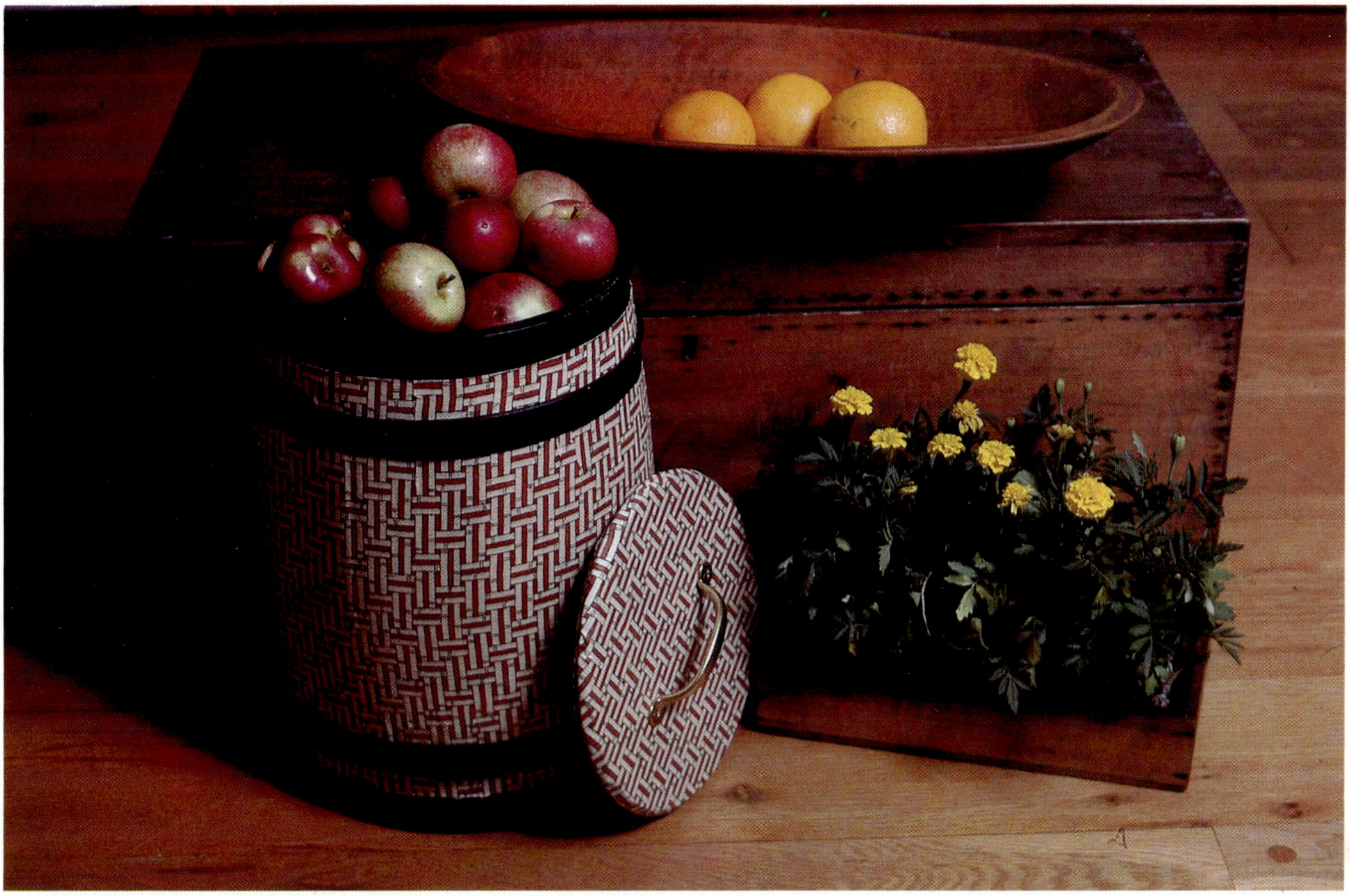

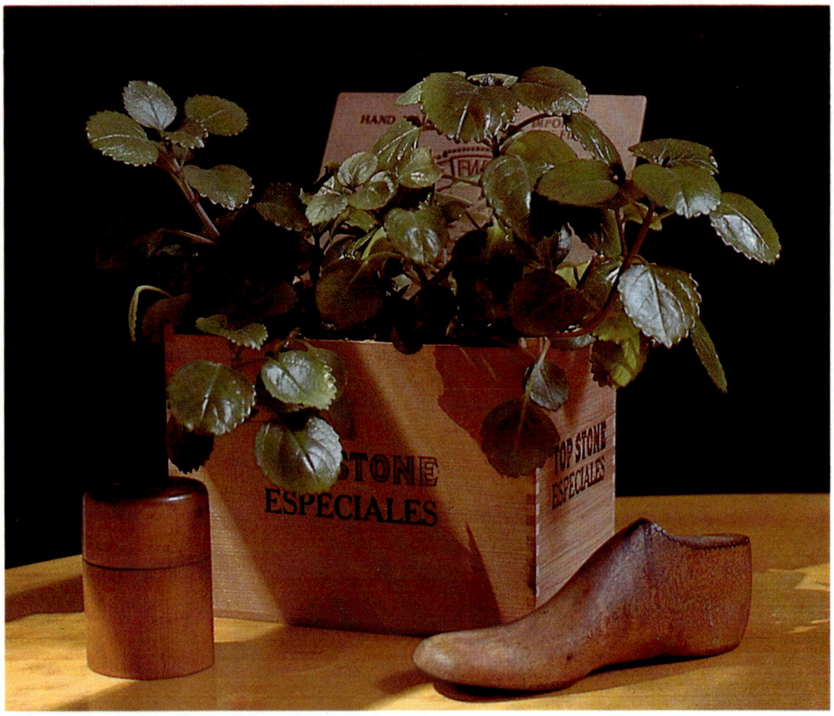

Cigar-box plant holder.

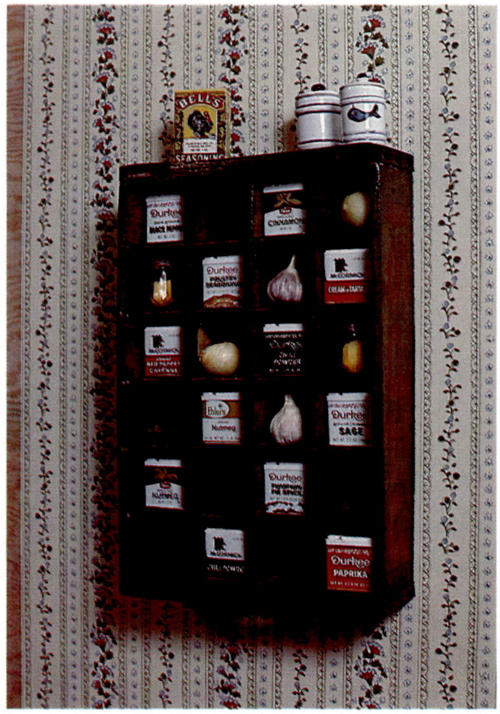

Pepsi-carton spice rack.

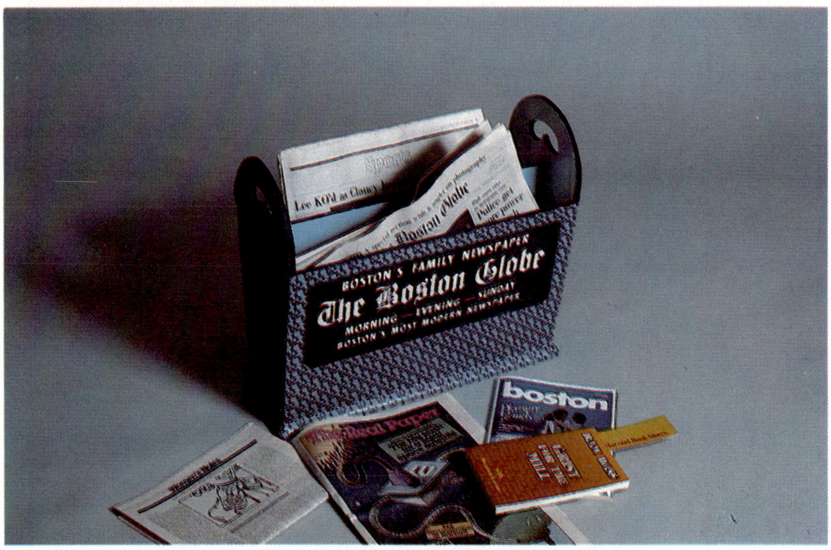

Wallpaper and old sign give new life to magazine stand.

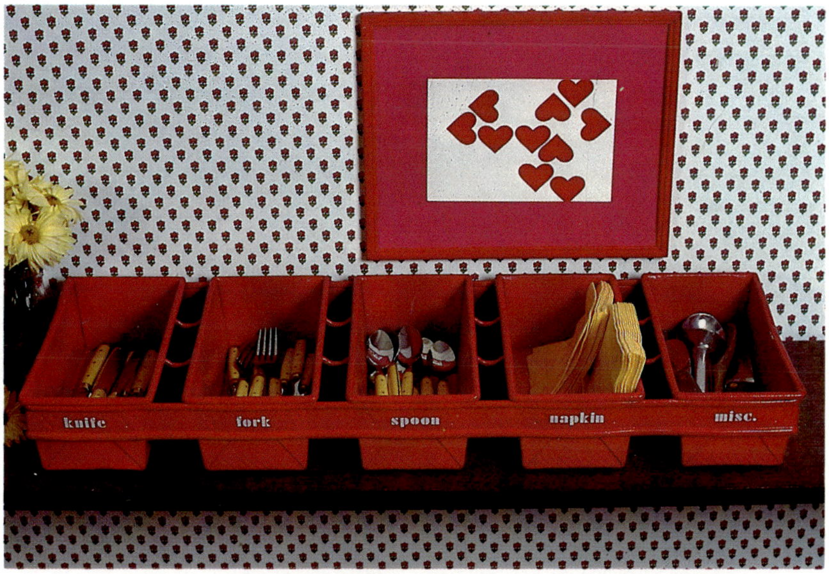

Baker's loaf pans transformed.

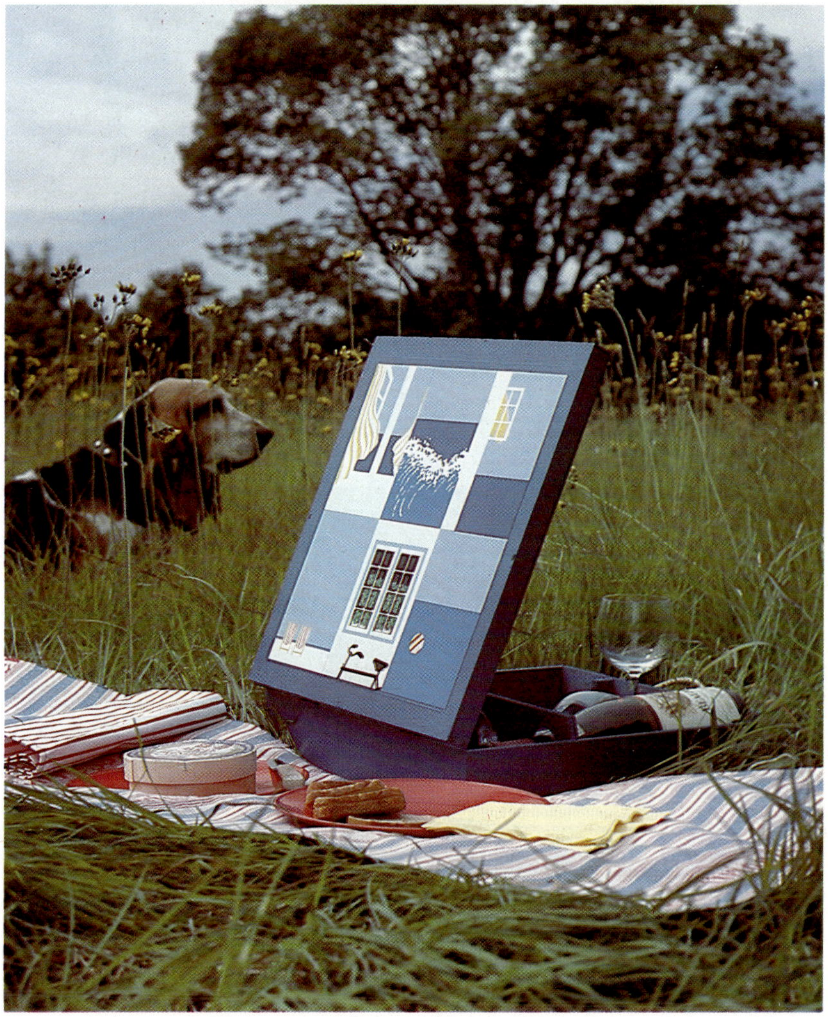

Wine-box picnic basket decorated with postcard art.

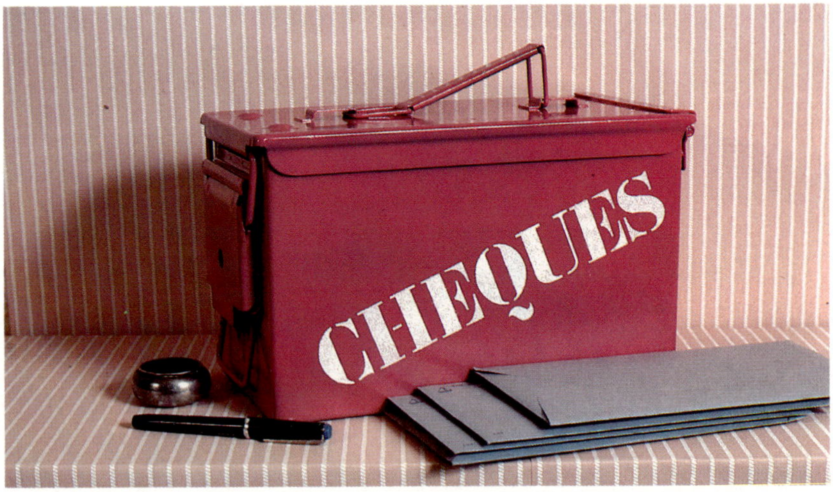

Fifty-caliber ammo box has many uses.

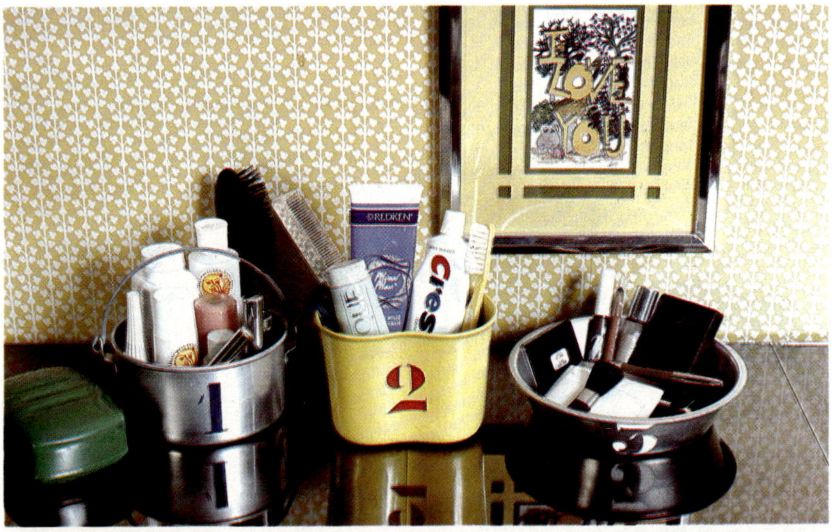

Double life for a canteen mess kit.

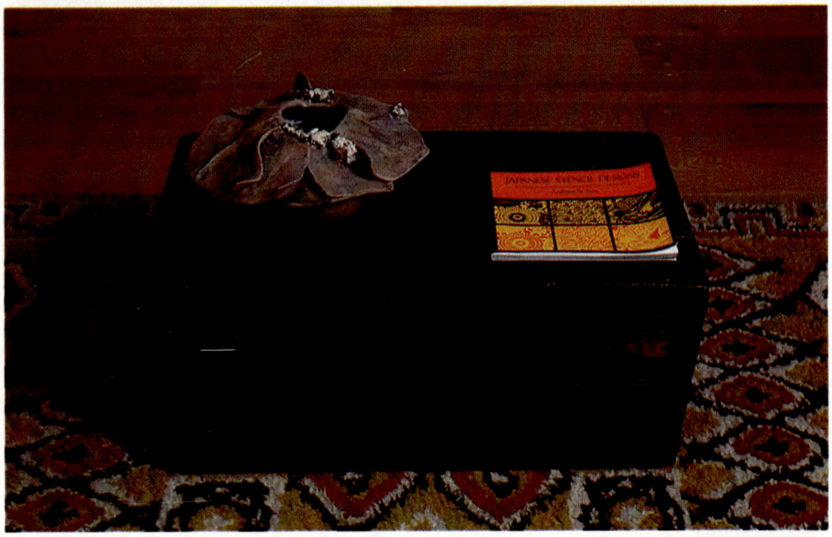

Stained pine box made into a table.

Pint-size milk bottles for starting plants.

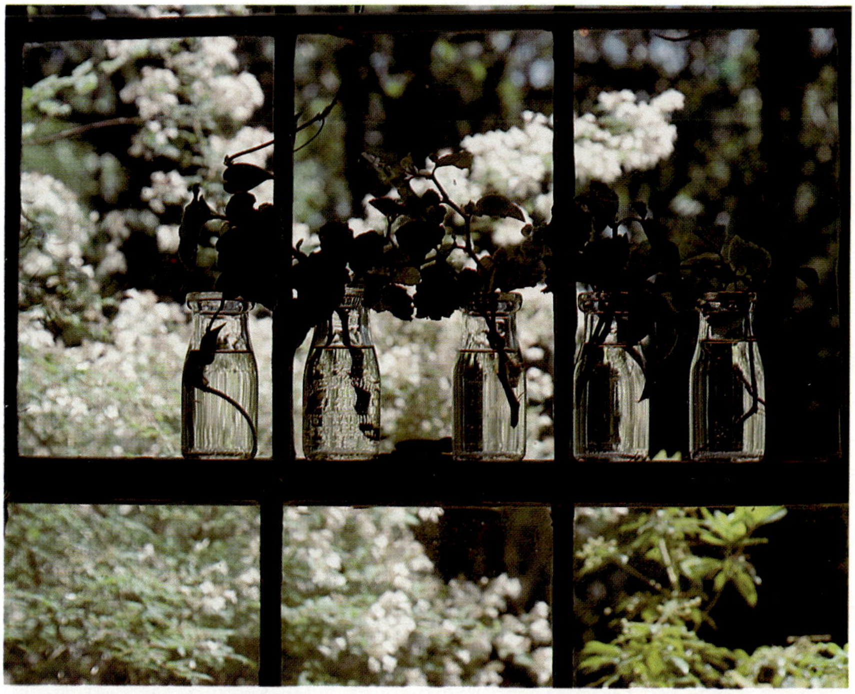

Wash basin, dish towels, and found objects for table setting.

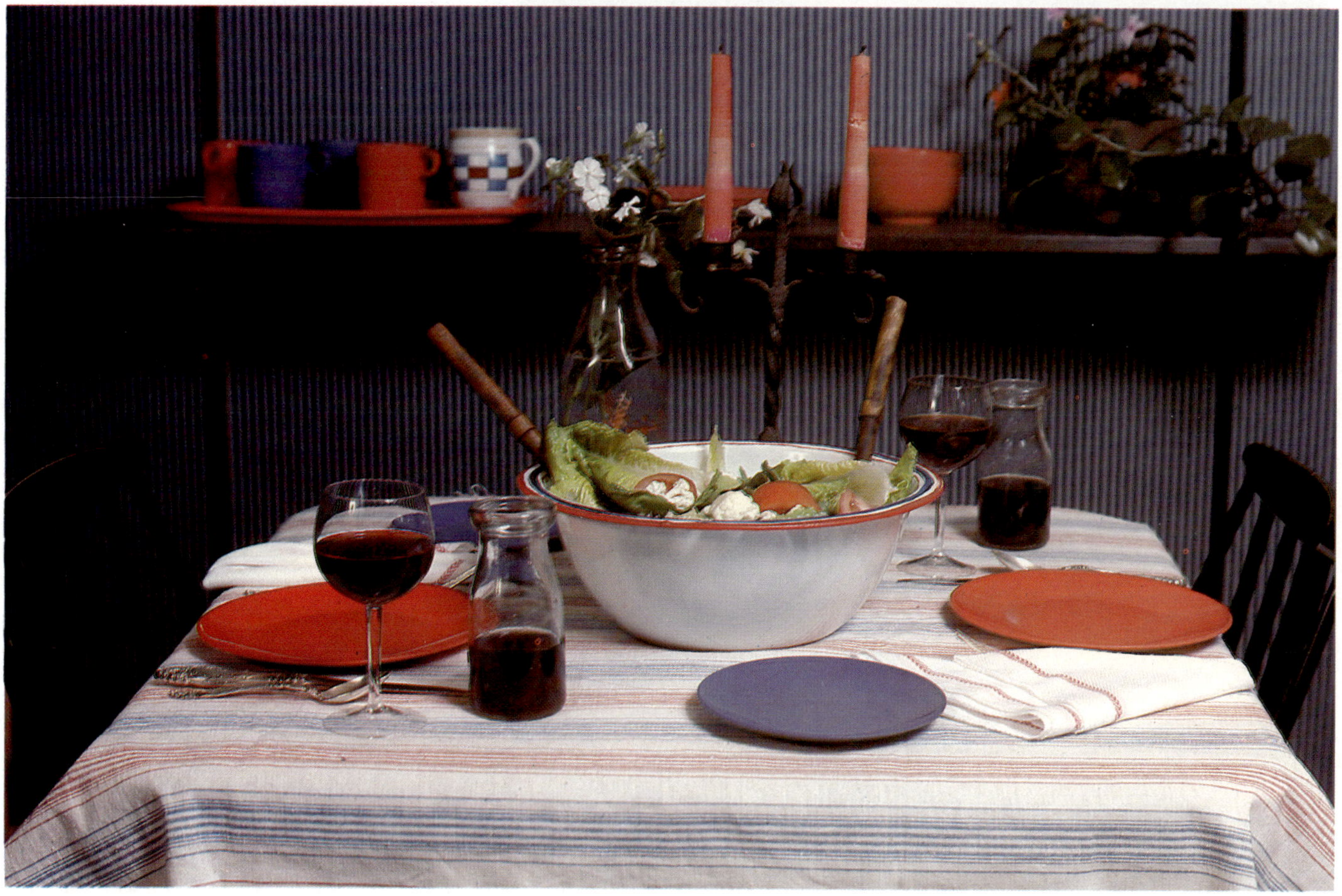

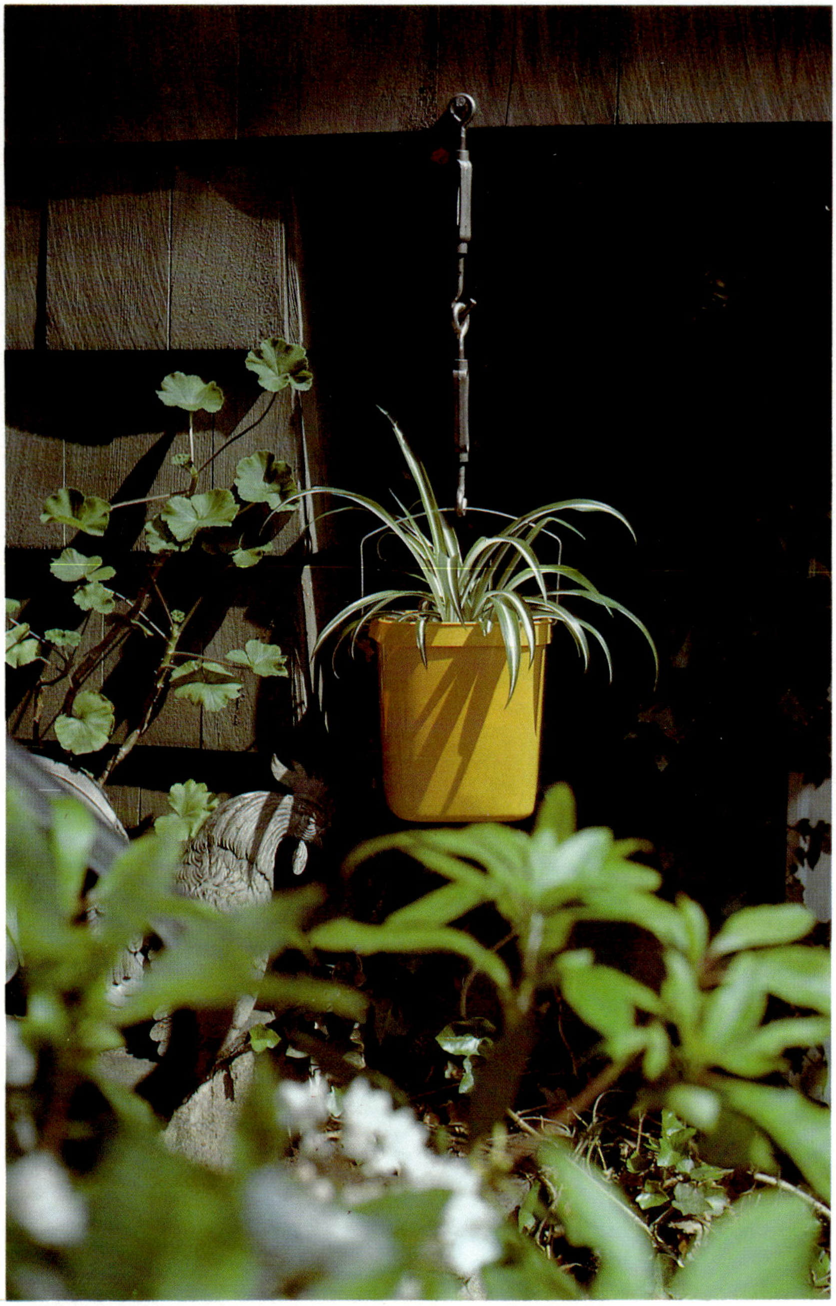

Paint-bucket plant holder hangs from tension hooks.

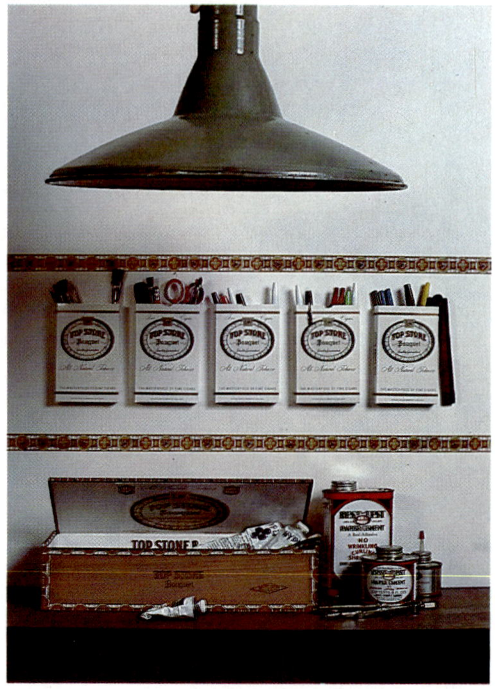

Decorative cigar-box storage.

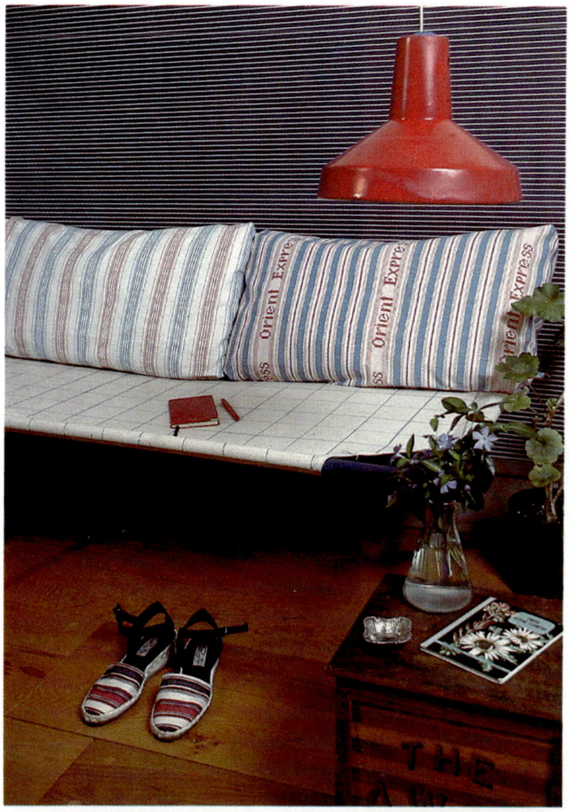

Spruced-up cot for inexpensive seating.

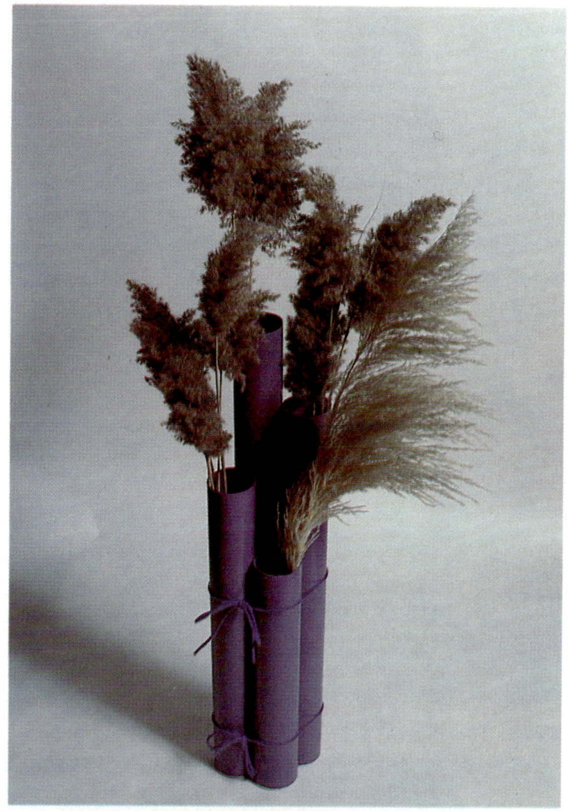

Plastic plumbing tubes hold dried weeds.

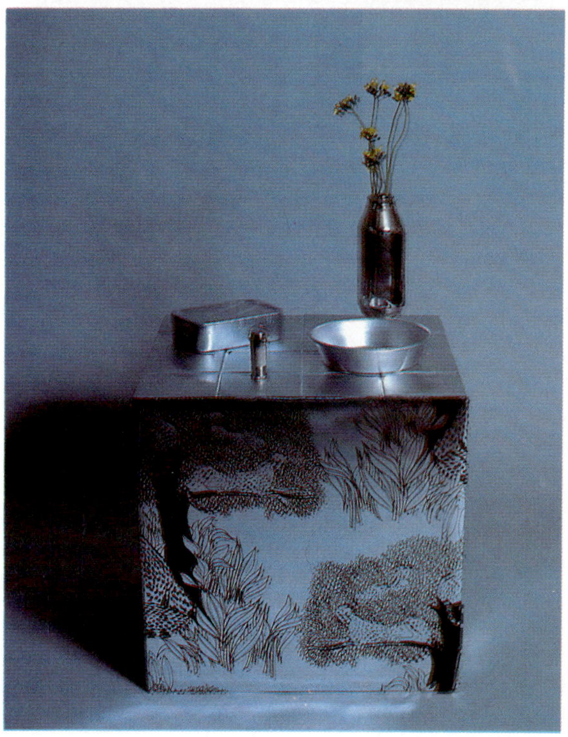

The elegance of simple items.

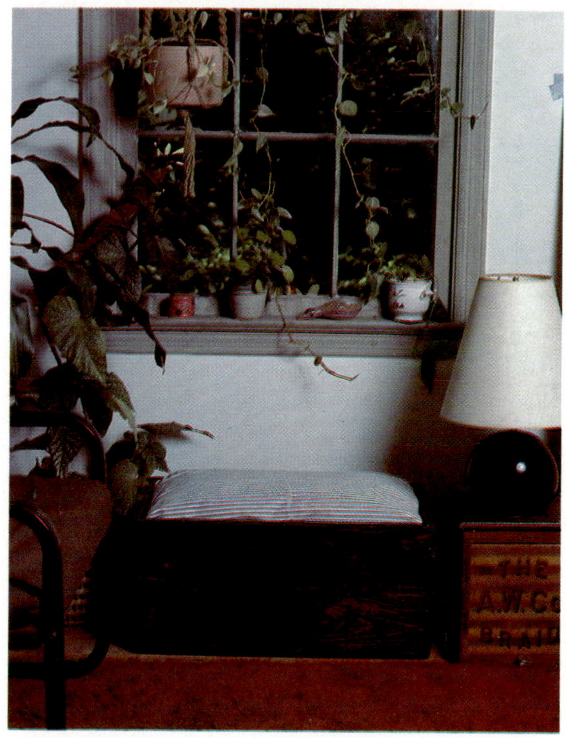

Pine box and army pillow seat.

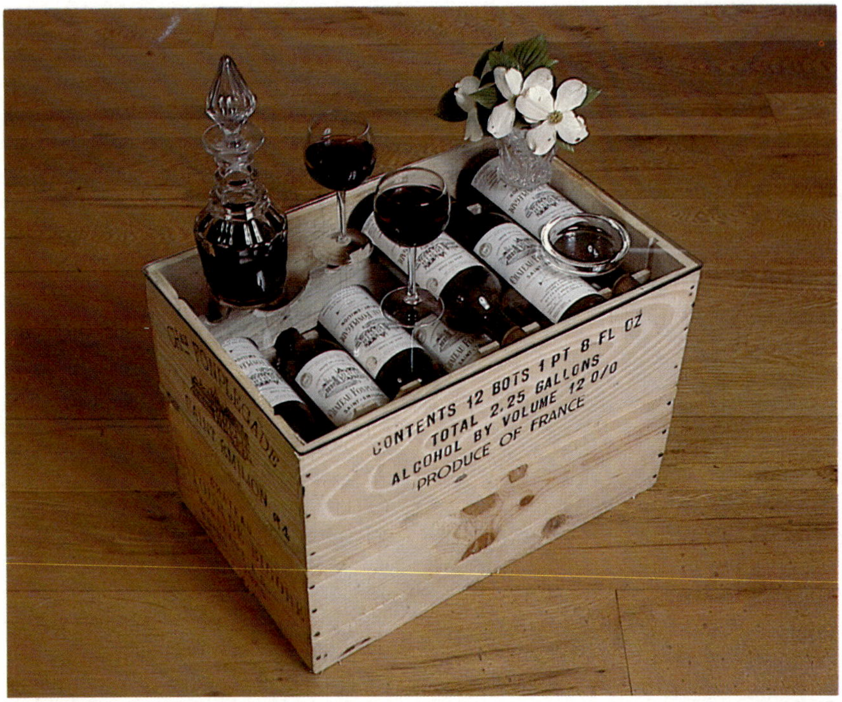

Wine-carton coffee table.

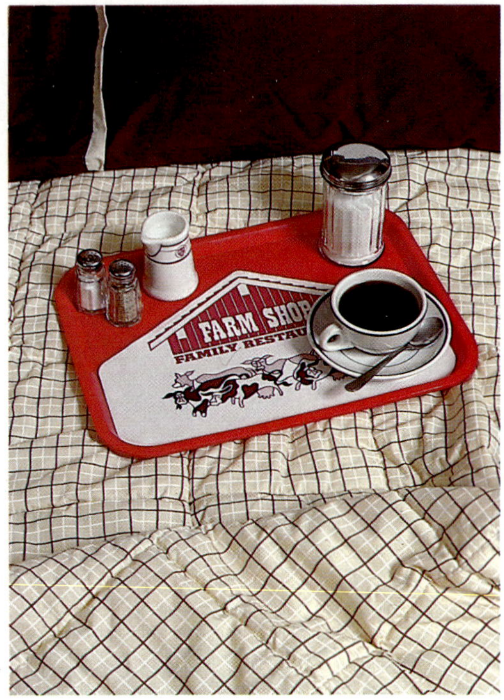

Restaurant supplies are sturdy and basically good looking.

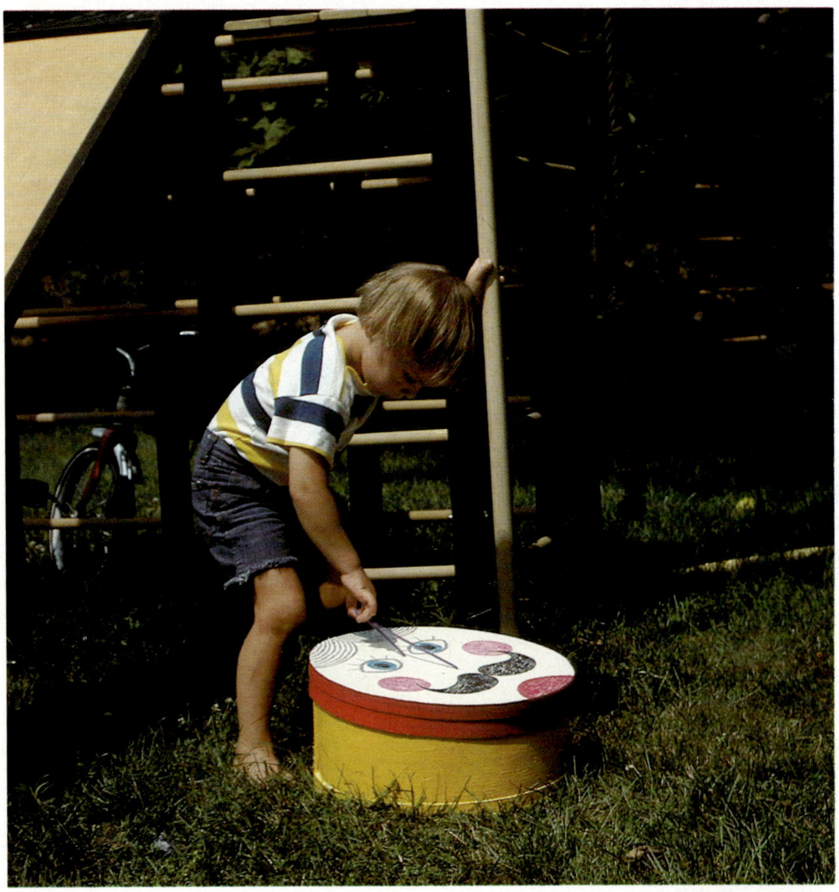

Old cheese-box toy organizer.

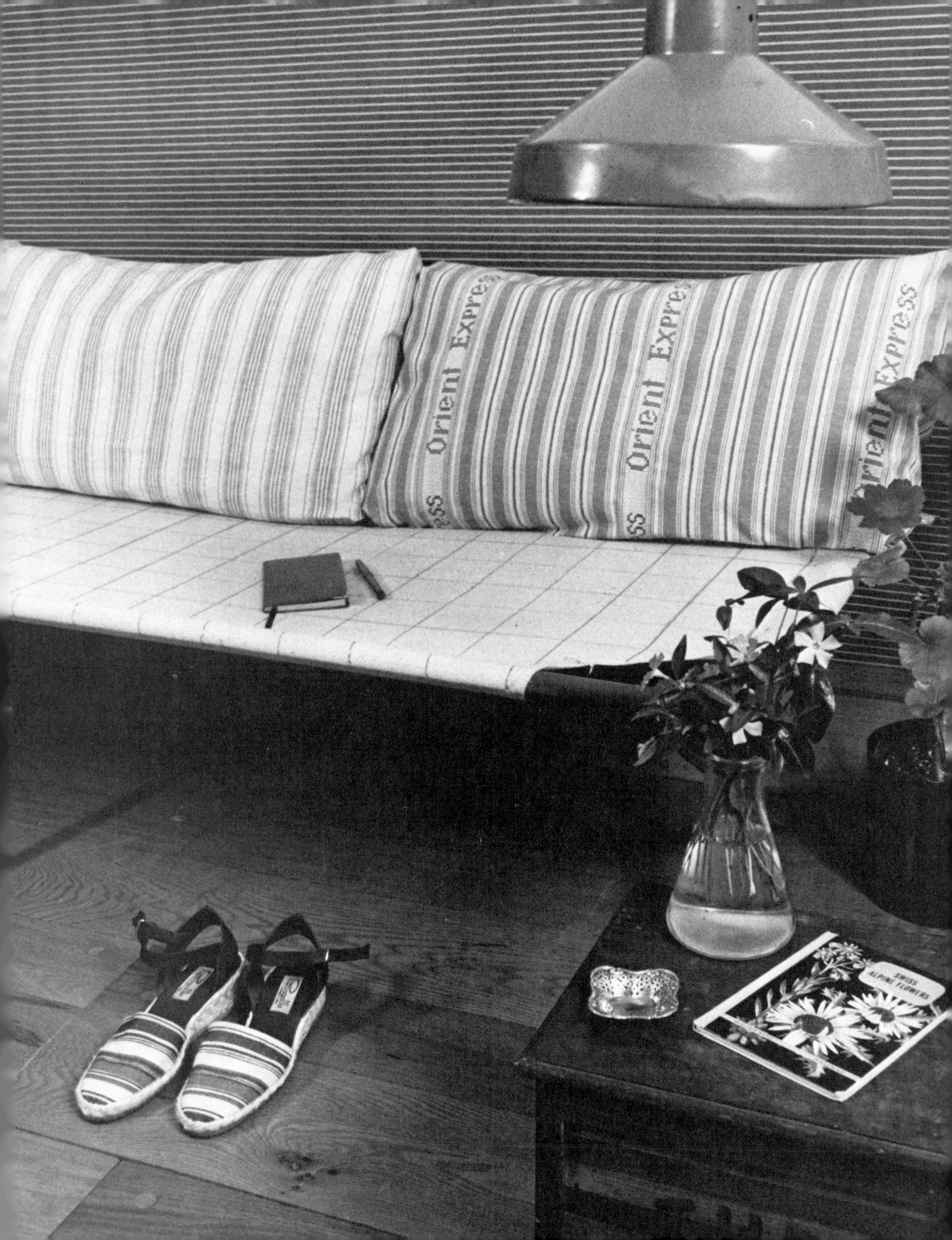
Orient Express
SWISS ALPINE FLOWERS

ing as a home decorator item. However, potential exists, and without much effort this standard object can be transformed into a very attractive addition to any room where light furniture and a short budget exists.

The duck covering may be called a slip-on cover, but it doesn't slip off. Therefore, one must be extremely careful when painting the frame. Cover the duck with newspapers and spray paint the frame. True blue enamel color was used for this cot frame. Let this dry thoroughly and recoat if necessary. The paint will immediately change the look of the cot so that it seems more respectable. Next, rule off squares with a pencil on the duck. Then place a long, flat stick on the cot running from one end to the other and resting on the ends. Use a fabric marker to color the stripes. Rest your hand against the stick in order to steady it as you draw the marker along the pencil line. Move the stick over as you do each new line. Then turn the stick so that it rests on either side and repeat the process. The marker color should match the painted frame.

For the pillows, select fabric that has the same feeling in design as the cot. The French dishtowel fabric, delicate stripes, or a small calico print are all good. Either cover pillows that will fit on the cot or make cases and stuff them with shredded foam rubber. Place the finished cot against a back wall for support, and there you have the ultimate in inexpensive couches. For another space-saving idea, replace pillows with the sea bag bolster (see page 111).

The hanging lamp was purchased for 50 cents at a junkyard, where a lighting manufacturer had discarded a number of dented or scratched lamp parts. A quick coating of Flame Red spray enamel, a bulb, socket, and wire made it as good

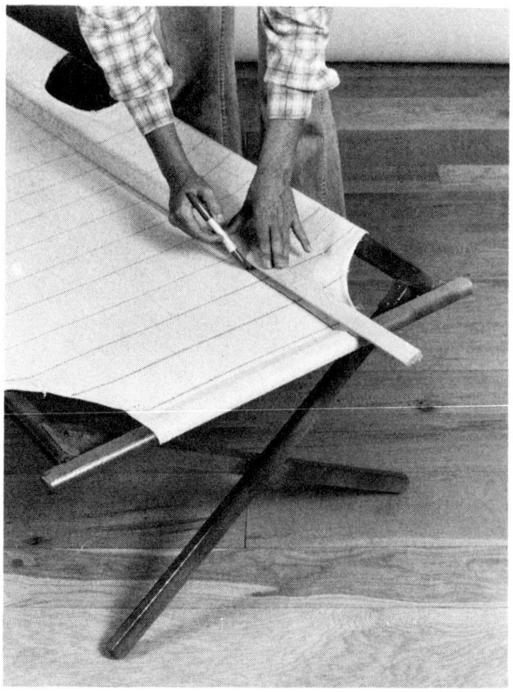

Rule off lines and draw with colorful marker.

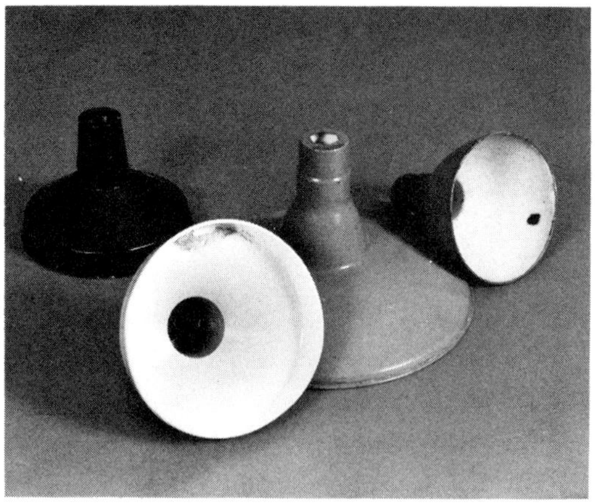

Damaged lamp hoods are retrieved and restored for hanging lamps.

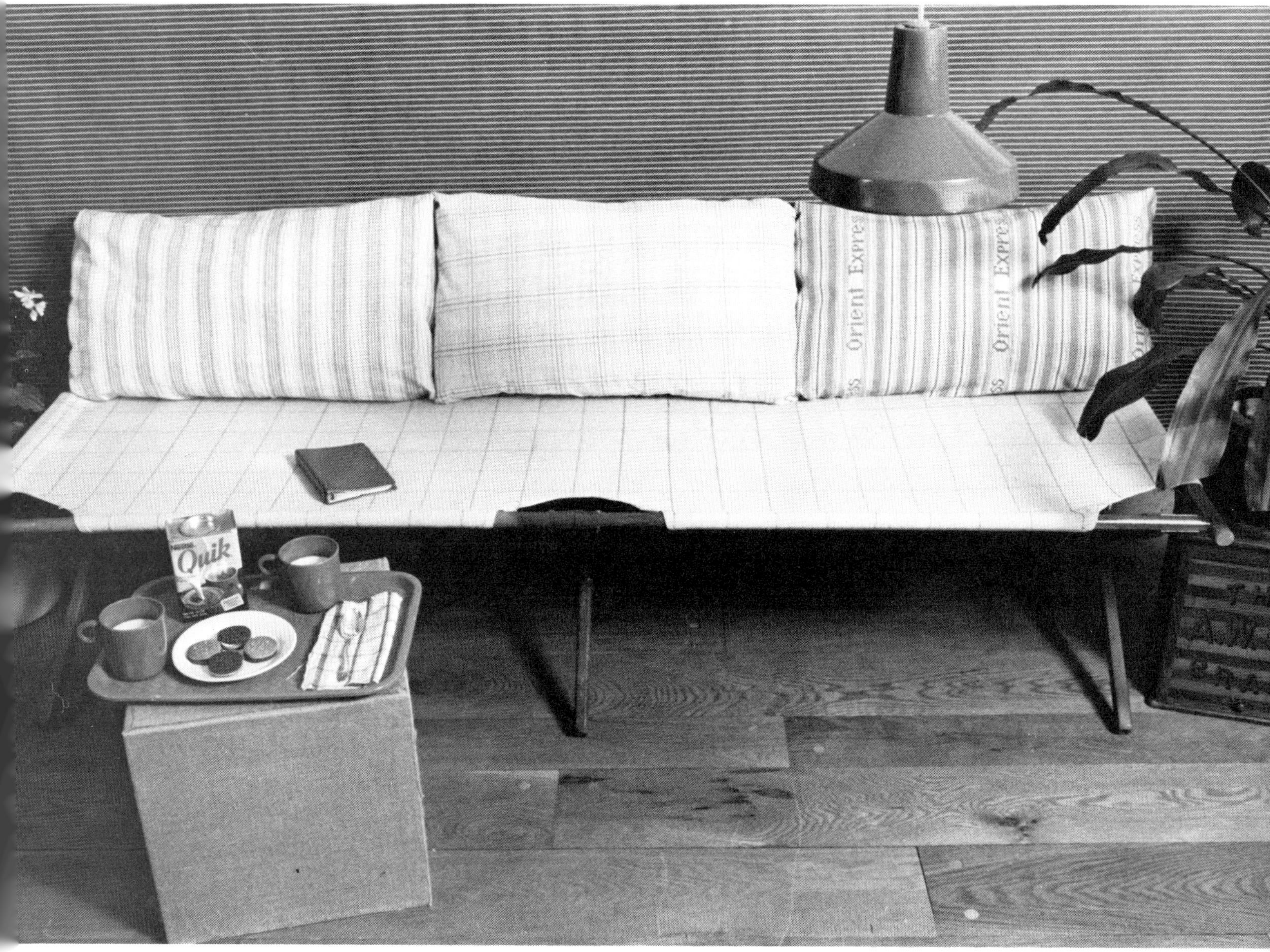

as new. A royal-blue plastic grommet was used on the top, through which the wire cord was threaded. A red plastic tray from a fast-food cafeteria and red-and-blue plastic mugs complete the effect.

CAMPY SEATING

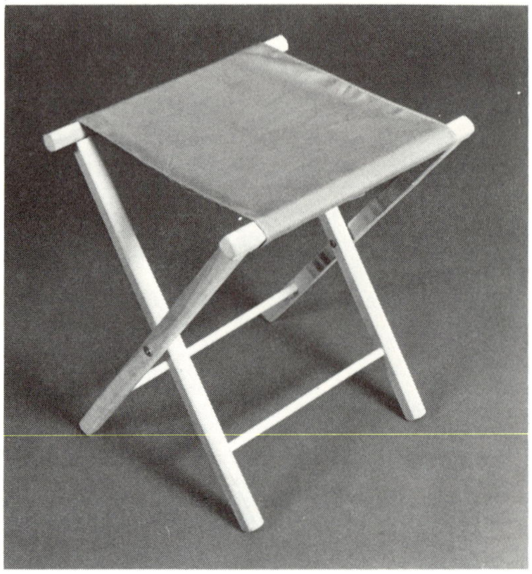

There is nothing more basic than the fold-up wooden camp seat often referred to as a "Maine Woods" stool. This is a two-dollar seat that hikers and campers carry with them on trips. It is not as fancy as its more contemporary version, the golfer's folding seat, which is more sophisticated in both design and price. The frame of the camper's seat is made from seasoned hardwood in a natural finish. A strip of canvas duck is stretched across the top and stapled under the wood. Weighing only ten ounces, the seat folds flat for easy storage. Since the wood is natural and the canvas is usually a neutral color, there is nothing particularly outstanding to commend this item as a home furnishing piece. However, like the cot, it has a lot of potential for a little time, imagination, and money.

The piece of canvas is easily removed and the frame can be spray painted in a bright color. With the smashing designs found on canvas today, it isn't difficult to find bright, bold material to replace the old. Less than half a yard is needed. By redoing several frames, you can create extra pull-up seating for an outdoor patio or to carry with you to an outdoor sports event. It is not especially comfortable for any length of time, but it is perfect for a child to use at the beach.

The seat area is about the size of a needlepoint pillow canvas. If you do needlepoint, this would make an interesting project. Paint the frame to match the design and use the seat as a stand for a lucite tray. Since the tray is clear, the needlepoint will show through when not in use.

I especially like the seats when grouped in a child's room. Either line them up along the wall or gather them around a small table. Our seat is designed so that the balloons continue right up onto the wall. You might consider a similar

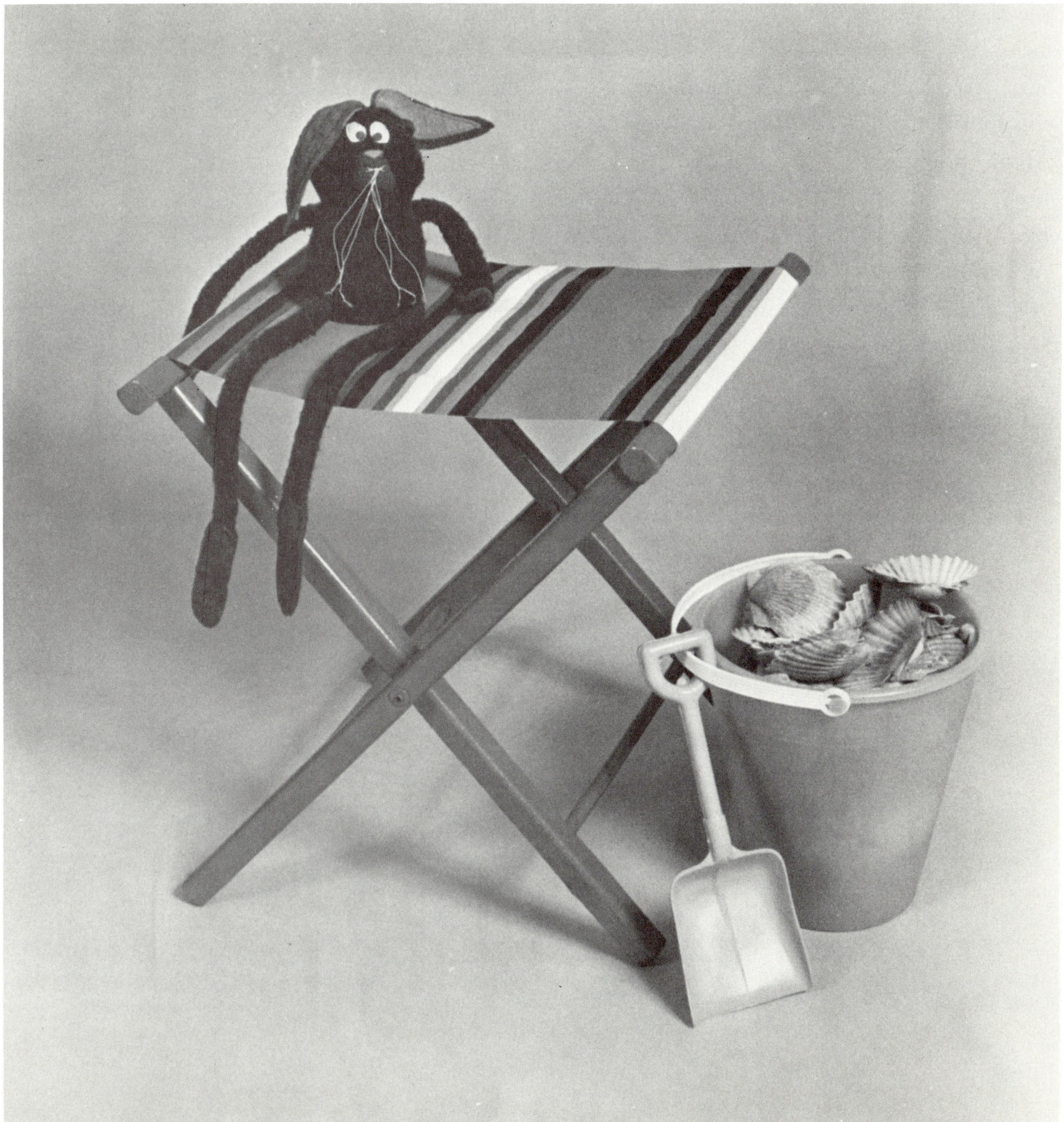

design, which is very easy to do. Cover the frame with white duck. Heavy-duty staples hold the fabric onto the frame. Next, trace a design and transfer it to the seat. Color it in with fabric markers. The ones used here are made by the Sanford Company. If the markers you are using do not specify use on fabric, test one on a scrap to be sure that the color won't bleed. The continuation of this design was done with the markers as well, but you could apply it with an artist's brush and acrylic paint. The clouds were added after the balloons were colored in.

For a variation line three or four camp seats along a wall and create a design that starts on the first and continues on the next. The color of the frame and the seats can be changed as often as you like, as it is simple and inexpensive to do.

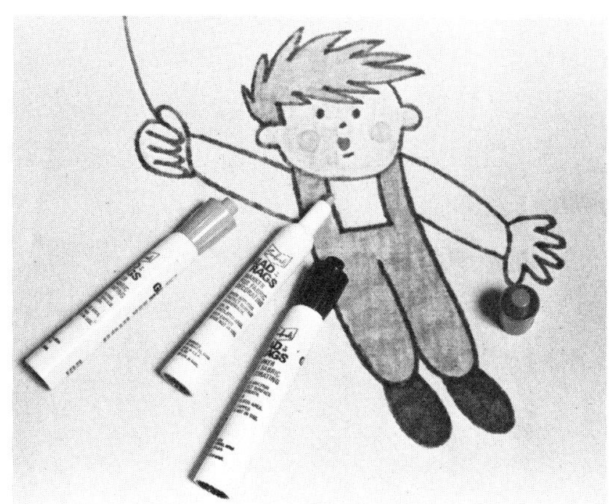

Color in design with fabric markers.

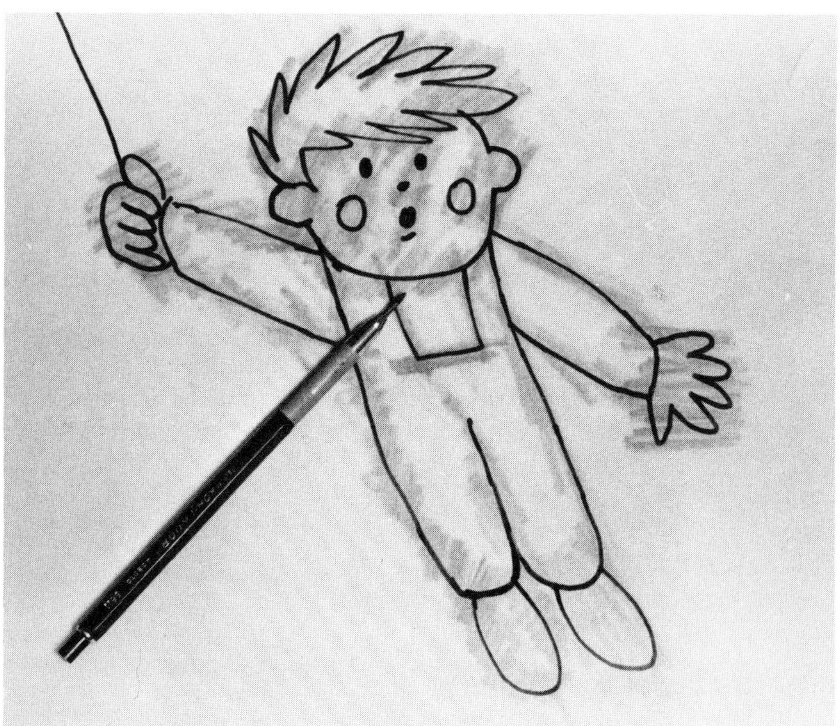

Trace and transfer design.

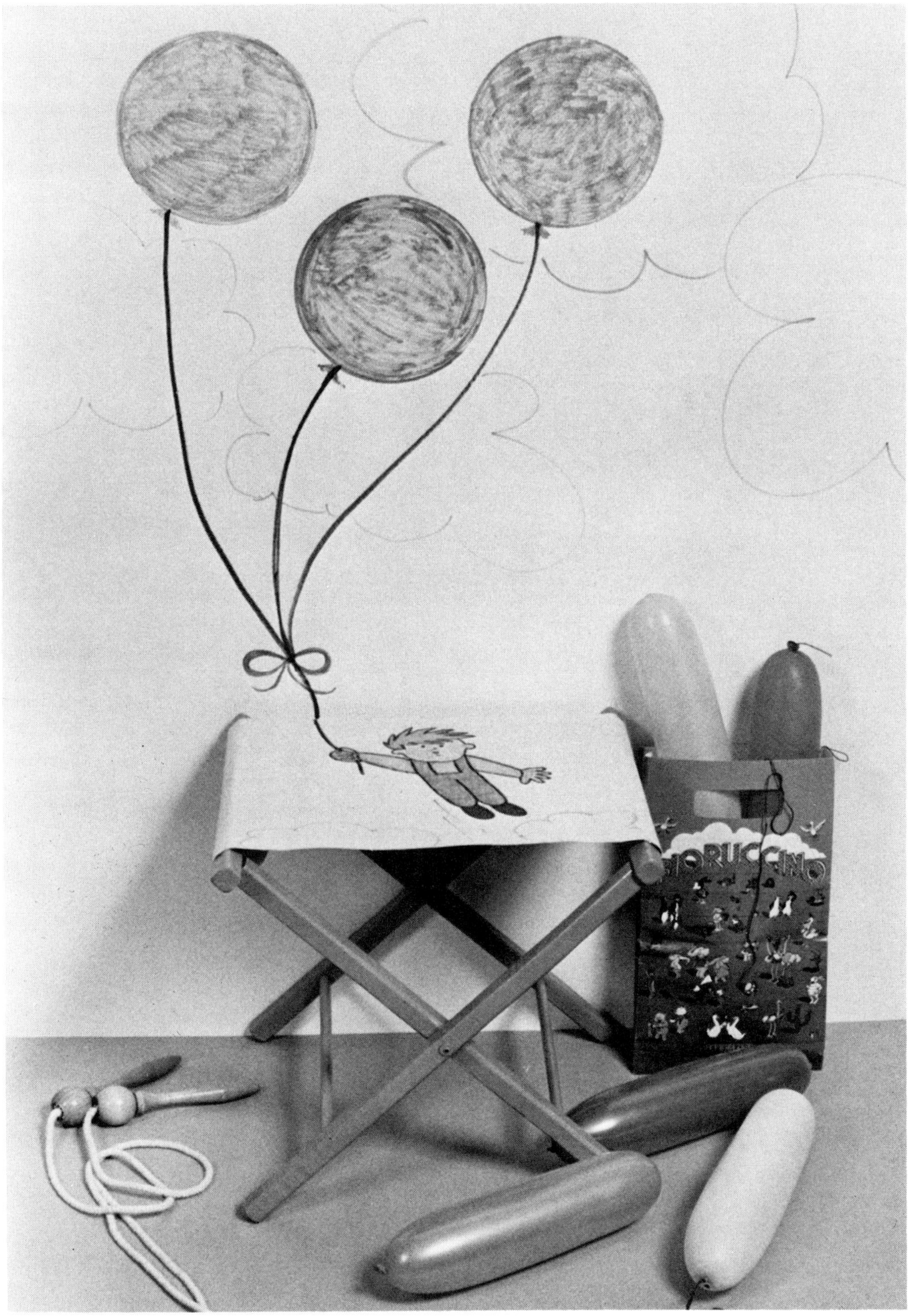
IORUCCINO

A CASE FOR BASKETS

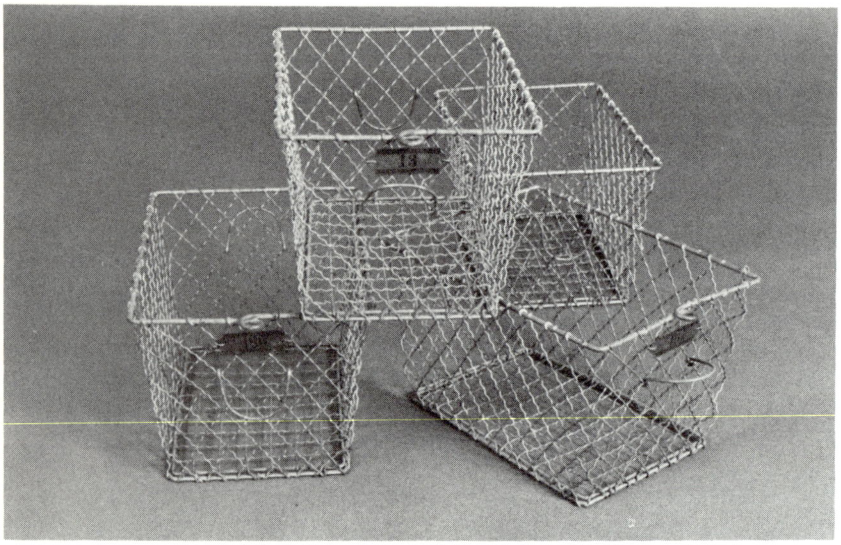

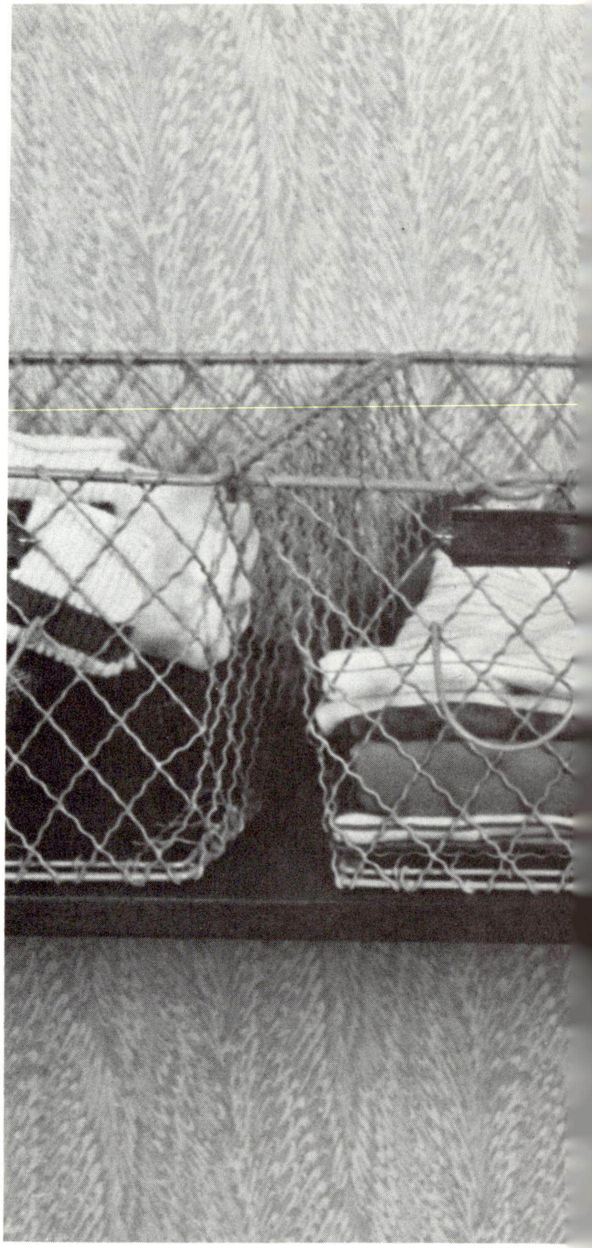

Wire YMCA baskets are excellent for clothes organizers on a closet shelf. But they needn't be tucked away out of sight. They are so good-looking when spruced up with a coating of spray paint that they should be displayed on an open shelf. These baskets were dirty and rusty and the metal number tags were blackened with age. A bit of steel wool and elbow grease refurbished them as good as new, and they were then painted a subtle beige. They can be stacked one on top of the other or lined across side by side. For more decoration, each could be woven with ribbon and lace trims until the sides are covered. Wrecking companies may be a good place to locate them. Or ask at your local YMCA. These baskets are often replaced with individual lockers. If you can't find the wire ones, wicker baskets can be used the same way. You might paint each a different color or corresponding colors. Plastic garment boxes are another way to organize clothes and shoes in the closet. Try labeling each container with large press-on type found in art-supply stores.

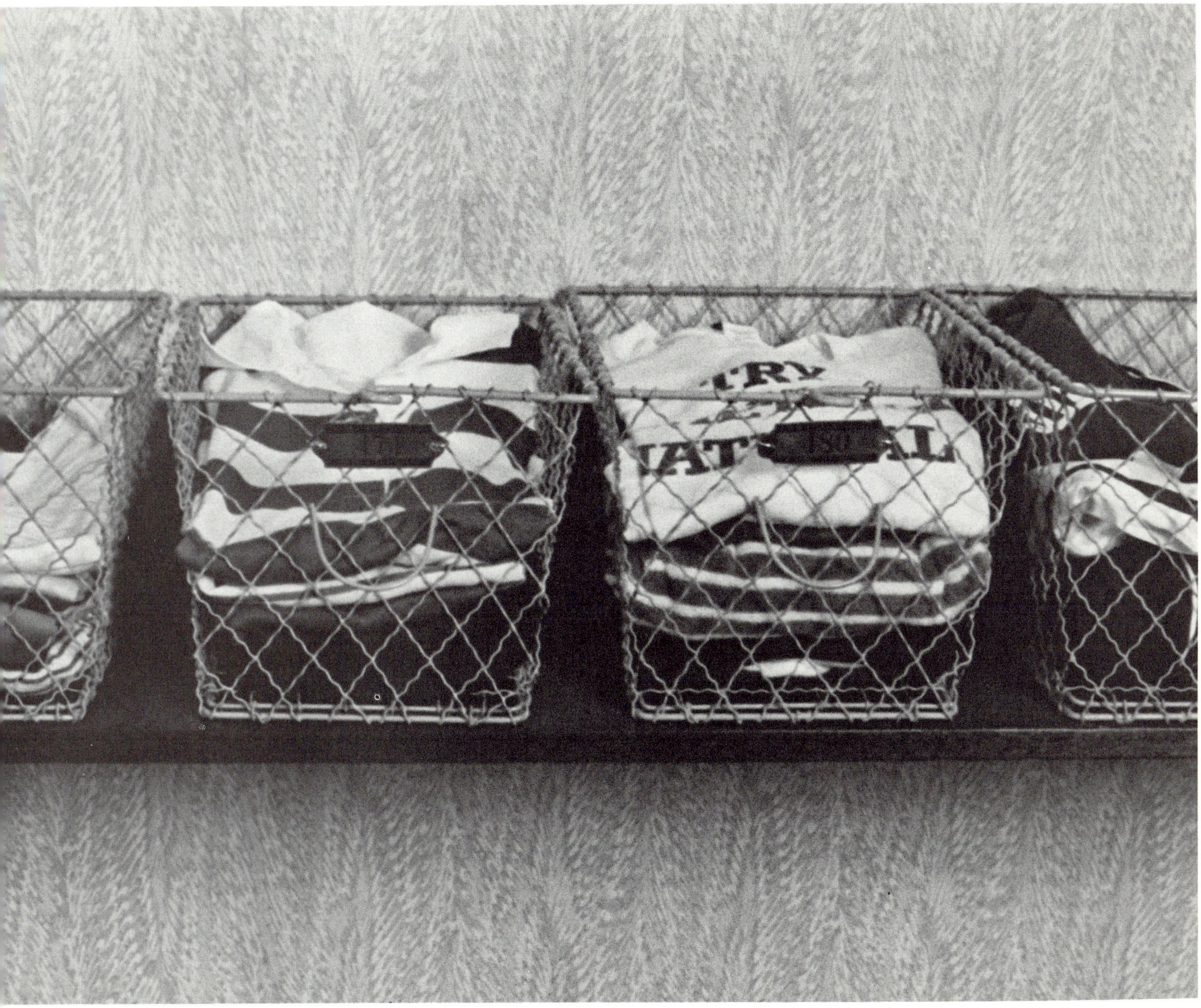

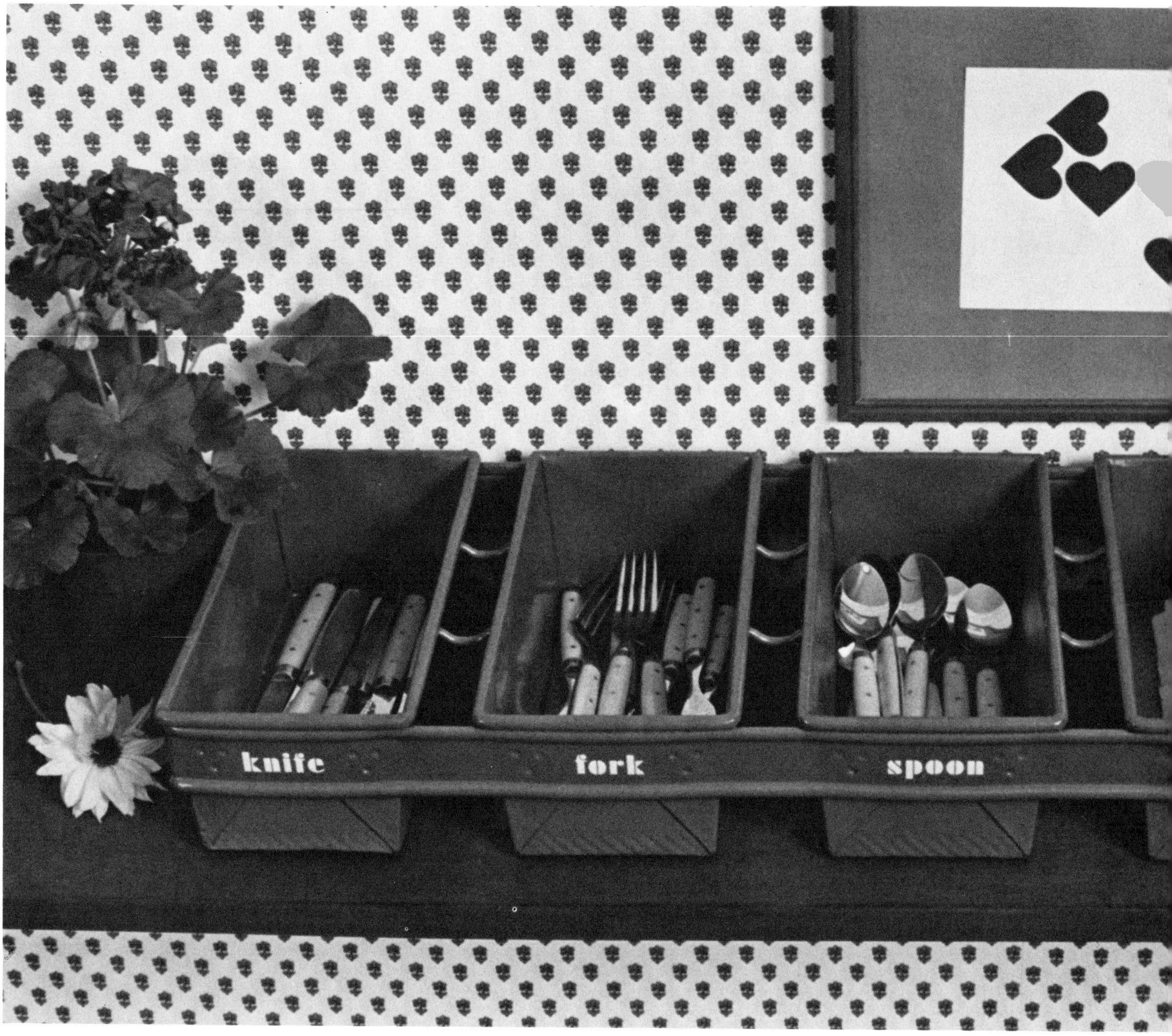
knife
fork
spoon

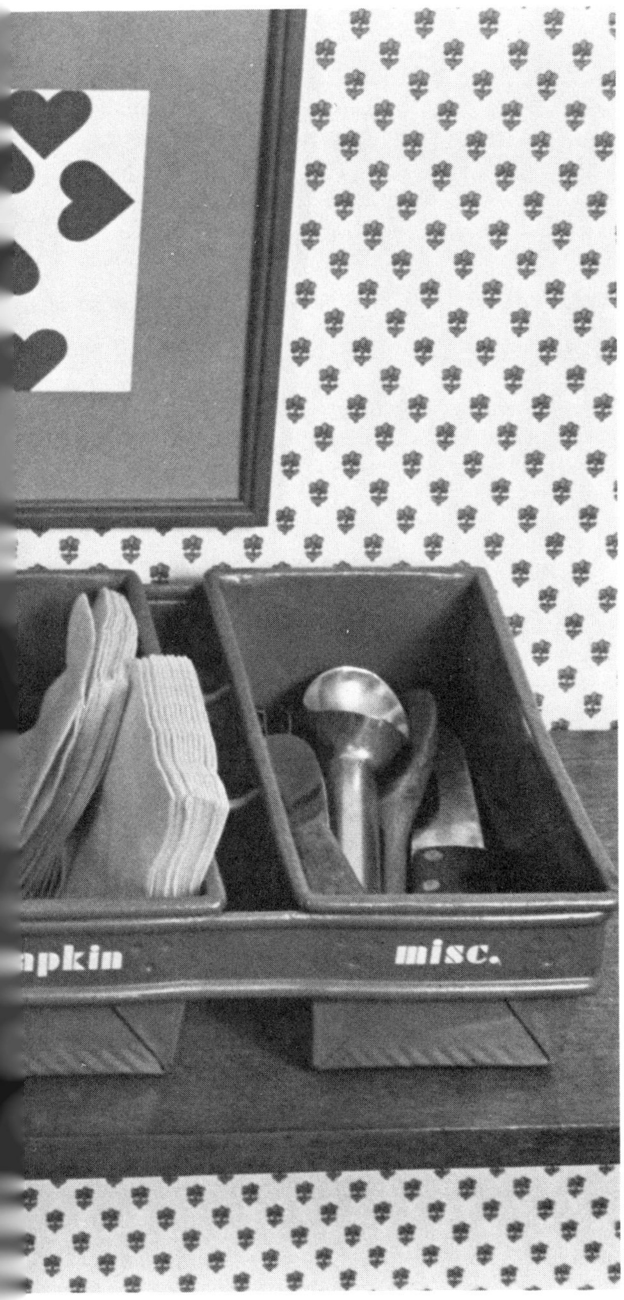

NOT FOR BREAD ALONE

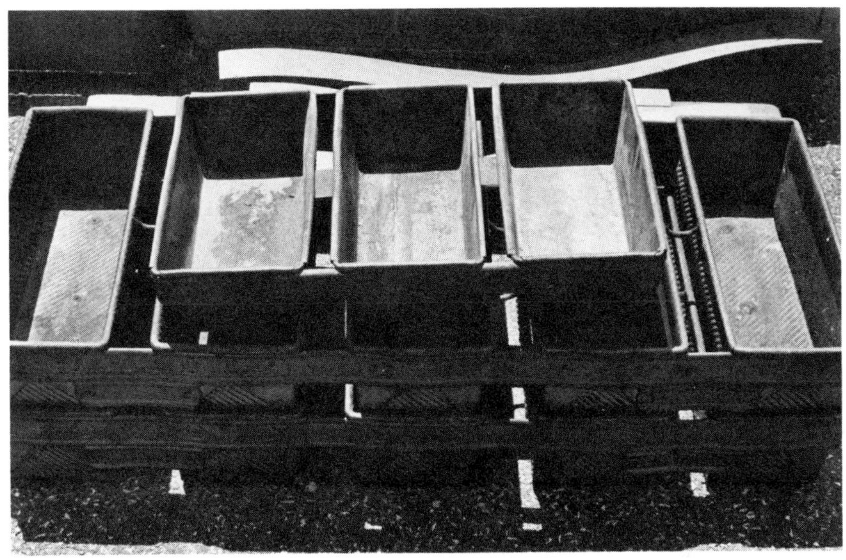

Restaurant supply houses sell everything you can think of for restaurant use and lots of things you can't. Pots larger than any you've ever seen, soda fountain equipment, baking materials for assembly-line production are but a few. The new equipment is most appealing, but outrageously expensive, if you aren't opening a restaurant. However, you can usually find used items that are often reasonably priced. You will need an open mind in order to think creatively on the spot since there is no telling what you will find. It isn't as though you go out one morning with the idea of finding a ten-gallon soda pump. If you run across a stack of pie-cooling racks selling for a dollar apiece it might be a terrific find, but if you can't begin to imagine what to use them for you will surely pass up such a bargain.

Bake shops use metal loaf pans that are attached so that five loaves can be put in and taken from the oven at once. When I stumbled across some of these, I couldn't think of a use for them. However, their shape and character were such that I knew an idea would come if I had them at home. Sometimes an object is not as appealing when there are many, many other things fighting for attention. Take it home and suddenly it becomes more interesting. The size of these loaf pans is handy for office use, as a tool holder, for craft materials, sewing equipment, or to organize small items in a child's room. For an open kitchen shelf it's also a very convenient space saver for holding silverware and cooking utensils. The graphic design is created with press-on letters that fit neatly and add a note of practicality.

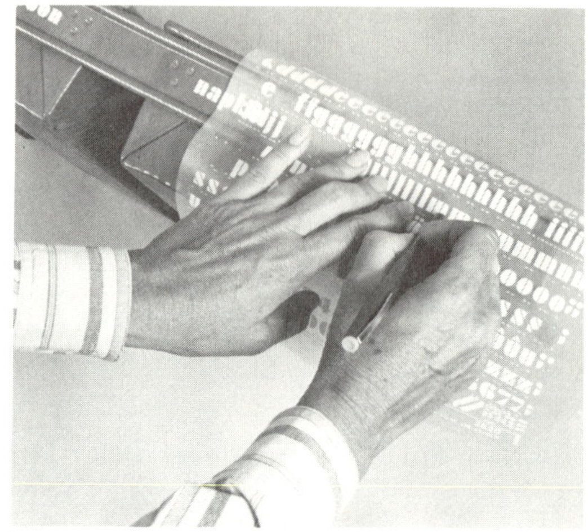

Applying press-on letters.

The pans desperately needed to be cleaned. They were dirty and rusty. First, they were left to soak in a regular household cleaning solution. Next, they were rubbed with a steel wool pad, then sanded. At this point they still weren't perfectly clean, but they were ready to be painted. Several coats of Krylon's Flame Red spray enamel were applied to give the pans a shiny, bright new look. Each coat dries in minutes so it is easy to reapply another coat of paint as needed. Press-on type is available in all art-supply stores and you can pick the typeface of your choice. Be sure to get a size that will fit the front of each pan so that it is readable. The press-on letters come in white or black so that they can be used against a pale or dark background. Protect the words and the painted surface with a final coat of clear spray varnish.

FIBER DRUMS

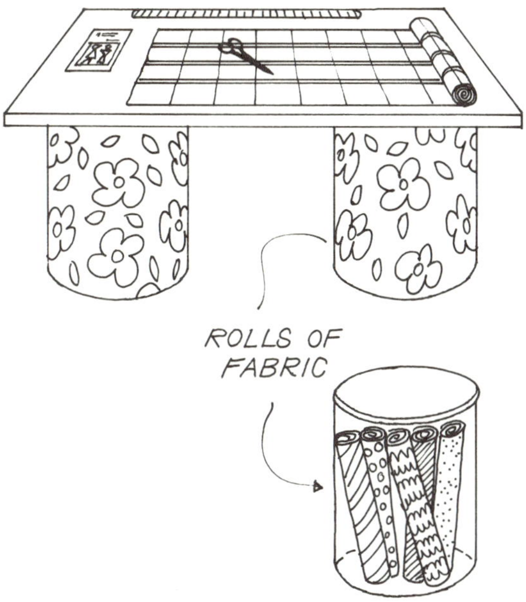

Fiber barrels or drums, which come in many sizes, are used in factories as waste baskets, by movers for packing, and if you think about it, in many other ways. You can use them as table bases, as plant pedestals since they also come with covers, or for storing large bolts of fabric and so on. They can be covered with fabric or wall-covering very easily with a spray fabric and paper adhesive such as Spra-Ment. A large drum is $16\frac{1}{2}'' \times 20\frac{1}{2}''$, and you will need approximately $1\frac{1}{2}$ yards of fabric to cover it. If you cover the drum with boat decking or similar weatherproof material found in Army & Navy or marine stores, you can use it outdoors. The small, low ones are terrific for patio side tables. In order to put the rubber material on the drum, you will also need a contact cement. Be sure to cover the bottom if you plan to keep it outside. To make a table, cover a hollow-core door with the same material and use two large drums, one under each end. When not in use, the table is easily disassembled for storage.

An offshoot of the fiber barrels is the kind of packing containers used in factories as bins for moving materials from one area to another. These are among the many kinds of containers that can be utilized for the home. Tote boxes, cases, barrels, baskets, pans, display units, mail bins, all are designed to keep the work flow efficient, reduce handling of material, free floor space, and protect materials during manufacturing, warehousing, and shipment. Why not take advantage of these specially engineered products to save you wear and tear and for a little home industrial chic?

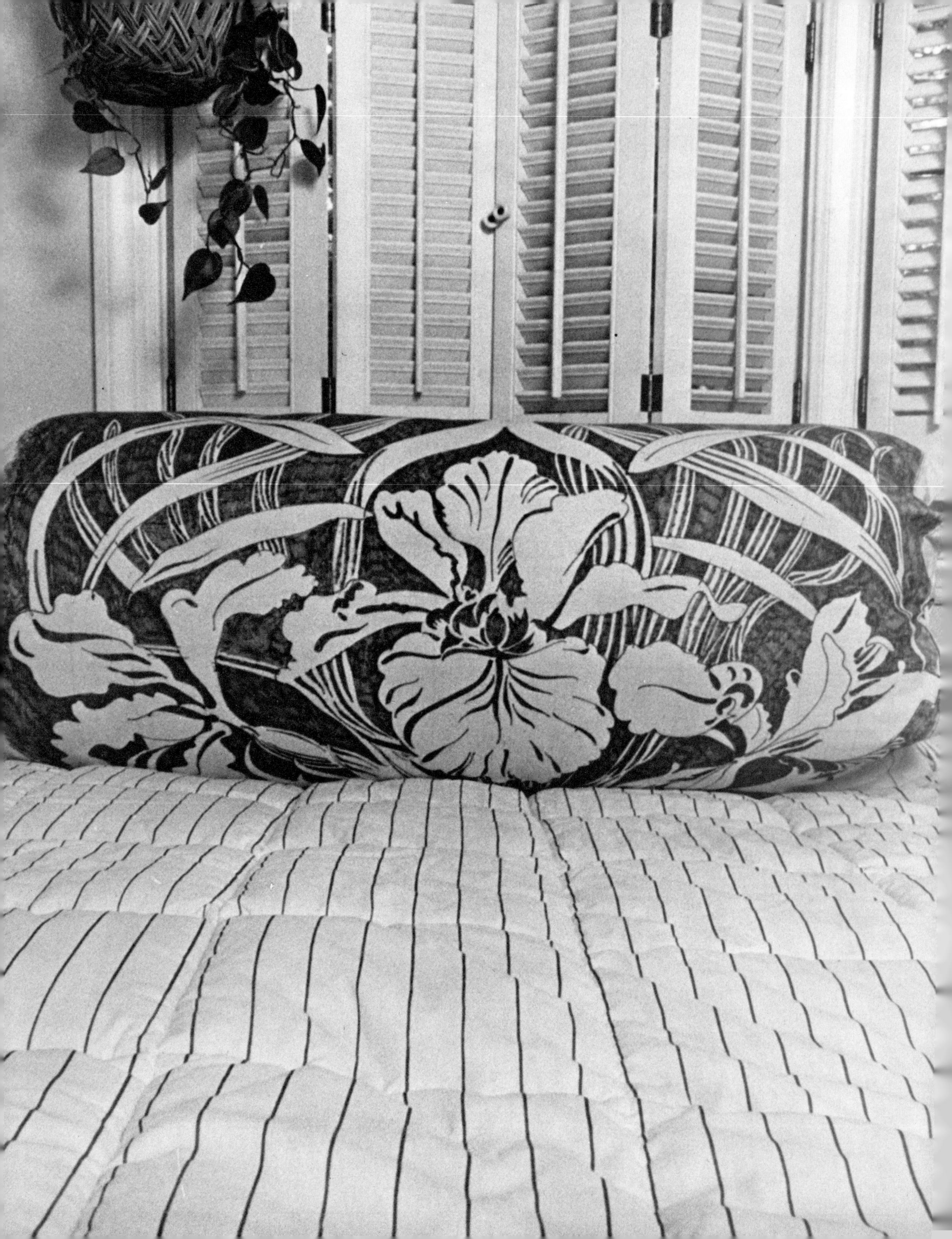

BOLSTERED UP

A Navy-style sea bag is constructed of heavy, water-repellent white duck. Rustproof grommets are set around the top, which measures 15 inches around. There is ample room in this duffellike bag to store bulky supplies. If you have limited space, team the sea bag up with a day bed or cot and convert it into a bolster. Use the bag to hold extra blankets, bedding, and pillows. One sea bag has plenty of room for all of this, and for a sleeping bag as well.

Decorate the bag with a design that is the same shape. In other words, a vertical design will not work as well visually as one that is horizontal. An overall pattern looks best because it conceals the fact that this is a sea bag. You can use the design provided here, or if you can draw, you might want to try some original sketches to create your own design. If you have an interesting bedspread, the motif might be continued on the bag.

To copy this design, use a pencil to rule a grid onto the sea bag. Each square represents 2 inches. Copy each square

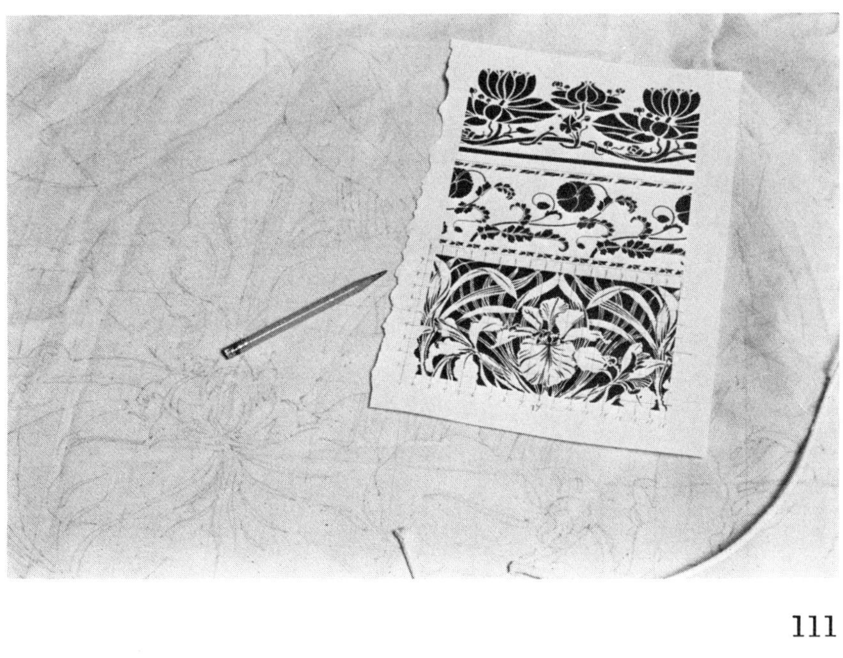

Scale design to size.

from the book until the design has been filled in. To insure accuracy, start in the center of the design and work outward. While this design may look complicated and, when finished, very intricate, it is really easy to copy.

Use one permanent marker to do the entire design. Begin by outlining over the pencil marks. In this case a rust-brown marker was used. Fill in everywhere with this same color. If you prefer, your design could be executed with many different colors, but a simple color scheme looks well with a complicated-looking design. In this way you don't have to figure beforehand which colors will look best where. Also, one color scheme will usually look well in the room without fighting for attention the way a multicolored project might.

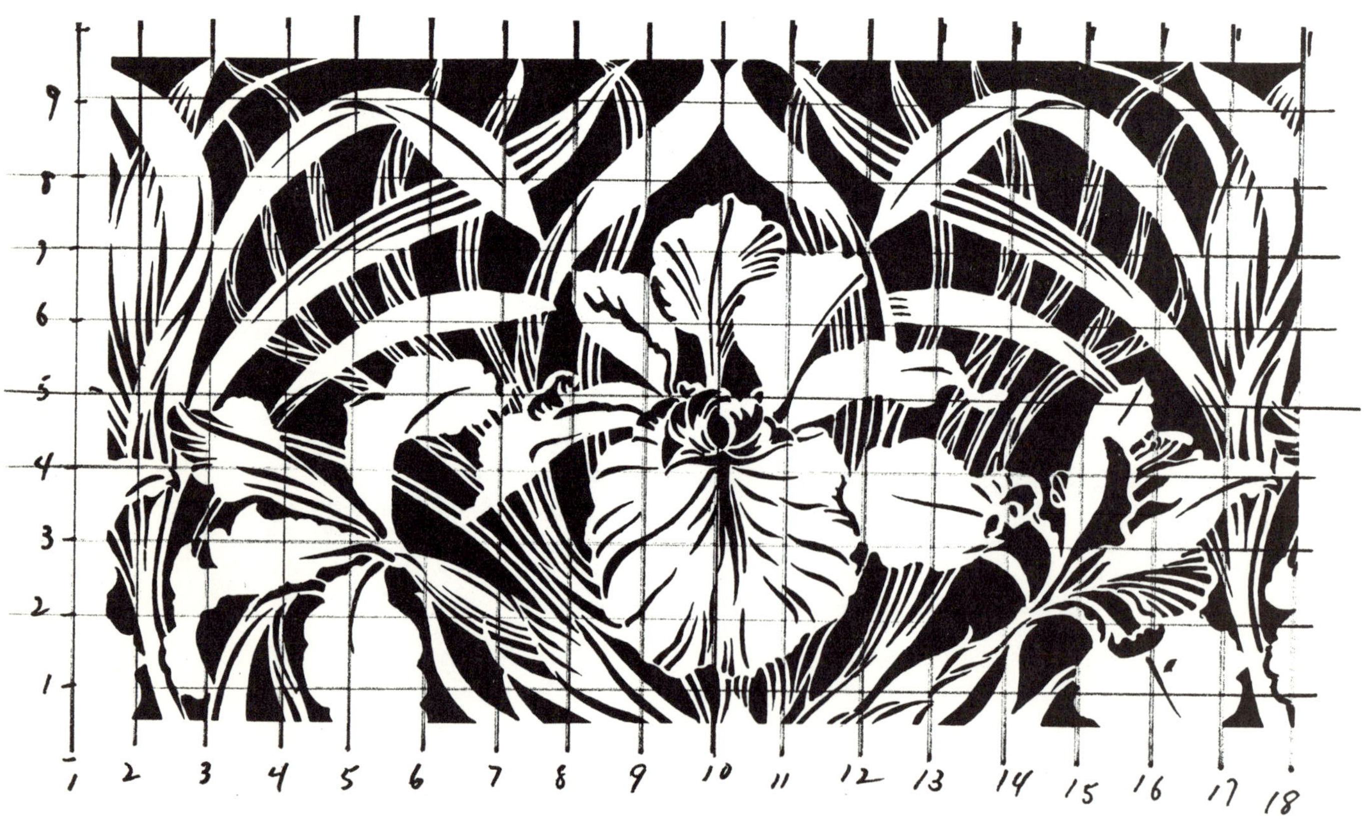

Make grid and enlarge design to desired size.

The markers tend to dry out quickly, but they regain their moisture when recapped. For such a large area you will need two or three markers of the same color. Switch from one to the other while working in order to maintain an evenness throughout.

Stuff the bag and use it at one end of a bed as the bolster, or make two to place along a bed or cot. When set against the wall you will have a backrest, thus creating a more comfortable seating area. If you do the cot project on page 96, the sea bags could be decorated with the blue stripes to match. This could be the space saver of the year for a total cost of around twenty dollars.

Outline design with marker, then fill in.

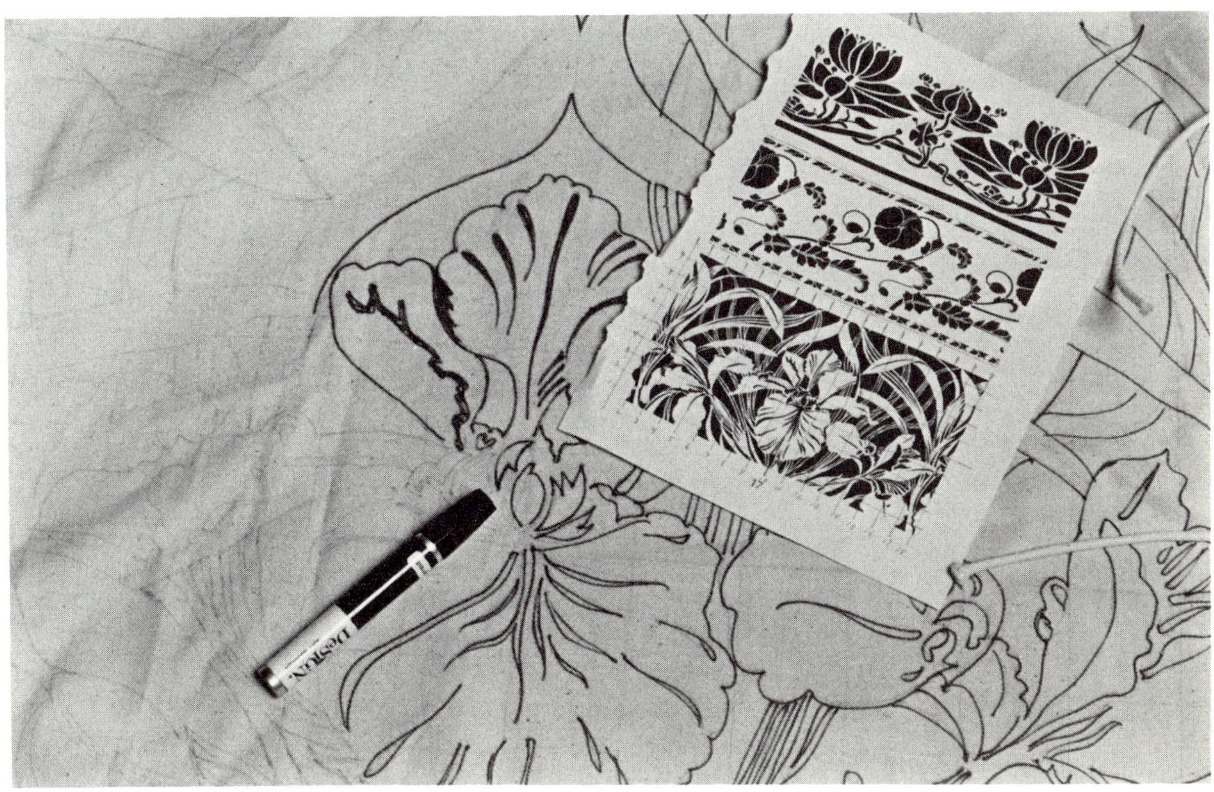

COOPED UP

Would you believe a lobster trap or a chicken coop could actually look stylish in your kitchen or living room? Decorators suggest the use of chicken coops as storage units, and they look pretty good. They are light and airy and when stacked and hung can hold anything that won't fall through the slats. Some are being used as wine racks, bookcases, storage units for fabric in a sewing room, and more. It isn't even necessary to uproot a family of chickens to obtain your coop. There is a company in Chicago that will send you a brand-new coop which they claim is "the latest decorating idea that isn't for the birds!" The ones that are used here are for transporting chickens in trucks, and each measures approximately 23″ × 35″ × 12″ high and has a hinged door opening.

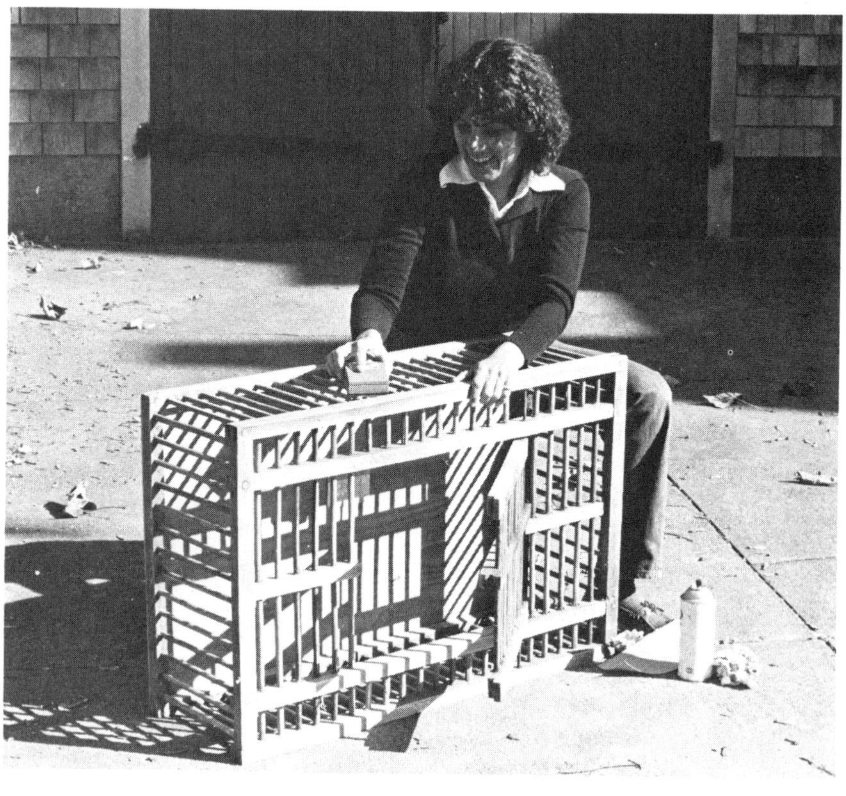

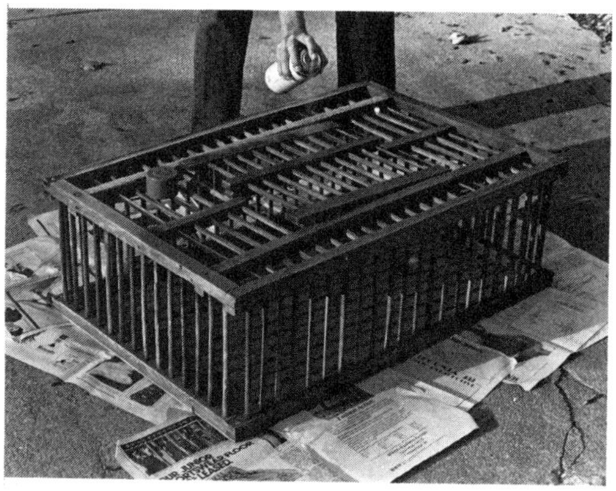

First sand chicken coop, spray with enamel paint, then protect with varnish.

The lobster traps aren't as easily available. They are seen around sea towns and sometimes work their way inland. Similar wooden crates are easier to come by. Apple crates, for instance, are the perfect size for holding record albums, and when stained and turned so the opening is to the front the top can be used as a small occasional table. College kids have been using them in dorm rooms for years. (See source list for coops, wooden boxes, and crates.)

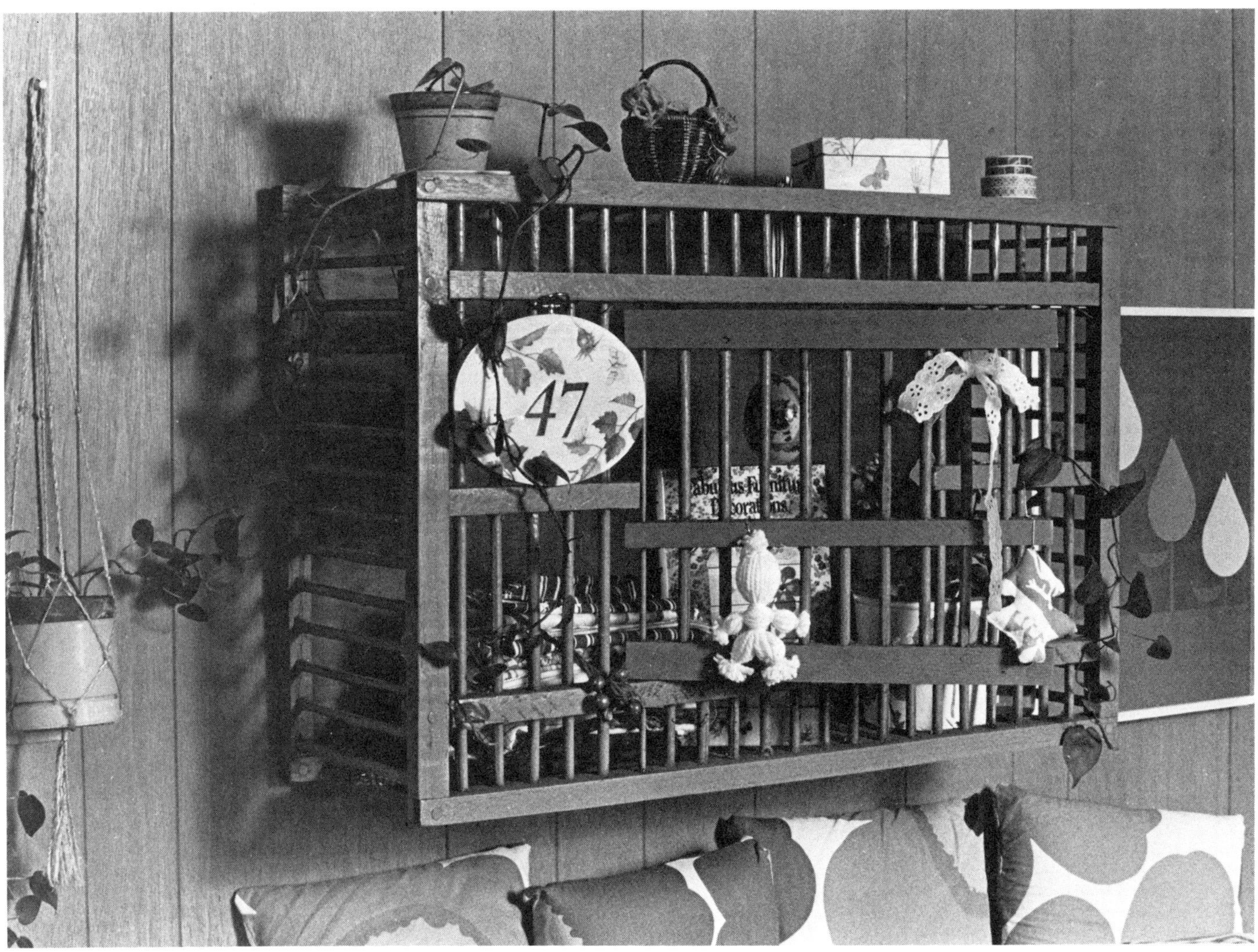

OFF THE RACK

Movable clothes storage racks used by department stores to hang and move garments are good for a "plain pipe rack" closet. These can be outfitted with colorful garment bags for shoes and hanging clothes and are excellent where extra hanging space is needed. You don't have to talk your favorite store owner out of one either. They can be purchased through the mail-order catalog service of J. C. Penney Co.

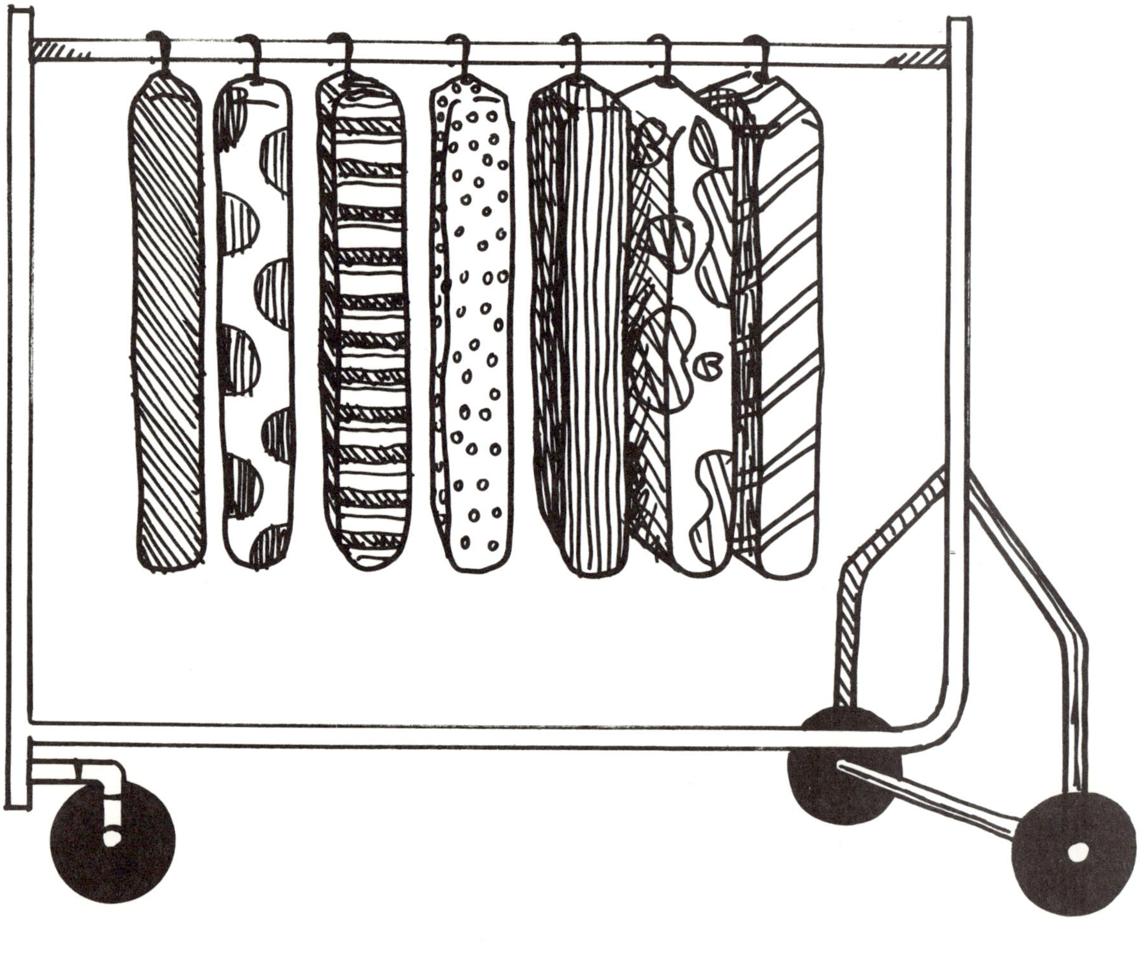

LOCKER ROOM SPRAWL

Gym lockers are a wonderful solution for a storage problem in a small area. If you can find used ones in a junkyard, it's a good deal; the new ones, though easier to get, are quite expensive. A single steel locker is good in a pantry area for cleaning supplies; one or more can be lined up in a hallway for sporting equipment and coats or for extra closets in a child's room. Because they are narrow they don't require much space, but the storage area within is quite compact. When coated with spray paint in bright colors, the lockers will take on a decorator look. If you are creating a new wall, consider building the lockers in for built-in customized storage.

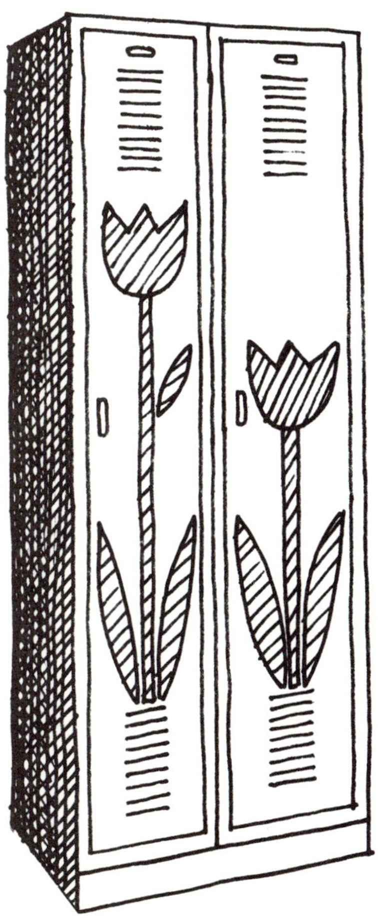

Steel lockers are made in a wide variety of widths, depths, and heights, so you can purchase them to fit your space exactly. They range from the small ones, one foot high and eight inches wide, to the very large 72-inch-high ones. Made of baked enamel finish, they are treated for maximum corrosion resistance, and when ordering new ones you do not have to be limited to the dull school colors. They come in a colonial blue, beige, and peachy rose as well as gray and green. Whether old or new, you can decorate them further by adding a graphic design. It might be a geometric pattern or a stenciled design. Perhaps you'd like to use words in press-on letters or done with large stencil letters. Oversized numbers, one on each door, could be striking. (See source list for lockers.)

ON THE ROAD

Trunks are not just for use when going off to camp or school or for traveling performers. They are used for extra storage space as well as for seating, if you get the sturdier kind. These are inexpensive copies of the old metal footlockers, and they are less cumbersome because they are smaller, lighter in weight, and therefore more practical. However, they are not the best-looking item to have out in the open. Unless, of course, you decorate them to fit into the room. You can cover one with wallpaper to match a bedroom and leave it at the end of your bed to store extra blankets. In a hallway a small trunk becomes a low table for a small lamp and magazines. Posters and colorful tapes can combine to create an unusual covering. The large commercial show or advertising posters are inexpensive, or for a more formal design, cover a trunk with one of the New York Botanical Gardens posters, which are inexpensive at six dollars.

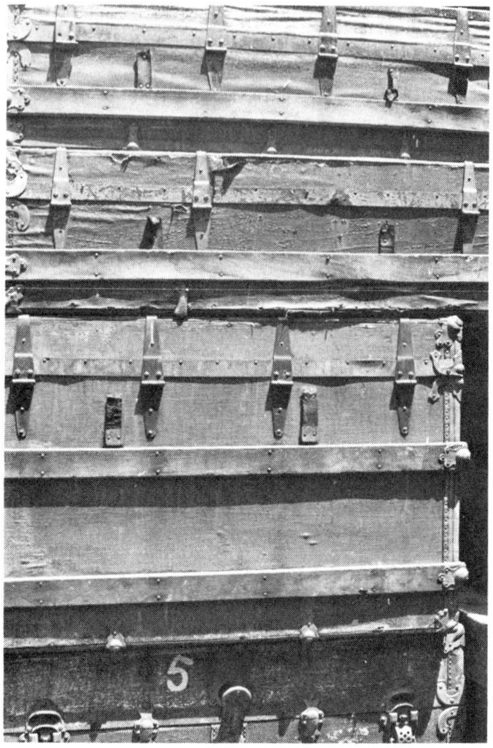

Old trunks demand attention: great potential here!

This miniature trunk is one I had as a child and in which I stored doll clothes. My mother saved it all these years, and I recently covered it with wrapping paper. I have also covered regular-sized trunks in this way; it is a lot easier working on a large surface. Vinyl wallpaper is best for this project as thin wrapping paper will wrinkle when glued down in large sections. It will take awhile to do this properly, as you should take the time to cover the trunk accurately, and measuring each area should be done with care. Use white glue for permanency. If you want to be able to change the paper or fabric covering from time to time, use fabric adhesive. The covering will hold firmly, but is also removable.

Give the surface a coating of semigloss polyurethane varnish for a long-lasting protective finish. Let the varnish dry thoroughly before using the trunk.

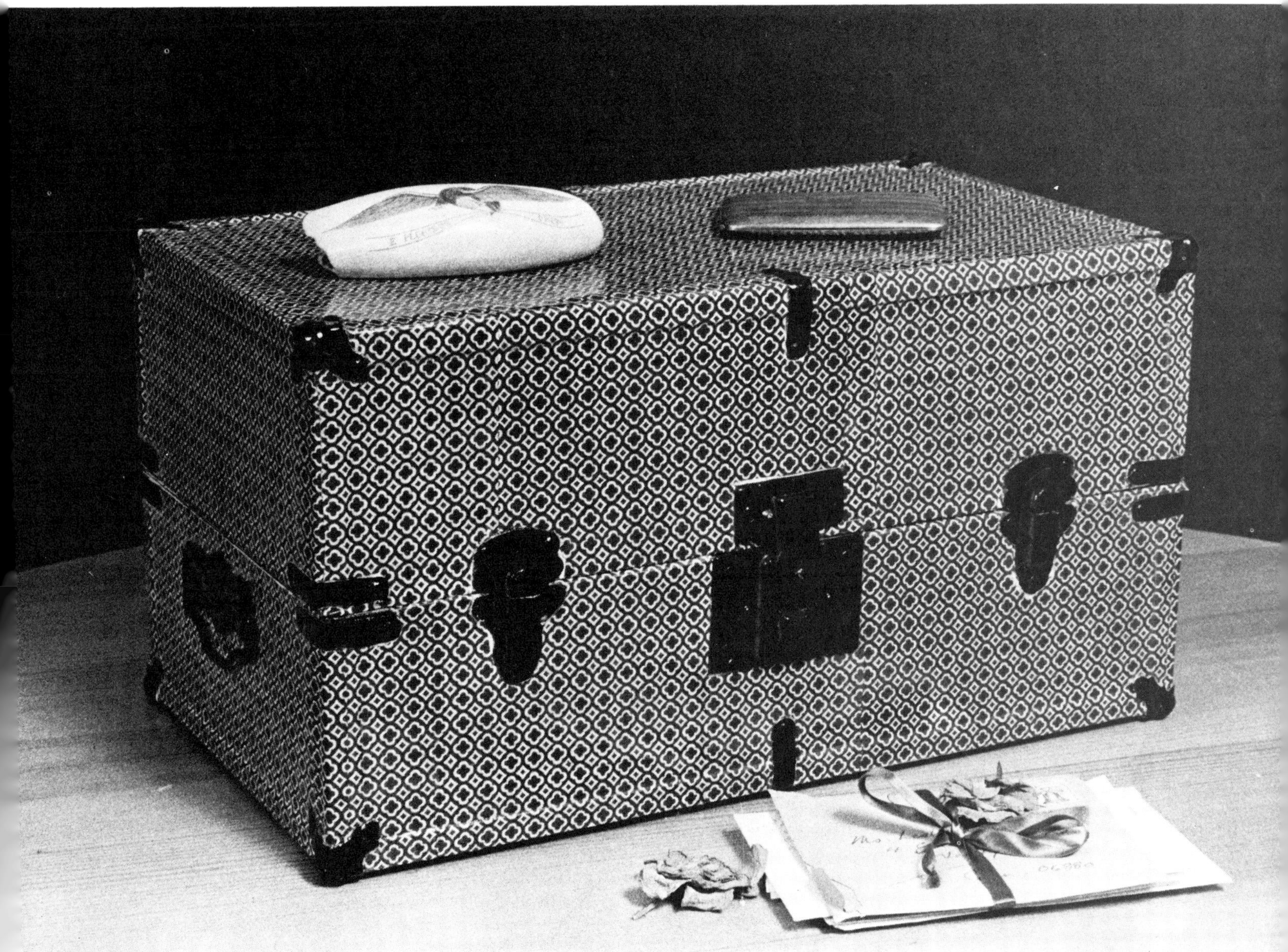

PLANTERS WITH PUNCH

A CUPFUL OF FLOWERS

There are dozens of cups that are used with the canteen plates and cooking pots. Some are collapsible, some are made to fit into other items for compactness. The aluminum field cup has a handle that folds and snaps under itself in order to pack easily and to support the cup when it is standing. The handle snaps open to provide a firm grip when scooping water from a stream. This cup is perfect for holding a plant because it is rustproof. Further, it hangs a good four inches away from the wall, allowing room for flowering or full-leaved plants to sprawl naturally over the edges. There is a hole in the handle for easy hanging. The metallic cup is attractive as is or you may prefer to paint it a bright color. Spray enamel will cover evenly. Use a decorative screw, hook, or knob on which to hang the planter on the wall.

If you have small items to organize, this cup idea is simple to adapt. Hang one in the bathroom to hold your brush, comb, powder, toothpaste, and so on. In the kitchen, several cups can be hung on a wall to hold utensils. If you are a craftworker, assemble brushes, ruler, pencils, scissors, and so on neatly and accessibly.

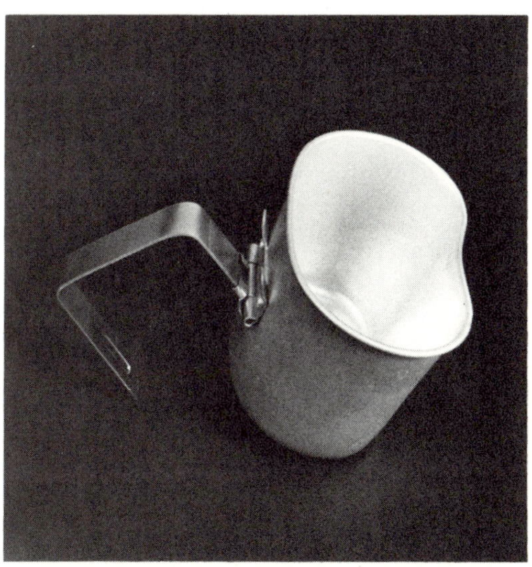

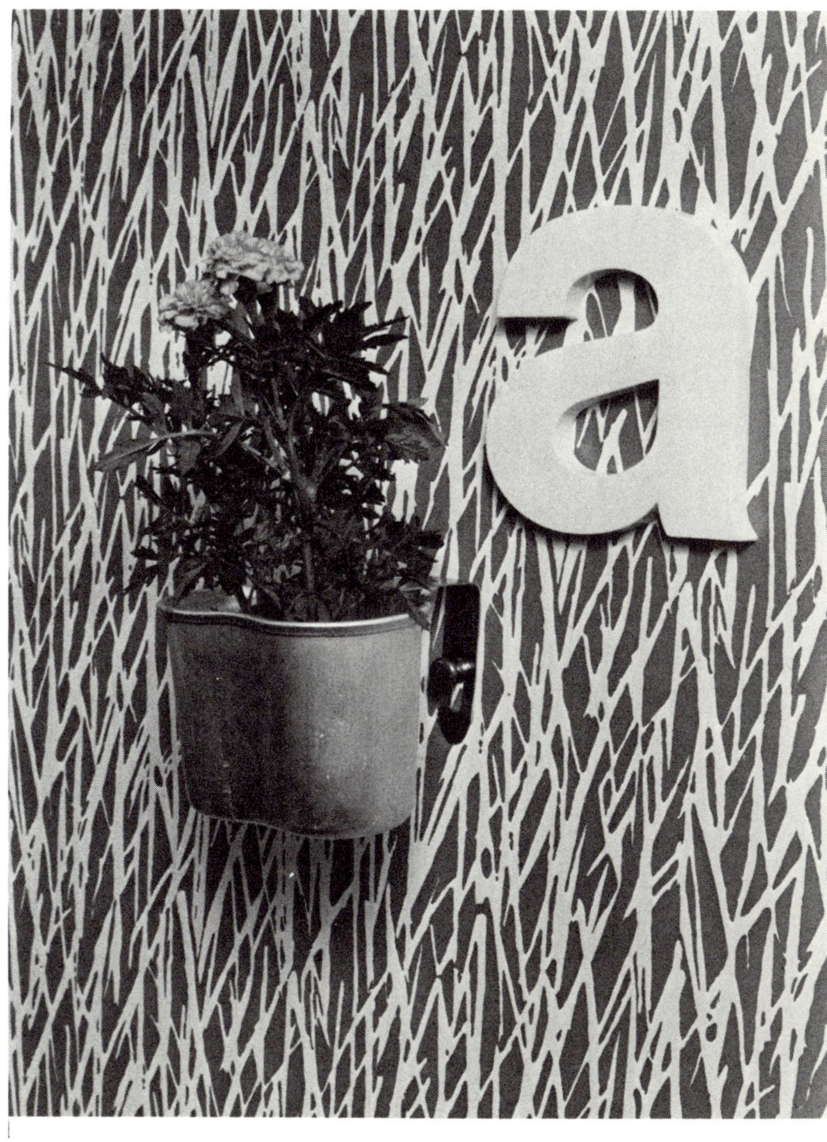

PLANT A GOOD IDEA

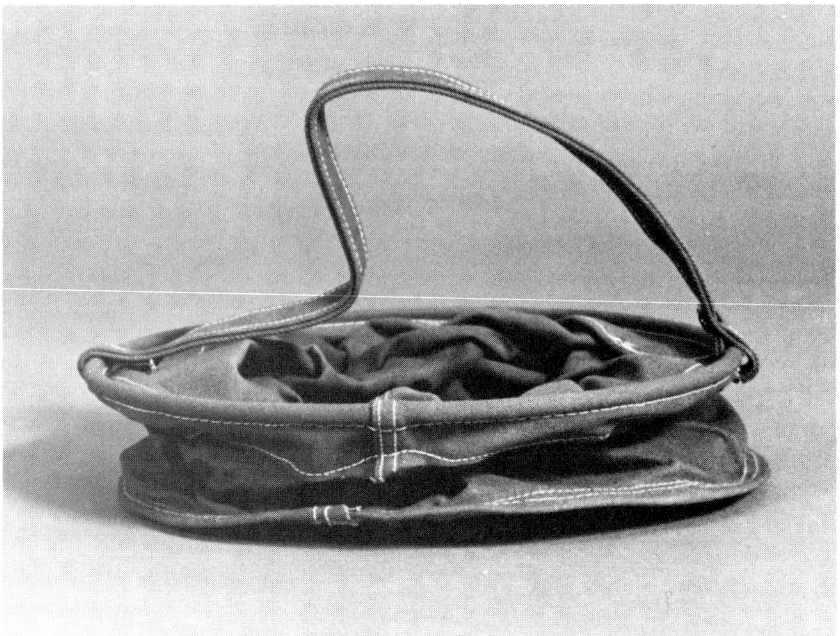

No responsible camper ever left home without a collapsible canvas water bucket. Made of heavy-duty waterproof canvas, the bucket has a steel frame and can be set down rigidly without losing the contents. It holds ten quarts.

These buckets, which are inexpensive and considered standard equipment in Army & Navy stores, are marvelous for hundreds of other uses. Any store that sells camping supplies will usually have them in a variety of colors.

Since they are waterproof and strong, they can't be beat as holders for hanging plants. The double-stitched, ample handle affords the means for easy hanging. Nylon cord or picture wire can be used to attach the bucket to a hook, or in this case, a curtain rod. For a more decorative planter, a design or words can be stenciled onto the canvas. The material takes acrylic paint quite well.

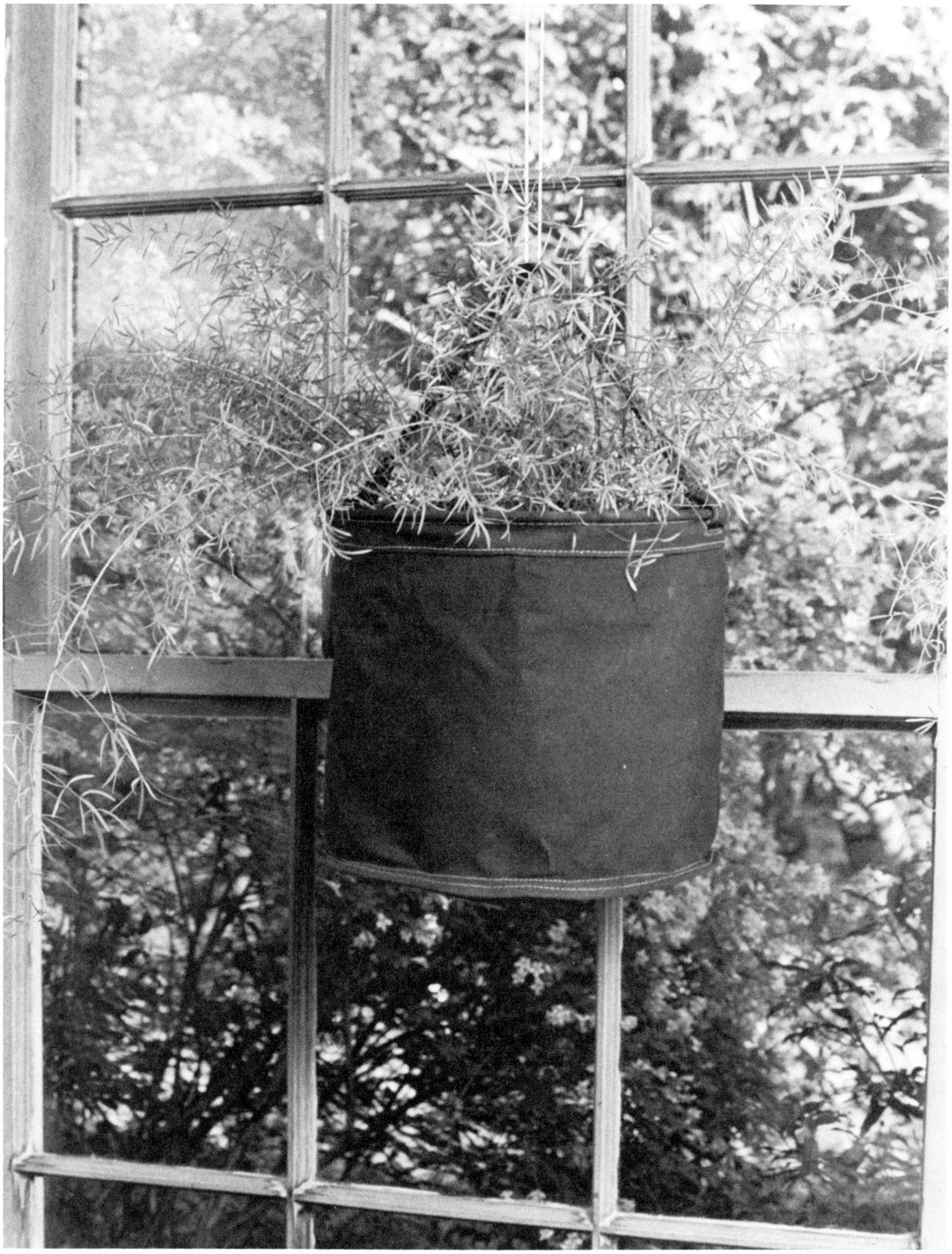

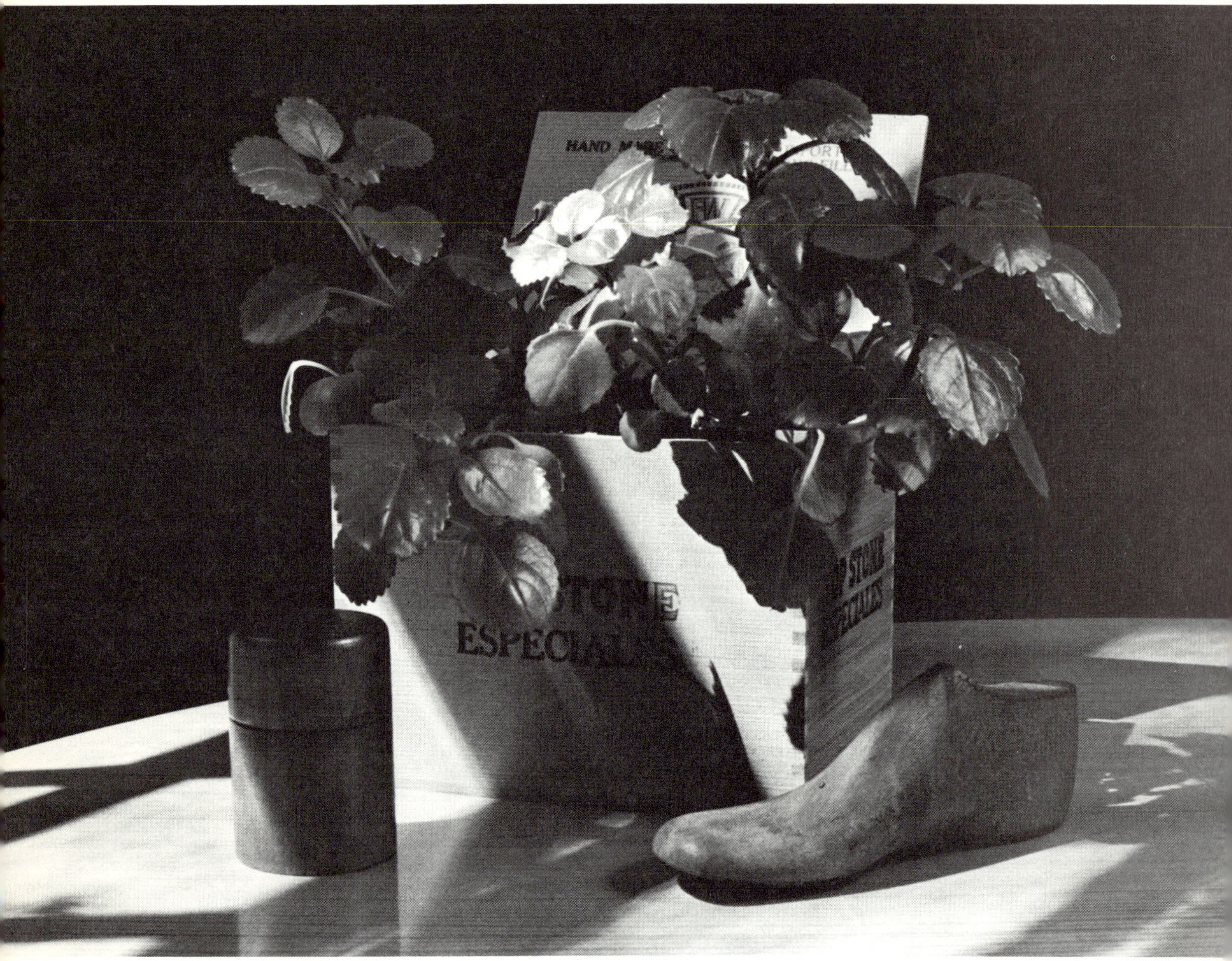
STONE

CIGAR BOX PLANTER

Another good-looking plant holder is a wooden cigar box. The wood is treated to absorb moisture in order to keep the cigars fresh, so it shouldn't rot from the plant moisture. You can use the box as is for a rugged, natural look, or you can perhaps paint it and line it with pretty vinyl paper. The wood takes stain well, if you prefer a dark, rich-looking container. This would change the exterior of the box so that no one could tell what it had originally been intended to hold. These boxes come in a few different sizes, but I found that the deeper ones were better suited to most potted plants.

The Top Stone Cigar Company is in my area. The people there were friendly and cooperative when I walked in, unannounced, looking for boxes. But you don't need a cigar factory to obtain the boxes, as they are everywhere. You needn't go farther than the corner smoke shop. The wooden boxes are a bit harder to come by as they hold fifty of the more expensive cigars, but if you put in a request where they are sold, the owner will probably save the boxes when empty.

The wooden boxes can be coated with polyurethane varnish inside and out for longer lasting protection. If you have used stain, the varnish will intensify the wood, giving it an impressive appearance.

Another use for these boxes is to hold desk accessories, mail, and tools in a workroom. Of course, using cigar boxes as containers is not a new idea—everyone has done so at one time or another. However, there are many ways to decorate them without much effort so that they can be displayed as well as used.

OUTDOOR HANG-UPS

A trip to the hardware store will always yield some interesting odds and ends that can be utilized for imaginative projects. Everything there is made of sturdy material, and the industrial nuts-and-bolts approach is refreshing for home decorating. There you will find hooks and screw eyes ranging from the very tiny to giant size; latch hooks for screen doors and door handles; hinges and grab bars; painting tools and hundreds of other utilitarian items. Paint buckets abound in metal, colored plastic, and paper. The sizes vary, but the cost rarely exceeds $1.25. Since they are used to hold paint, which is heavy and wet, these are excellent for holding outdoor plants.

You needn't buy expensive hanging hooks made especially for planters. Rummage through your garage or kitchen drawers. While cleaning my garage I came up with many unidentifiable objects that could be used for this purpose. I don't know how, but I seem to have acquired three tension hooks that, when linked together, are perfect for holding a plant-filled yellow plastic bucket.

The paper buckets are made of sturdy white paperboard and come in three sizes. When decorated with paint or a decoupage design, they dress up the potted plant they hold. Either line the bottom with waterproof material or place a small dish in the bottom. I also use these painter's pails to organize small items in the closet or bathroom.

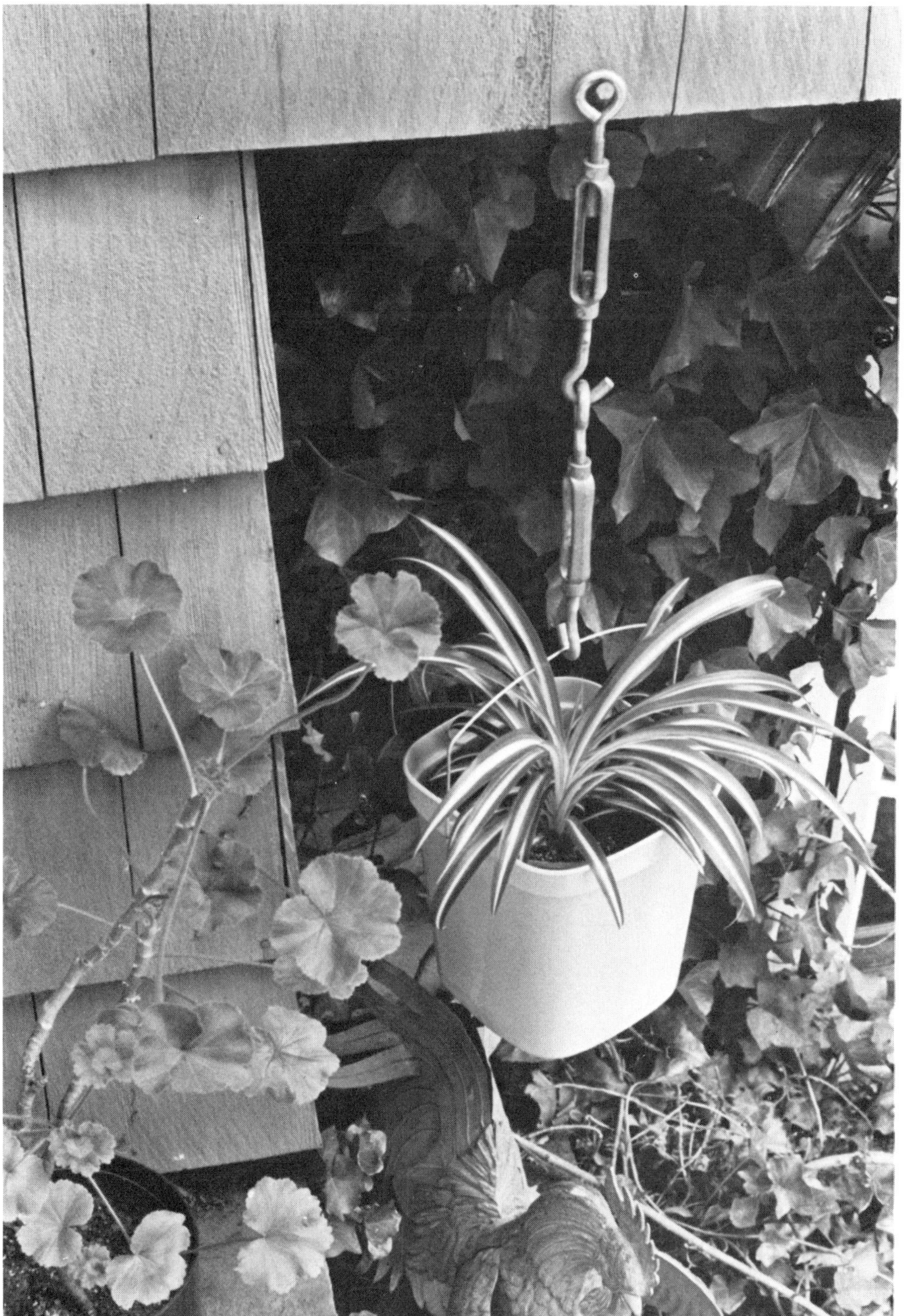

SOFT VINYL PLANTER

Ditty bags made of thin vinyl are among the many standard camping items found in all Army & Navy stores. These soft bags are waterproof and have a drawstring closing. You'll have to look for them as they are small and often hidden away in a box that one must rummage through in order to choose a color. They are made in surprisingly beautiful colors. Some are hot pink with deep purple linings, others are green with contrasting linings. The one used here is pale gray with a deep wine color inside. Since the bags have a drawstring top, they are perfect for holding accessories and useful as a shaving kit, to carry cosmetics for traveling, or to pack with suntan lotion, sunglasses, and other beach items.

A ditty bag is also an excellent covering for a flower pot. It has become increasingly hard to find pretty, practical, and inexpensive holders for clay or plastic flower pots. For 79 cents you will probably want to pick out several. Simply slip the bag over the pot and fold the top down to create a two-tone container. Tie drawstring around top of pot. Moisture will not ruin the lining.

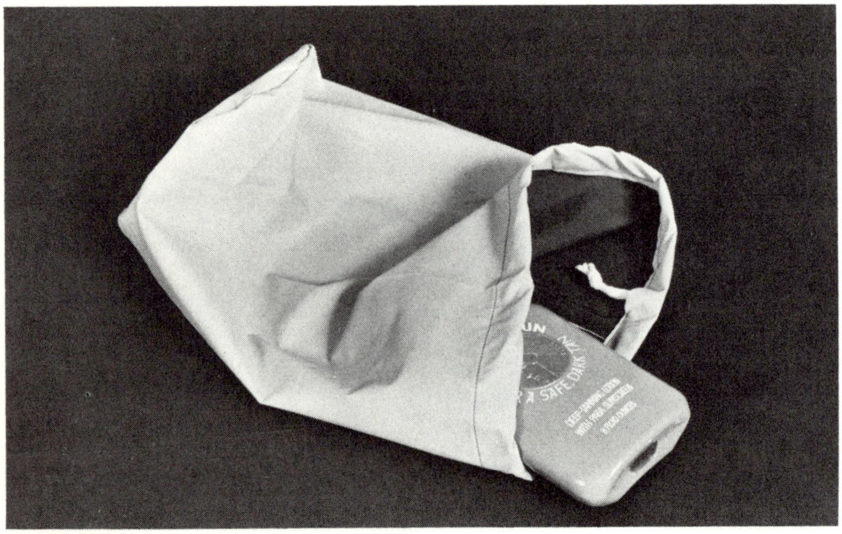

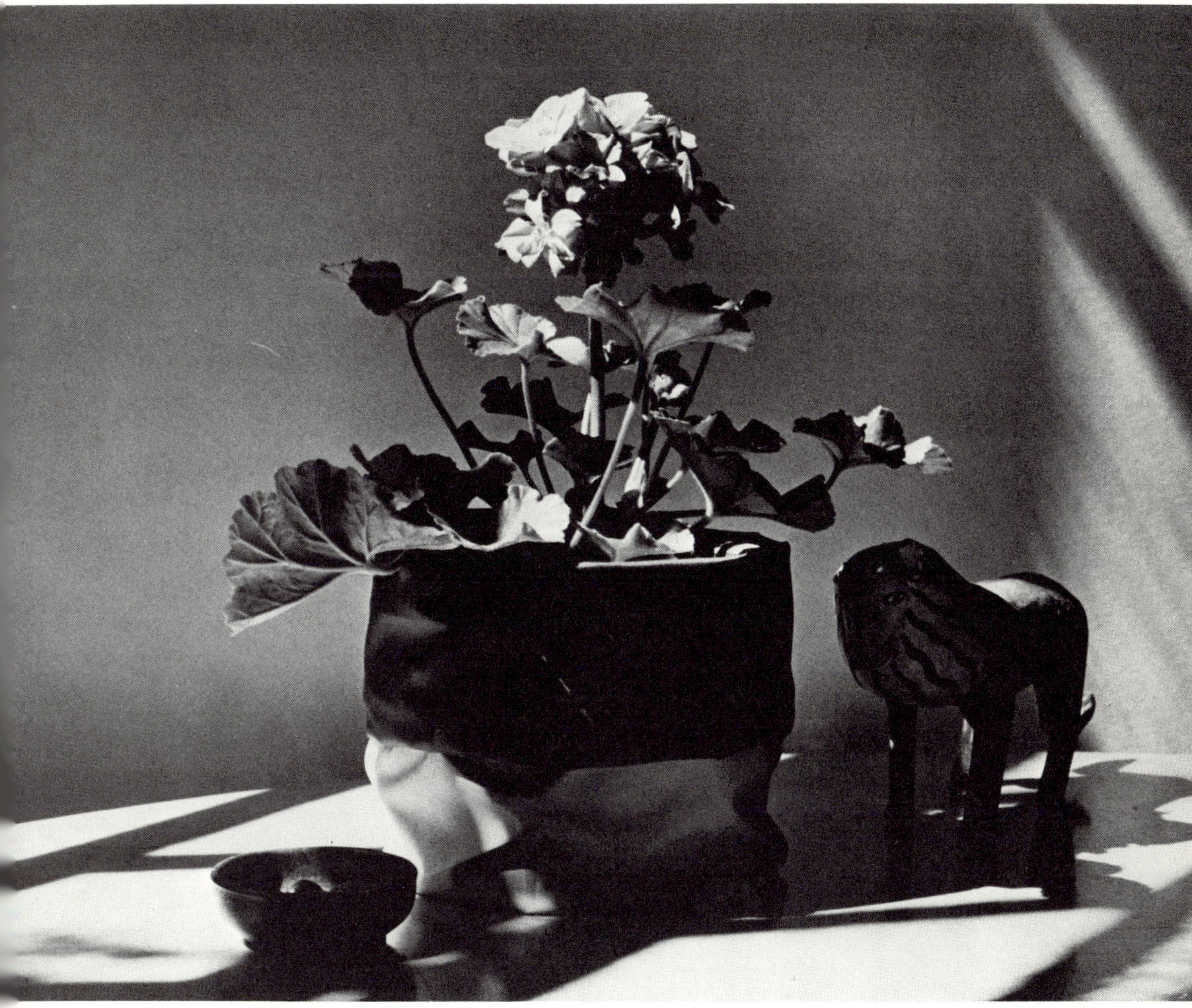

ALL BOTTLED UP

Small, pint-sized glass milk bottles are rarely used today, having been replaced by plastic and paper cartons. Even the larger, quart-sized ones have all but disappeared along with the milkman and home delivery. The small bottles are useful as well as decorative and can often be found in junk shops and rummage sales. Sometimes the name of the dairy is part of the glass imprint, which makes them all the more interesting. They are particularly appealing as starter plant holders. When small clippings are taking root, set them in separate bottles lined up on a windowsill. The light passes through the bottles and the delicate plant stems show through the water.

If you cannot find pint-sized milk bottles for this purpose, there are hundreds of other interesting bottles of varying sizes and colors that were once used for commercial purposes but are no longer made. They have become collector's items, which is evident if one takes a look in a few antique shops. Often those very things that were once considered commonplace are now nostalgia pieces. Many people find that the use of such collectibles is what gives their homes individuality. Bottles of varying sizes and colors are among such finds and not difficult to come across.

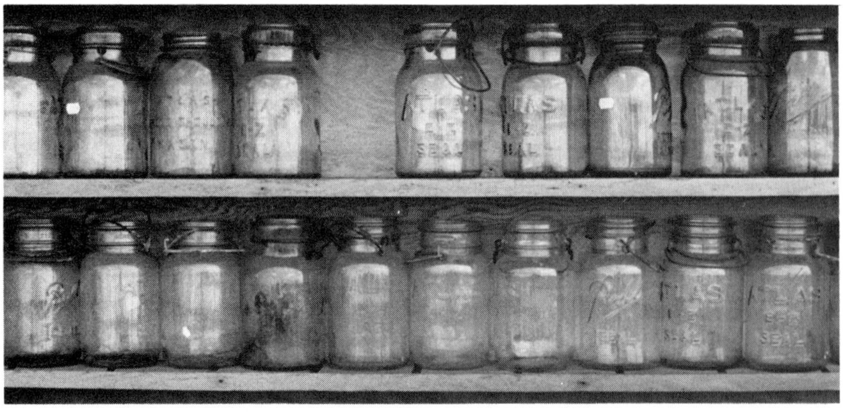

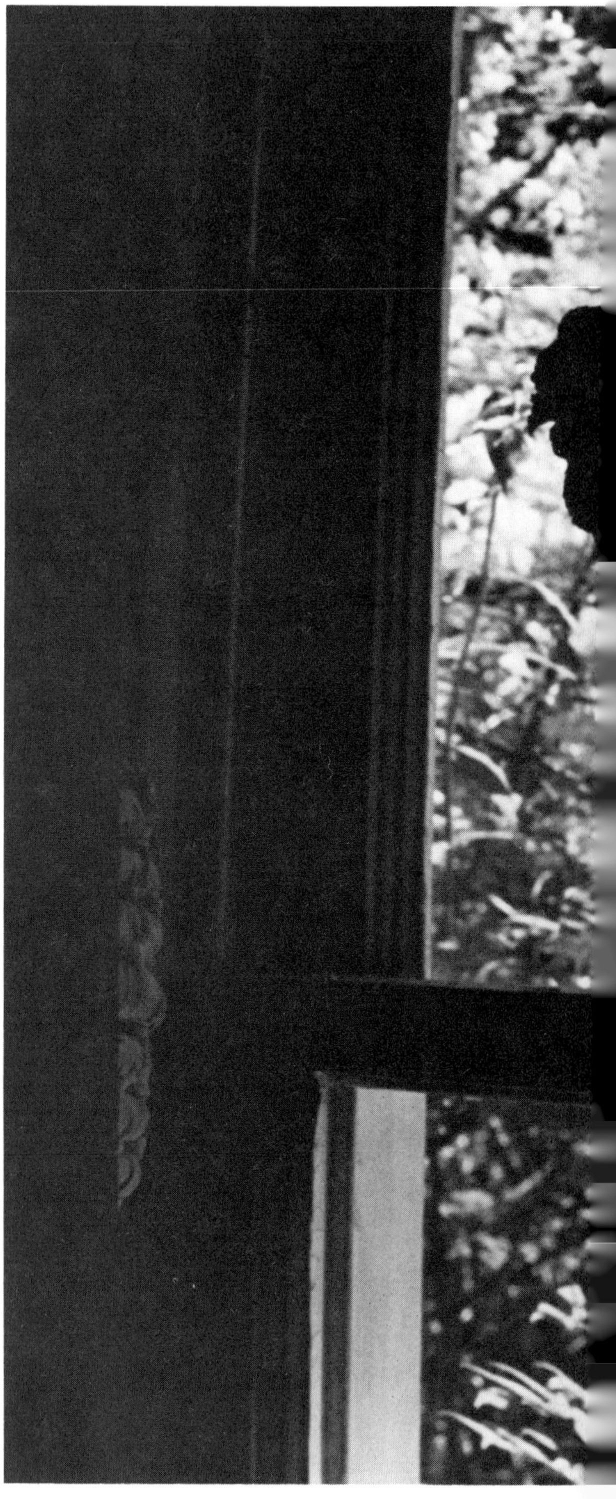

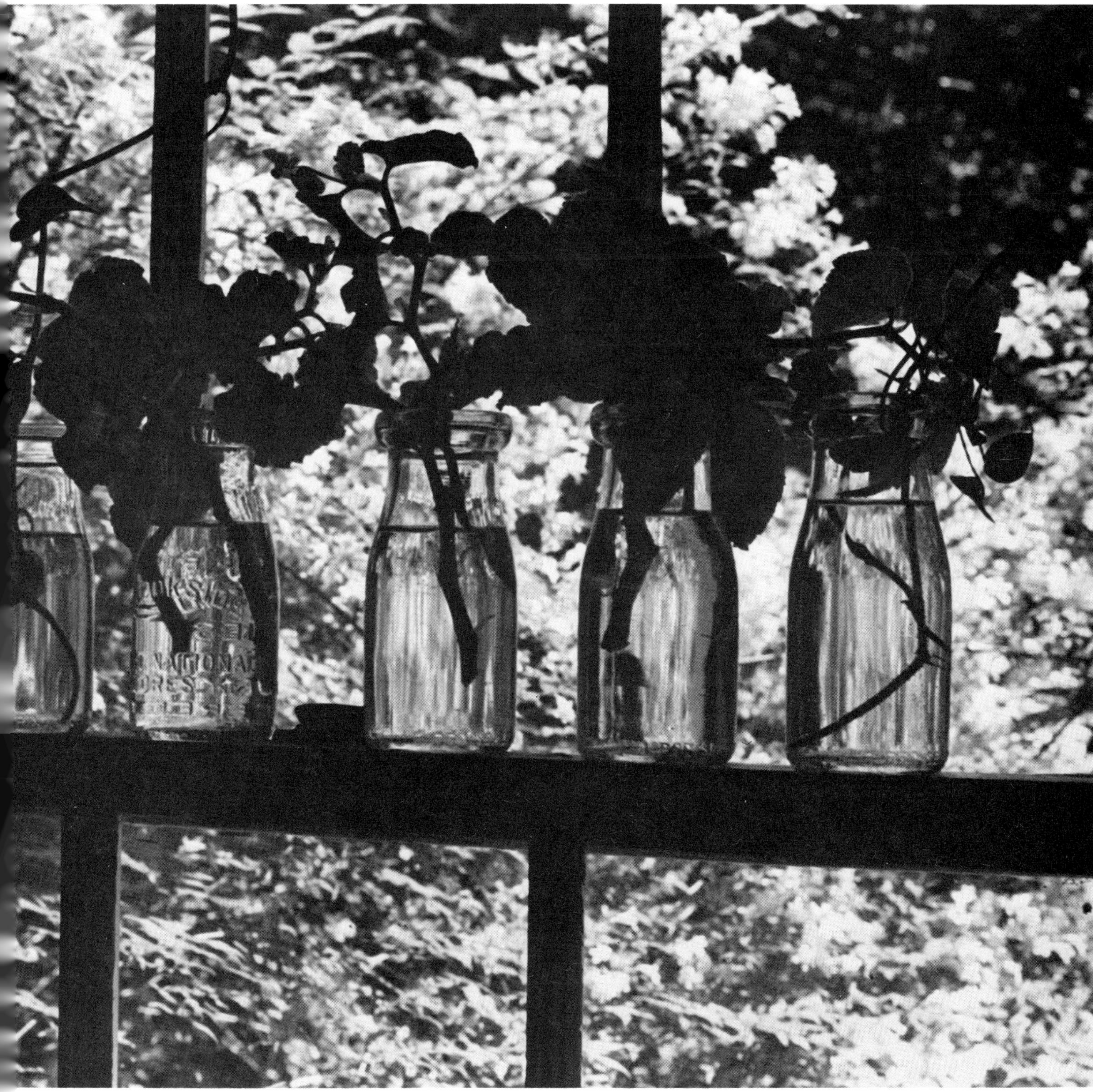

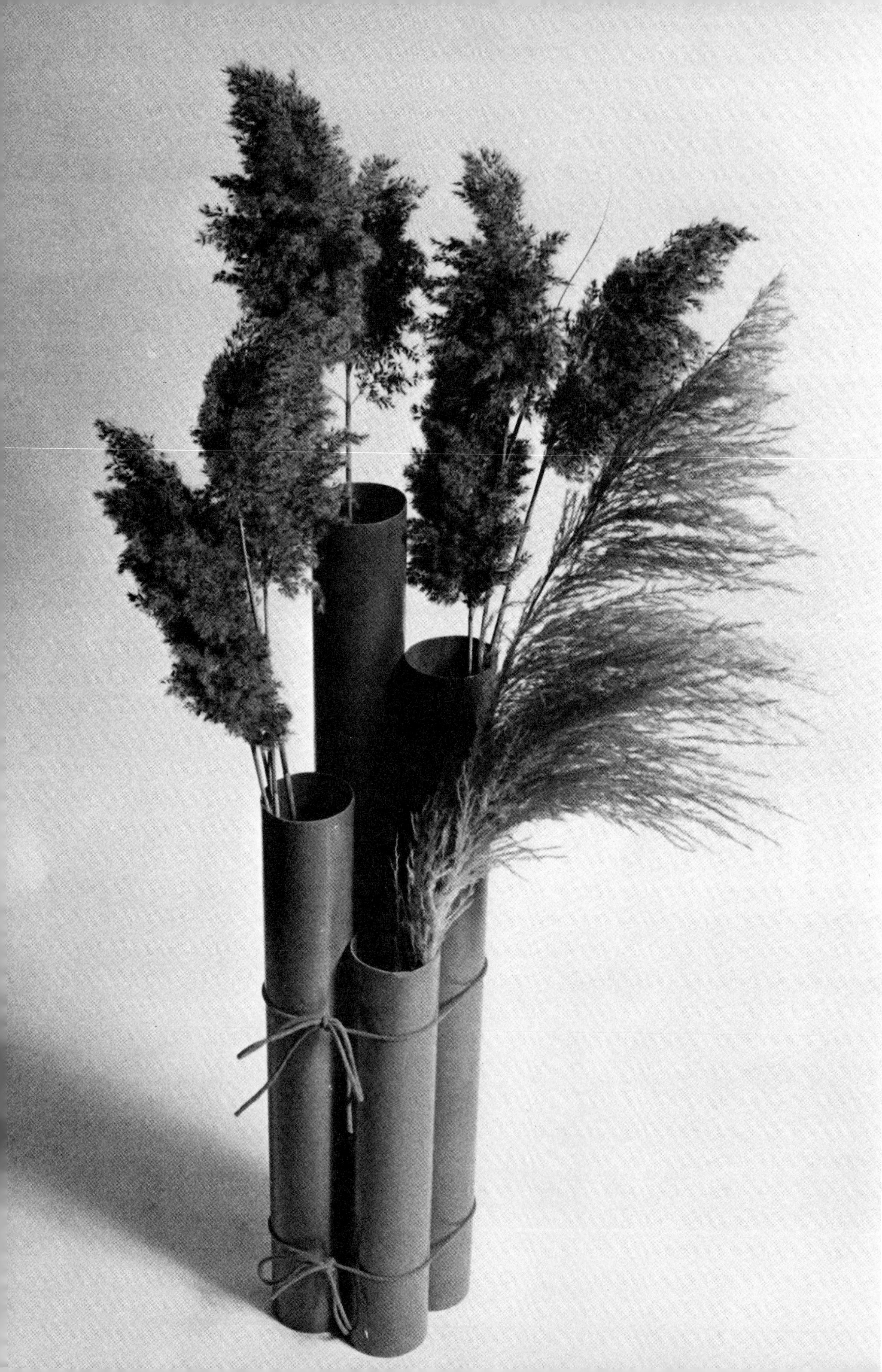

SEWER PIPE PLANTER

A plastic plumbing pipe that is 3 inches in diameter and 10 feet long is the basis of a tube planter. The pipe can be purchased in a building supply yard. Cut it in different lengths of 18 inches, 30 inches, and 36 inches. It will cut easily with a hacksaw. File and sand the rough edges. This planter has been spray painted with grape-colored enamel. The plastic surface takes spray paint beautifully. When the tubes are dry tie them together tightly with yarn or cord. This planter is a display unit for dried grasses and as such doesn't need a waterproof bottom. As these tubes are hollow, you can cut discs of cork or cardboard to fit tightly in the bottom of the tubes.

Map tubes come in long and short sizes. They are made of clear and opaque plastic and have capped ends. Cardboard mailing tubes aren't as pretty, but they can be covered with fabric or paper, spray painted or decorated, and used for the same purpose. They are also very inexpensive, ranging from 50 cents to a dollar. Look for them locally in your Yellow Pages under "tubes."

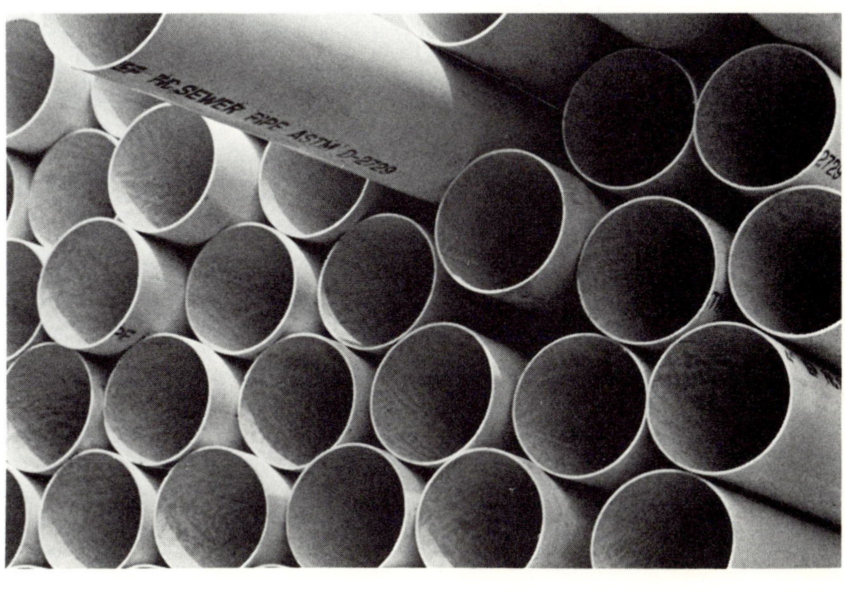

GIVE YOUR PLANT A LIFT

If you have very high ceilings or rafters from which you might like to hang a plant but feel it is impractical because you would need a ladder to water it, try hanging it from a marine pulley. The one shown here is used to tow a water skier. I replaced the rope with bright blue plastic-coated wire from which I hung an almost invisible nylon plant holder. The pulley is attached to a curtain rod with picture wire. It hangs in a spot that would normally be awkward to reach.

One end of the wire is attached to the planter; the other end, the excess, is wrapped around a boat cleat, most readily found in hardware stores. Screw this into the wall or window frame at a height that is easy to reach. When you want to water the plant, simply unwind the wire, slowly lower the plant, water, and hoist it up again to the desired level. Wrap the excess wire around the cleat once more to secure the plant in midair.

Water-skier's pulley.

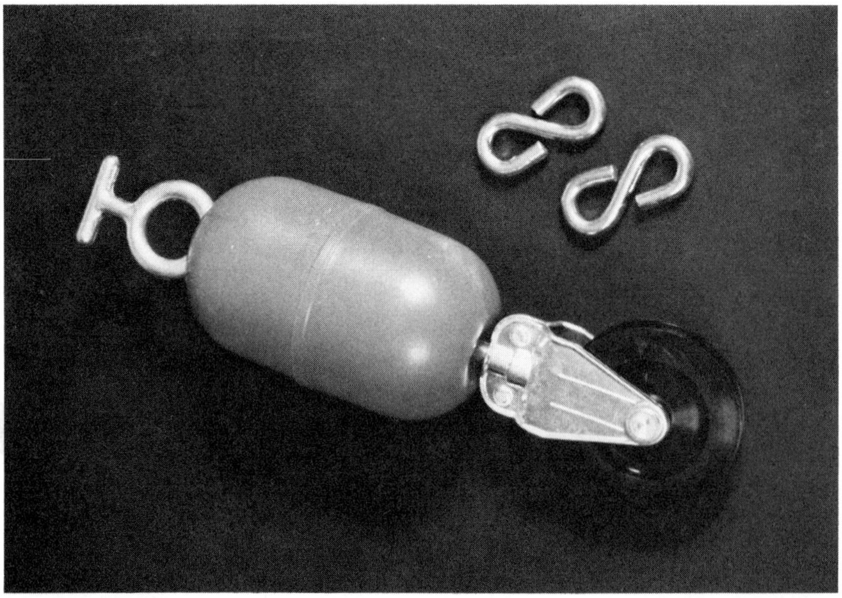

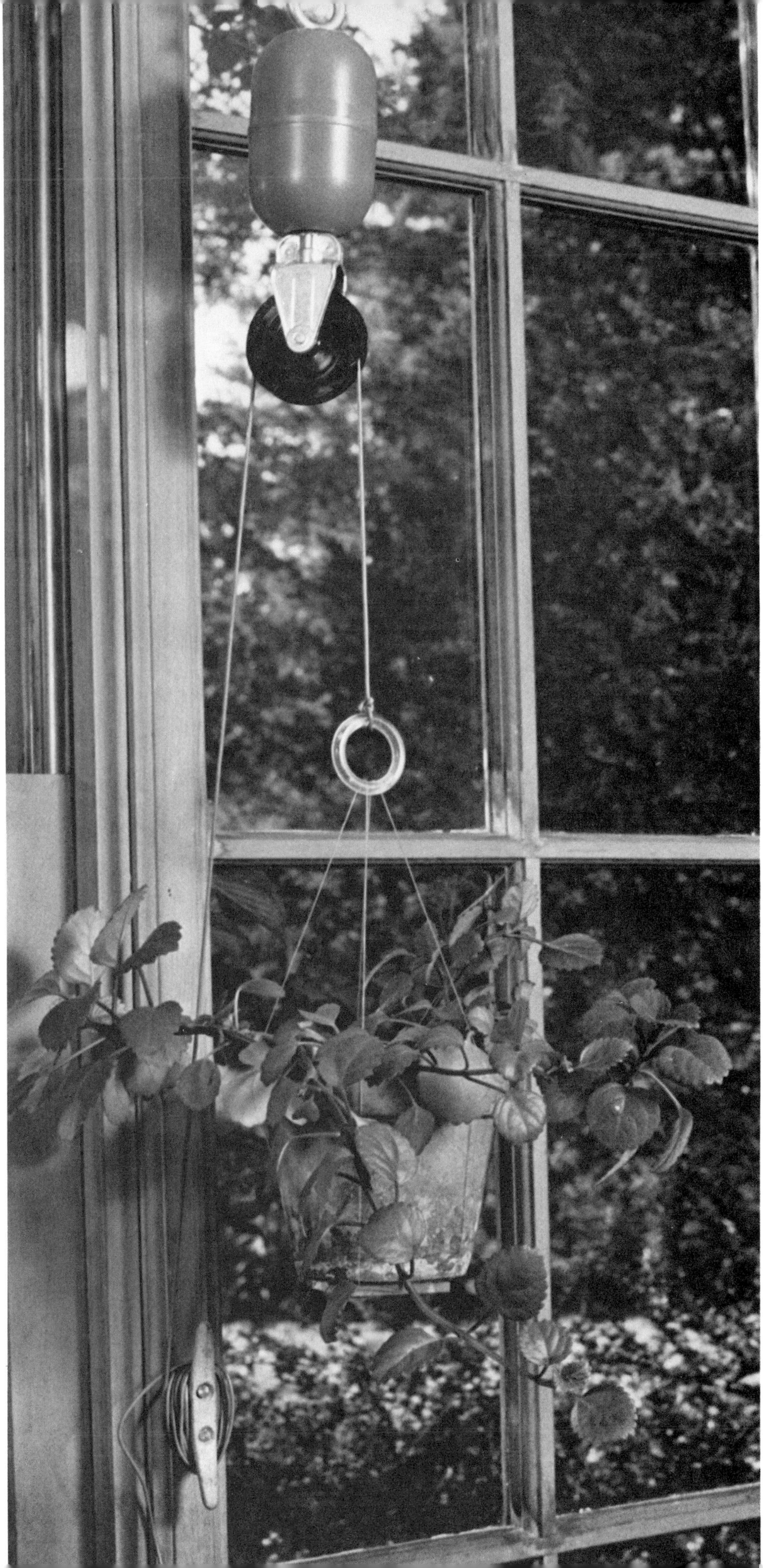

HANGING GARDENS

There are lots of industrial parts that are usable and interesting as containers for household decorating. Things that don't have any value in themselves are often discarded when there is a surplus. Molded plastic parts are just such items and it's anybody's guess as to what they were used for. I found these half-round plastic bowls in a plastic surplus store and couldn't identify anything else in the store either.

The soft plastic red, blue, and yellow cups make delightful holders for climbing vines. They are lightweight and hang easily from nylon cord. When the plant roots begin to spread out they can be transplanted to larger pots and new starter plants can be used.

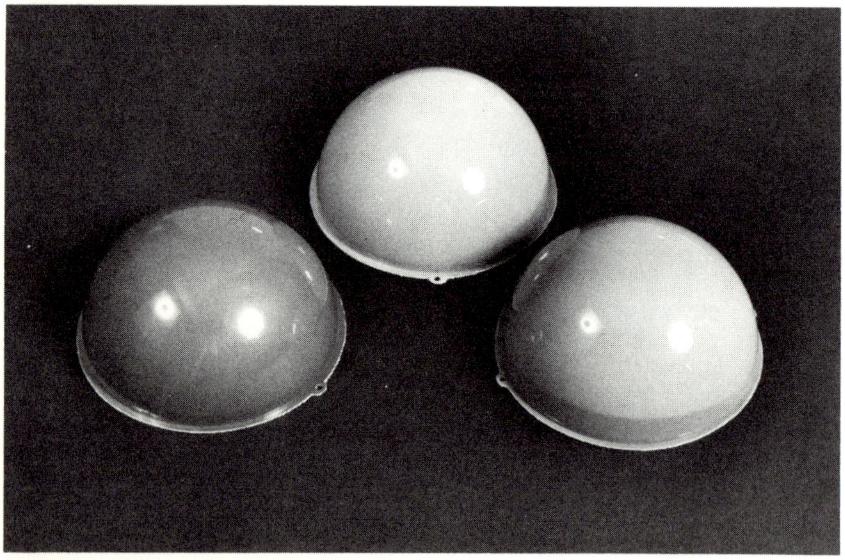

Molded plastic parts.

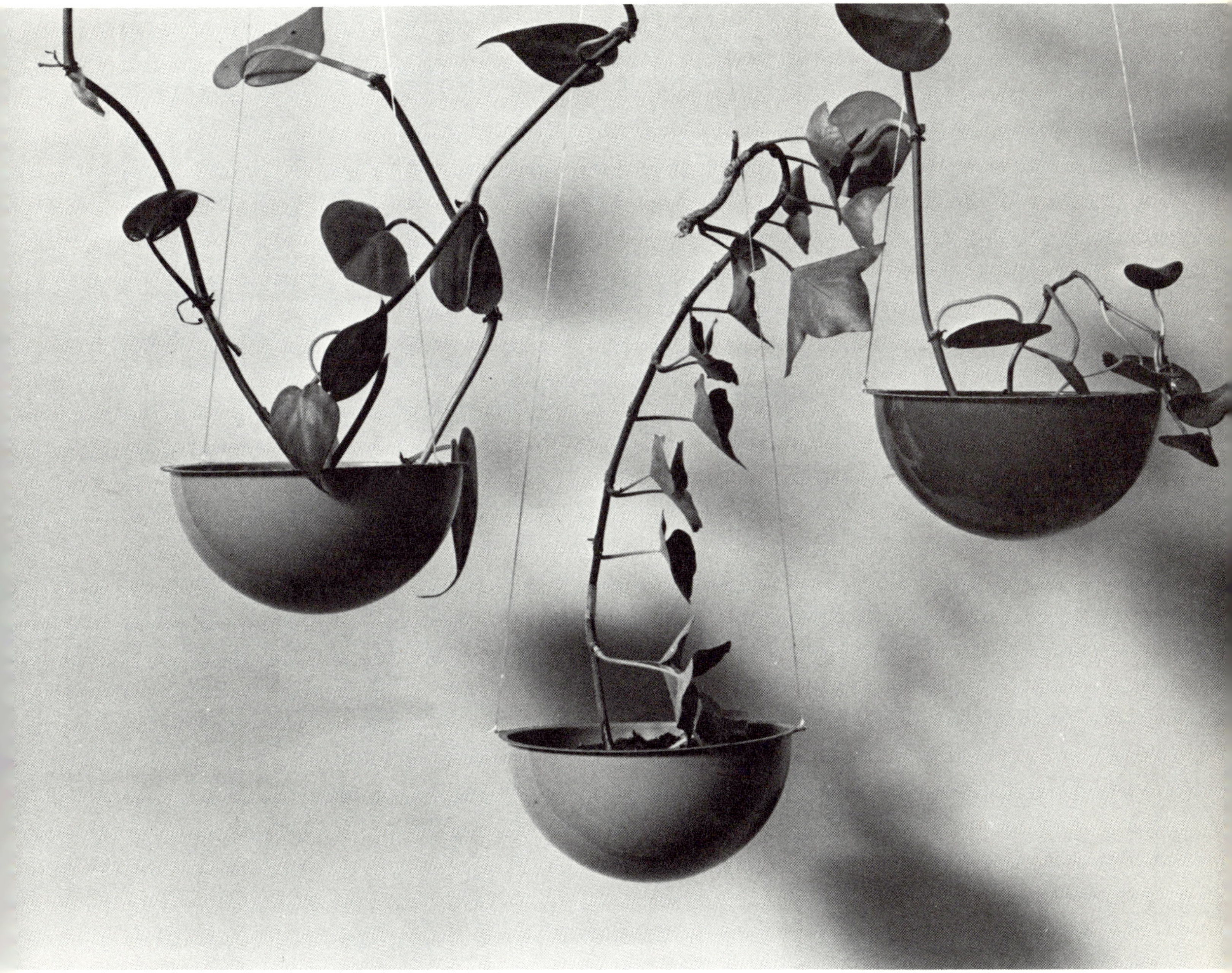

FLUE PIPE PLANTER

Inexpensive clay pipe is perfect for outdoor planters. The natural clay color looks beautiful outside on a patio, in a garden, or standing on either side of the front doorway. Use just one, or group them together in varying sizes. The chimney flue or clay pipe is readily available at a building supplier's and comes in a square or round shape. It can be cut to any length with a diamond-blade masonry saw. For this you will have to ask a building supplier or mason. If you can buy a length of pipe that is suitable for your use, it would be easier than trying to get it cut. Another way around this is to sink the long pipe into the ground until it is the right height. The cost runs from approximately 95 cents to $1.50 a foot.

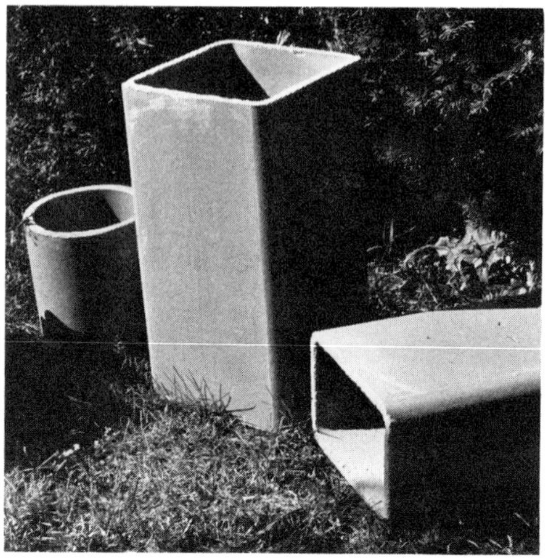

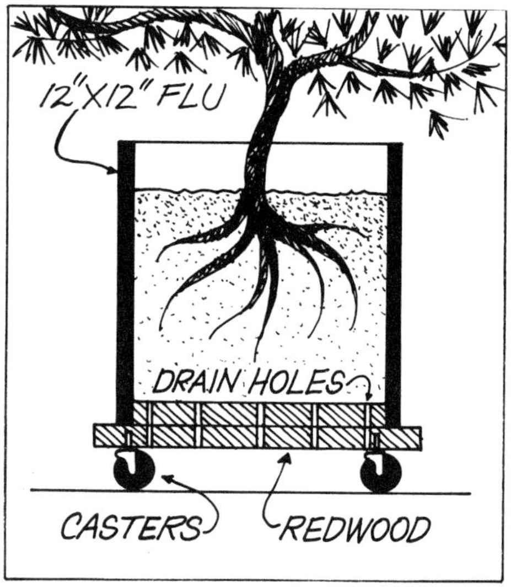

Make or have a lumberyard cut a 1-inch-thick redwood bottom. The redwood will not rot when used to hold the plant. Trace the opening of the flue and use this as a pattern for the redwood piece. Drill several holes in the wood for drainage. Insert the redwood into the pipe at the desired depth. Secure this in place with an epoxy.

Fill the planters with rich soil and arrange the plants. A small bush could be held in these pipes. If the plants aren't too heavy, the holders can be moved around from time to time.

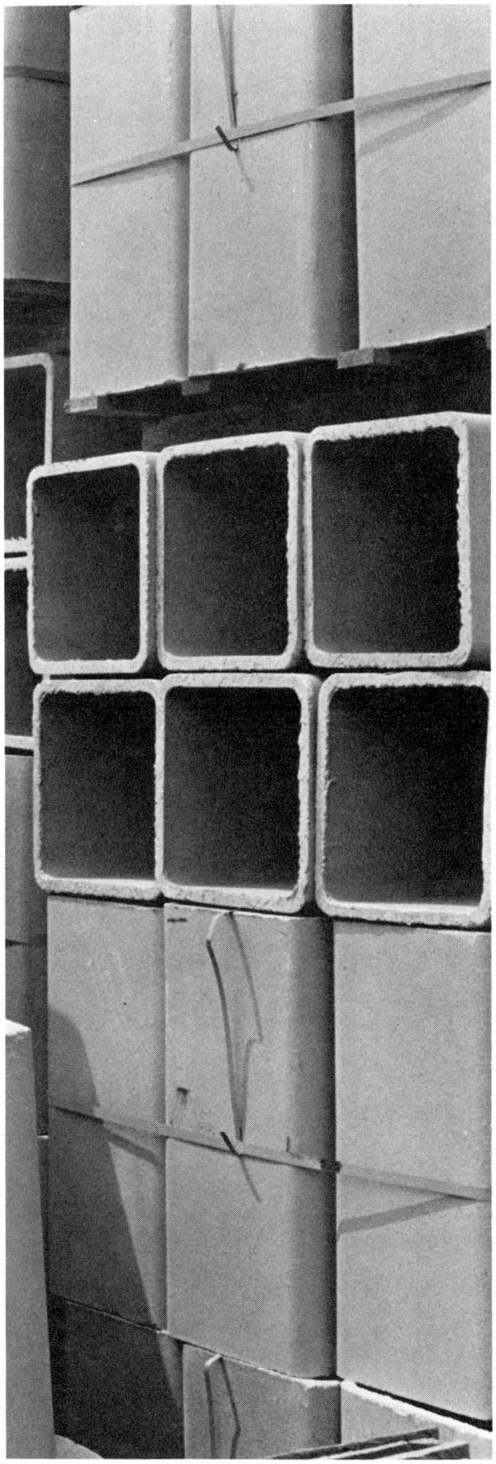

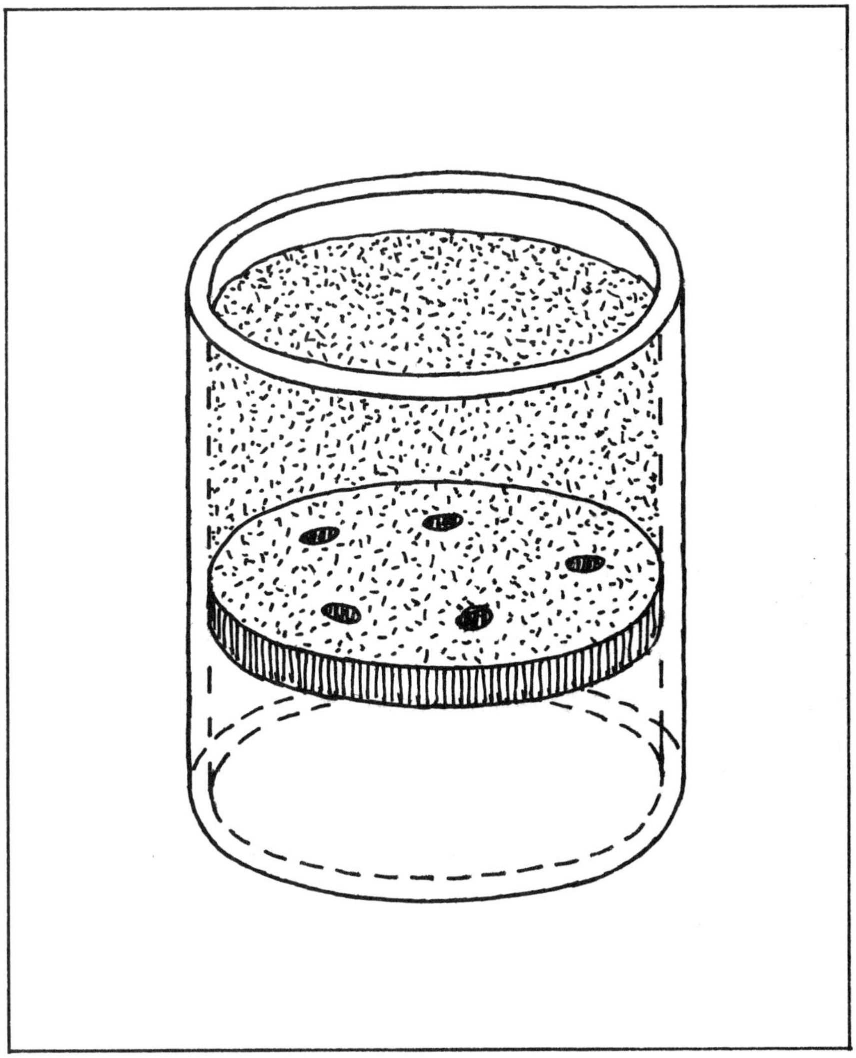

THE ART OF CONTAINMENT

A JARRING EXPERIENCE

There are many companies that make and distribute plastic and glass jars of varying sizes for many uses. If there is such a company in your area, they might be happy to sell you a few even though manufacturers generally take orders of considerable quantity. These jars are good-looking and airtight so that foods can be stored in them on open shelves in the kitchen. If each is labeled, the jars needn't be see-through. The ones shown here hold natural foods such as beans, rice, sprouts, grains, and so on, and were purchased from a plastic molding company. Added to these are three metal cans that once held snuff. They are coated with purple enamel spray paint. Some of the jars are clear, others are milk-white.

Press-on letters are used to create labels that look as though they have been printed. The labels, found in stationery stores, come in various sizes and are used for mailing

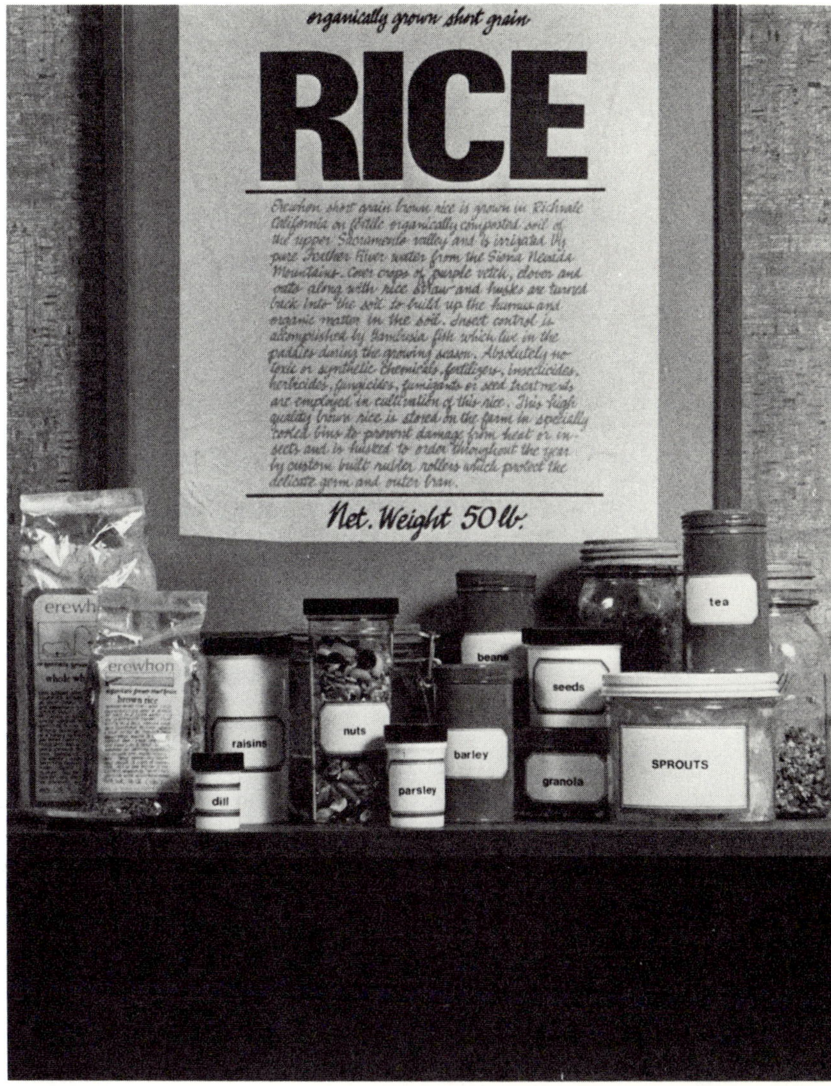

packages. While they have a gummed backing, they will eventually fall off if placed on a plastic or glass jar. They should therefore be attached with rubber cement or white glue. Old Mason jars are interesting as well and are cheaper than the new reproductions that are more readily available. Line them up in different sizes and fill with related foods such as macaroni, rice, and so on. The natural colors and interesting shapes of the food are decorative visual elements.

HIGH CALIBER

U.S. Army ammo boxes are made of steel and last forever. They seem to pop up with regularity wherever surplus is sold. They are fireproof, waterproof, and breakproof. What could be a better container for valuables? The boxes vary in dimensions, depending on the caliber size. Some open on the top and others in the front. All have a strong, collapsible handle for carrying. The front latch snaps the box closed by means of a massive spring that only the Army could have engineered.

Like all Army-issued supplies, these are olive green and not especially attractive. However, as a functional tool case they are excellent and no amount of abuse will ruin them in any way. This is an unbeatable value for four or five dollars.

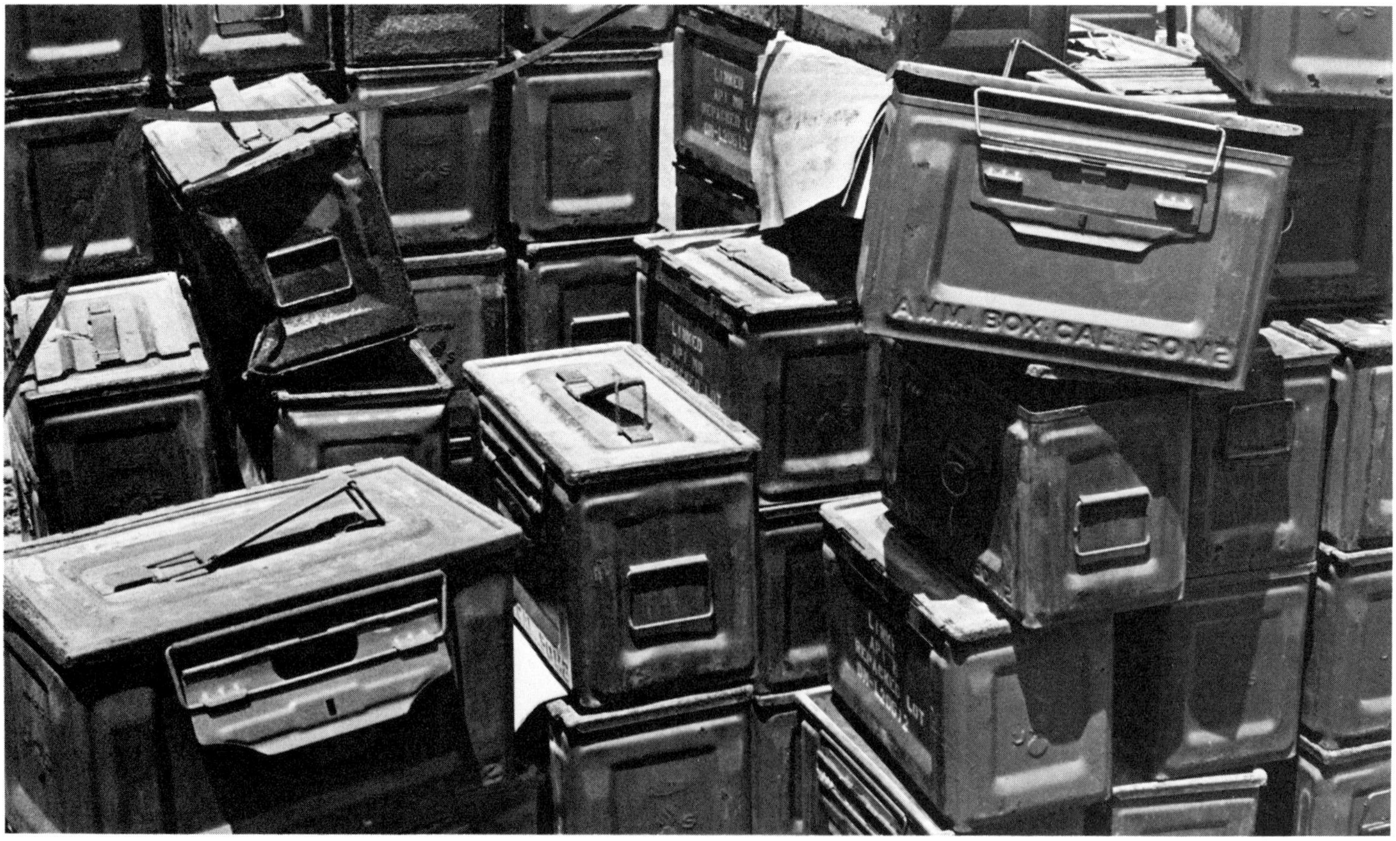

You can transform the ammo box into a chic-looking container for checks, important documents, or jewelry in minutes. This one was given two coats of hot pink color spray paint. The paint is permanent and takes minutes to dry. The stenciled letters dress it up further. These are individual metal stencil letters in a typeface called "Corbu." (See source list for stencil.)

Begin by placing a piece of masking tape across the box to create a straight line on which to place the word. Then apply white acrylic paint with a short-bristled stipple brush. Use very little paint at a time and tap the area until it is covered. Let this dry before reapplying the paint in order to completely fill in the letter. When this dries go on to the next letter. Care-

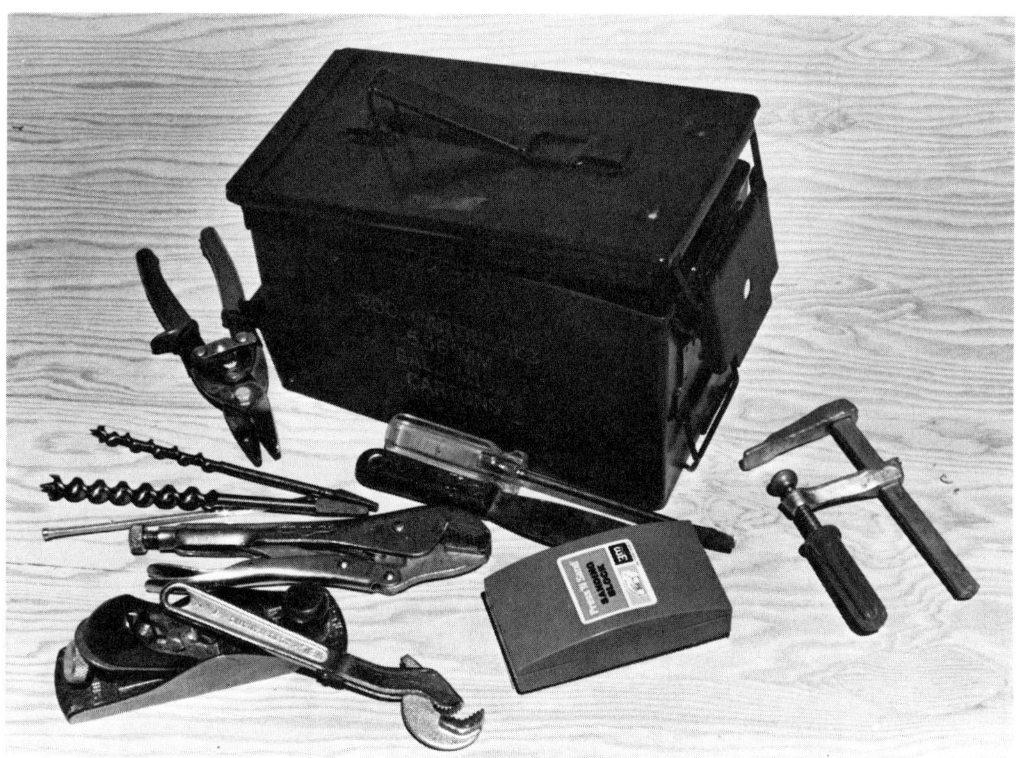

fully remove the tape so that the paint doesn't pull away from the box. To further protect the finish, you can either spray it with Krylon varnish or apply a coat of polyurethane varnish in a glossy finish. A piece of felt on the bottom will protect the surface of a table or desk top from scratches.

If the box is to be used for holding jewelry, a lining will soften the inside. This can be made from any fabric; however, felt or suede cloth is the easiest to work with. Simply measure and cut the pieces to fit all sides and inside the bottom. No hemming is necessary unless you are using a fabric that frays when cut. Brush a coating of white glue over the interior of the box and place each strip of fabric down.

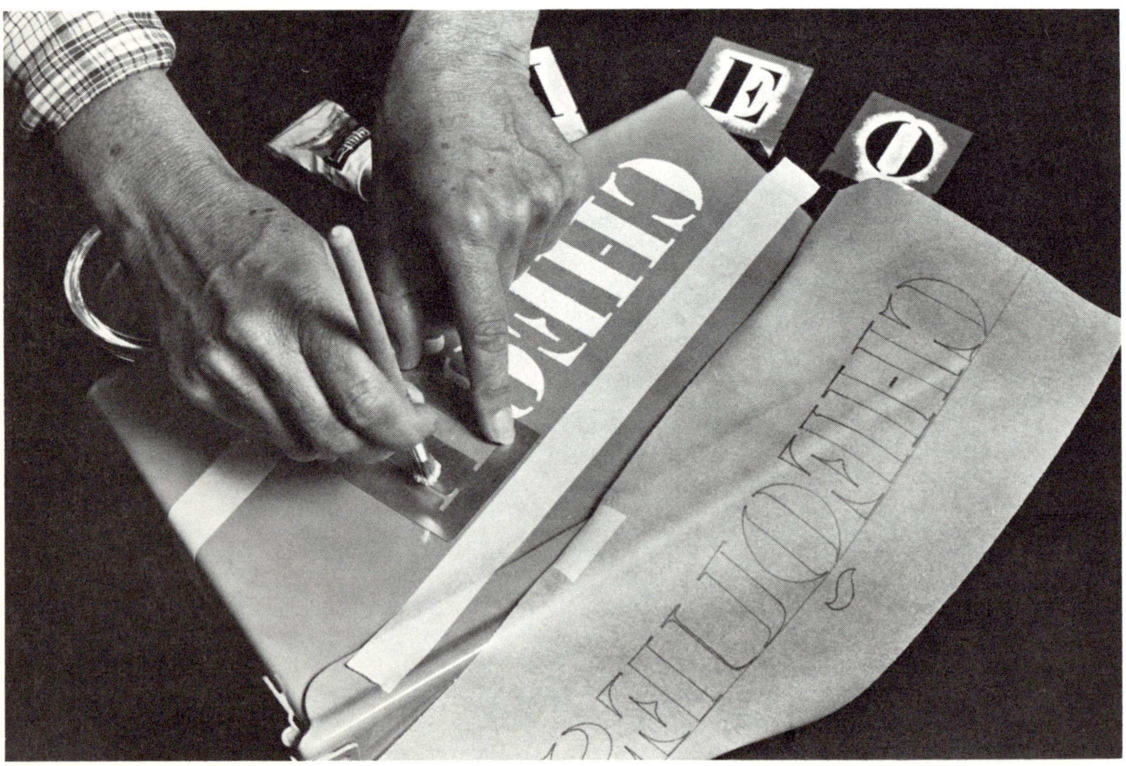

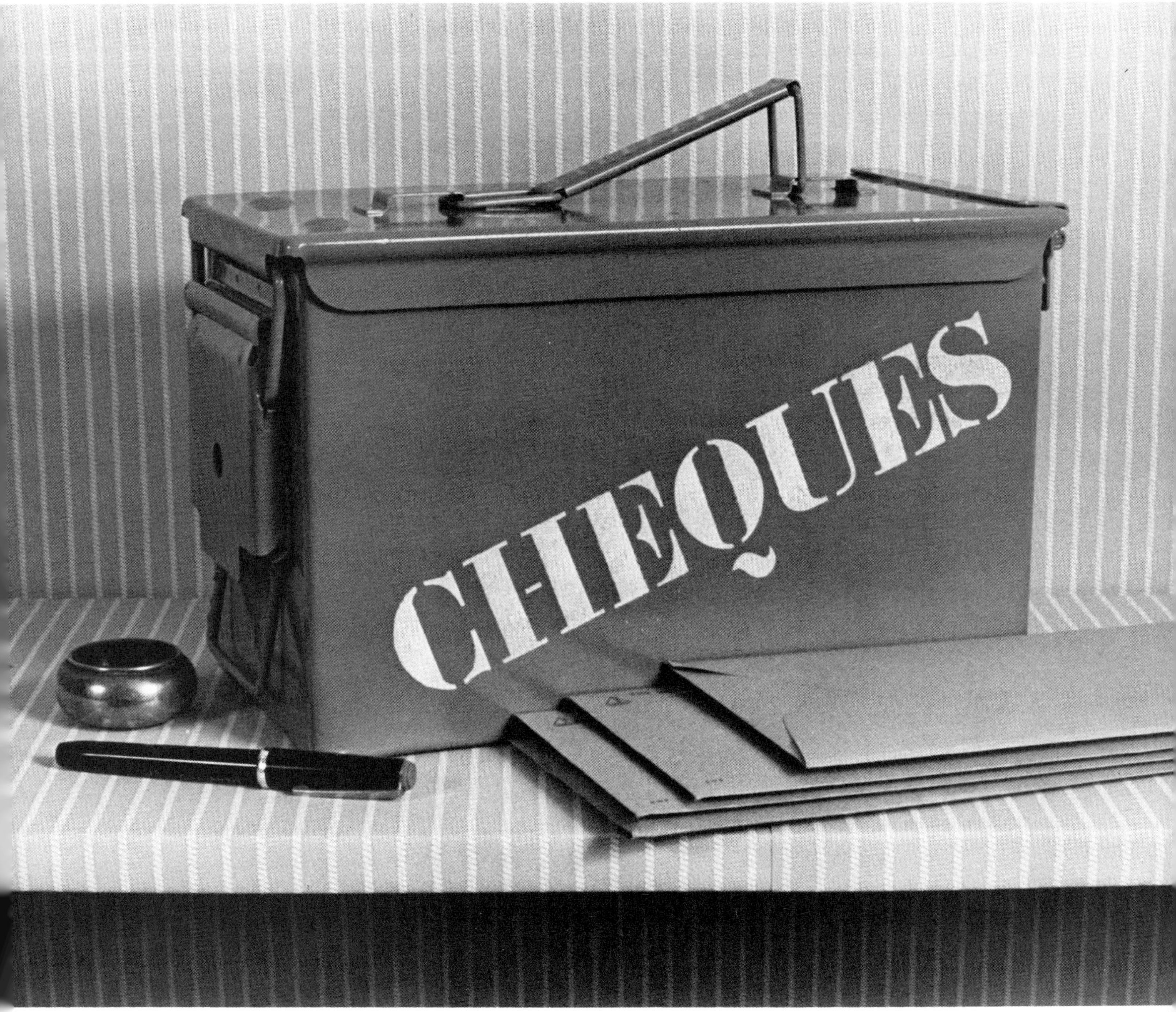
CHEQUES

DINING OUT

The wooden cases that contain four or five bottles of wine and have a rope handle are the perfect size for a picnic box. They can carry a bottle of wine and two or three glasses, which will fit safely into the wooden separator that holds the bottles in place. There is plenty of room for picnic plates, cheese, bread, and a few other goodies.

Sand the outside of the box and give it a coating of spray paint. True blue color enamel is used for this project. In order to completely cover the imprint on the box, apply two or three coats of paint. The design for the top could be found anywhere. You might create your own by cutting out pictures and glueing them to the front. This design is created with postcards from Design Research in Cambridge, Massachusetts. Arrange the cards so that they look well together and glue them in place. White glue is good for this project. To protect the surface give the whole box a coating of spray or canned varnish. Finish the inside with paint or line it with paper or fabric.

Other uses for the box might include a child's block holder for keeping a room neat or a box for sewing or for art supplies. Several manila folders will also fit inside the box for a portable file or briefcase.

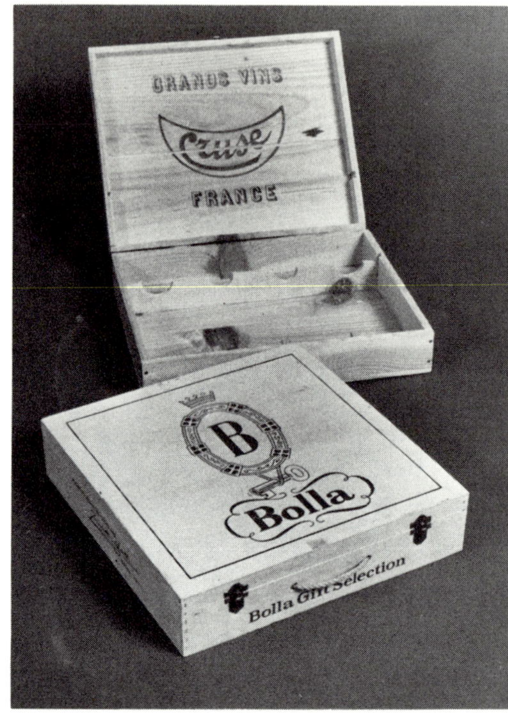

Wooden wine box is good for picnic fare.

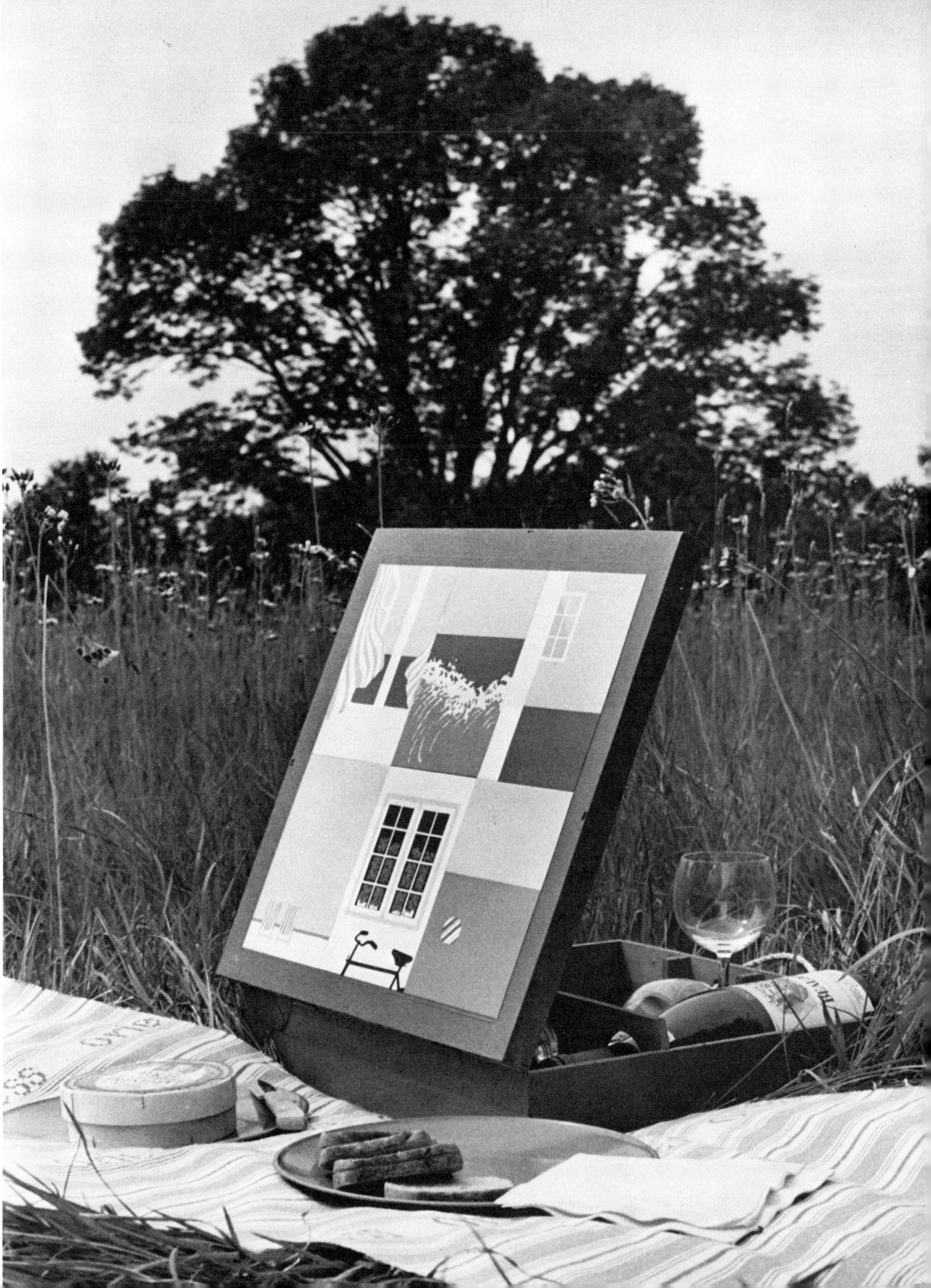

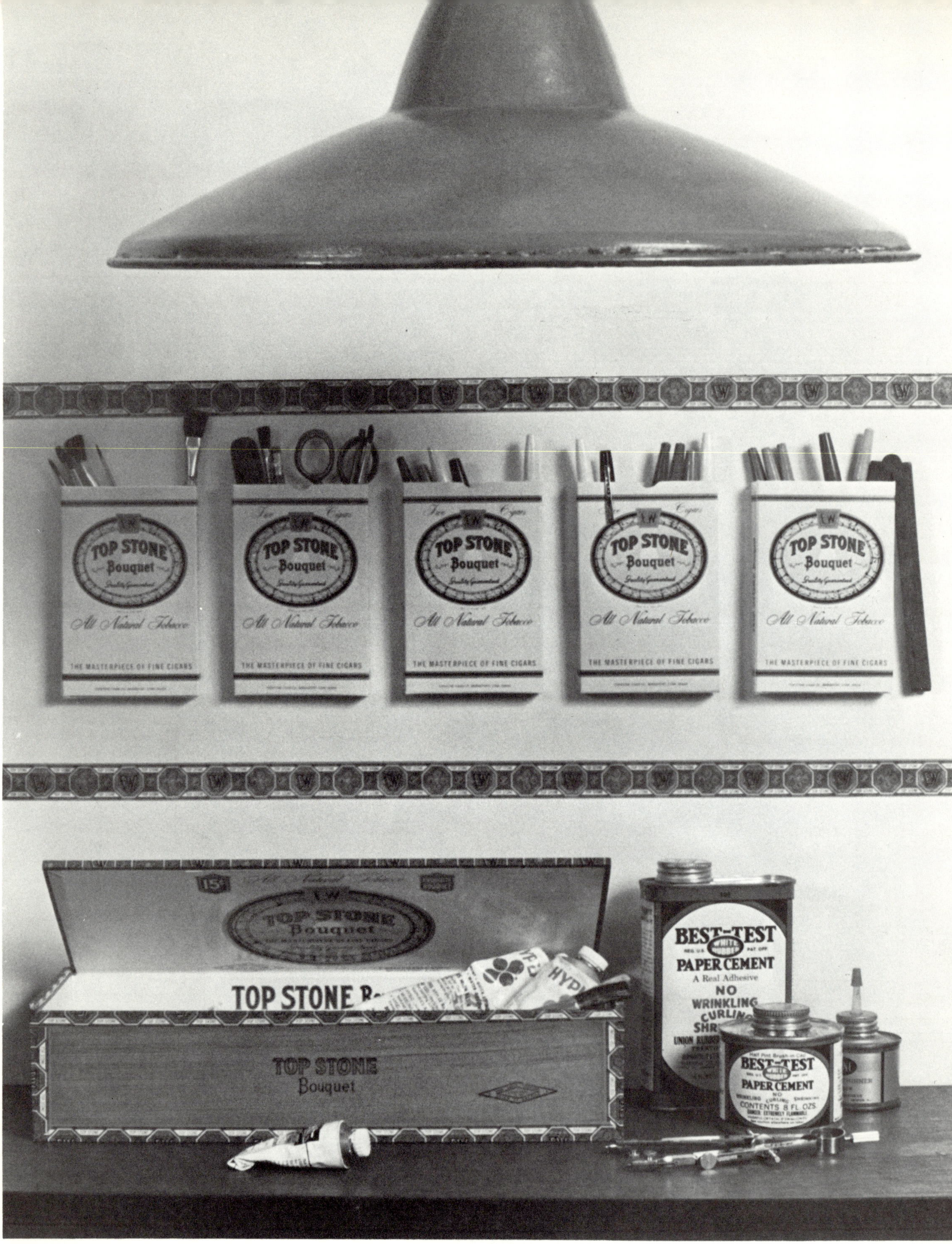
TOP STONE
Bouquet
All Natural Tobacco
THE MASTERPIECE OF FINE CIGARS
TOP STONE
Bouquet
BEST-TEST
PAPER CEMENT
A Real Adhesive
NO
WRINKLING
BEST-TEST
PAPER CEMENT
CONTENTS 8 FL OZS.

WHERE THERE'S SMOKES

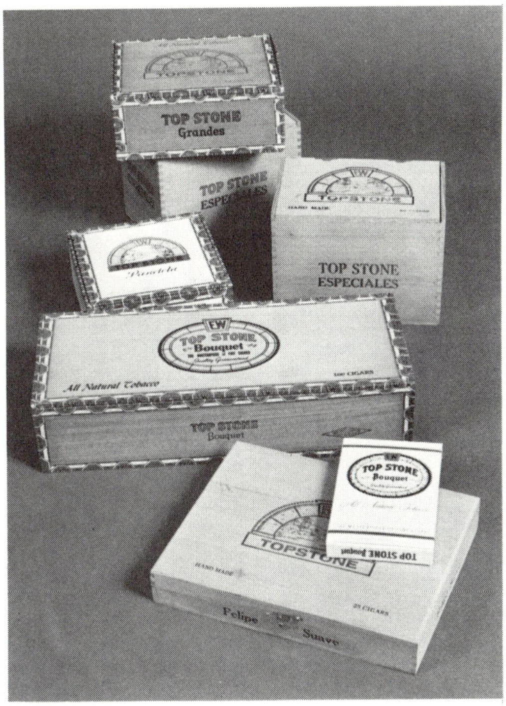

Paper boxes that hold five cigars are easy to get from a smoke shop if no one in your family smokes cigars. Or you may think of other commercial packages that are sturdy enough to use for this project as well. The white cigar boxes with a red-and-brown design are rather interesting as graphic art. In a kitchen area or over a desk the cigar boxes are perfect for holding pencils, artist's brushes, or lightweight tools.

Fold the tops in, thus creating a sturdy opening. Tape the bottoms closed. Use a yardstick to make a straight line so that the boxes will line up correctly on the wall. If you don't want to mount them directly onto the wall, you can attach them to a board or Fome-Cor backing and then hang them securely. Mount the boxes one inch apart. You can use rubber cement or self-adhesive squares to hold them in place. The border shown here is made up of cigar box border paper, which was obtained from the cigar factory mentioned earlier. However, cigar bands or decorative ribbon could be used. This strip was applied to create a decorative trim above and below the containers.

The large lamp hanging overhead was retrieved from a junk pile and was once used as an industrial light in a factory before it was replaced by fluorescent lighting fixtures. The inside is porcelain and simply needed a cleaning and re-wiring. It will take a coat of spray paint quite nicely when and if I use it elsewhere. These discarded lamp fixtures are easy to find. Often factories get rid of them when they modernize. And in the world of surplus, lamp manufacturers sell off seconds all the time.

AN UNMESSY KIT

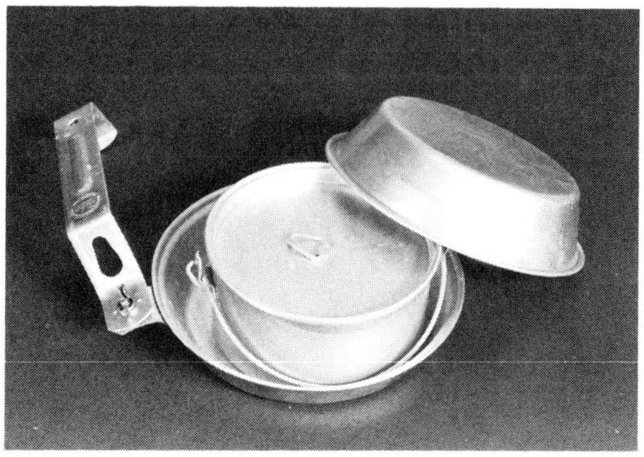

Mess kits, or canteens, used by campers, are sturdily constructed of aluminum. The utensils, which generally consist of a quart kettle with cover, a 7-inch fry pan, a 7-inch dish, and an 8-ounce polypropylene plastic cup, nest into one compact unit and fit inside a durable carrying cover with adjustable shoulder strap. All this costs approximately five dollars.

The canteen elements are good containers because they are well proportioned in size and unobtrusive in color. When lined up on a mirrored shelf in the bathroom, they look sensational. Fill each with cosmetics, toothpaste, comb and brush, and so on, for easy access. In order to liven them up a bit, each pot, plate, and cup can be stenciled with a number in a different color. The field cup that once held a plant on the wall on page 121 is now spray painted with bright yellow enamel. There are many similar utensils available separately. You can add any pieces to the basic elements in order to fill your needs. Aluminum provision boxes with rounded corners are nicely shaped and shallow for holding small, flat objects. A ladle hung on the wall could hold small cases of lip gloss. A compartment plate, which sells for a dollar, could hold various small items in each compartment. Salt and pepper shakers could be filled with dusting powder, and several tin cups could be lined up on the shelf and stenciled with successive numbers. These are perfect for lipsticks, mascara, color crayons, and any long-stemmed items. Most camping objects have handles or some way of hanging. Take advantage of this feature to save shelf space if needed.

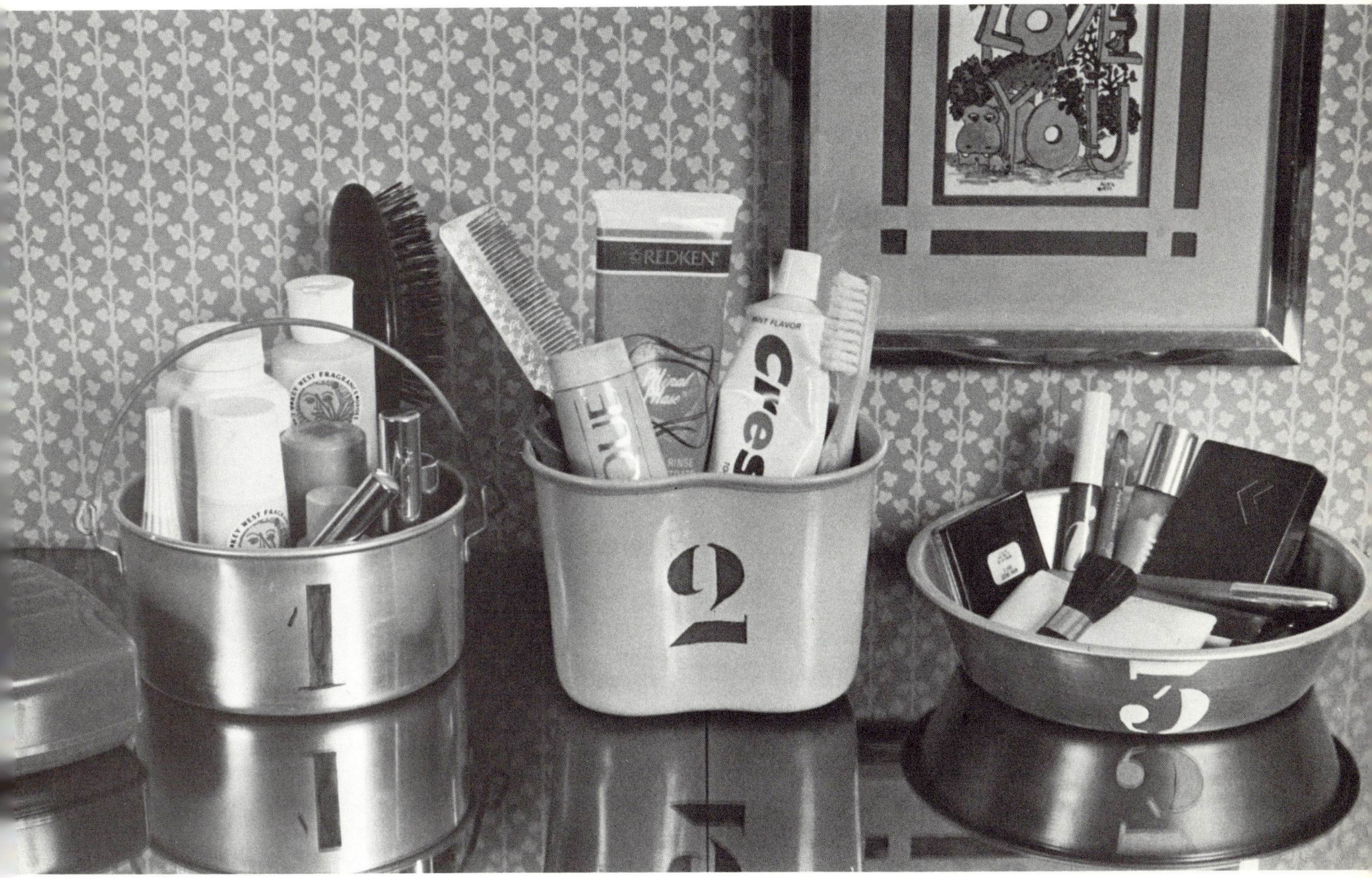

REDKEN
1
2
3

BARRACKS AID

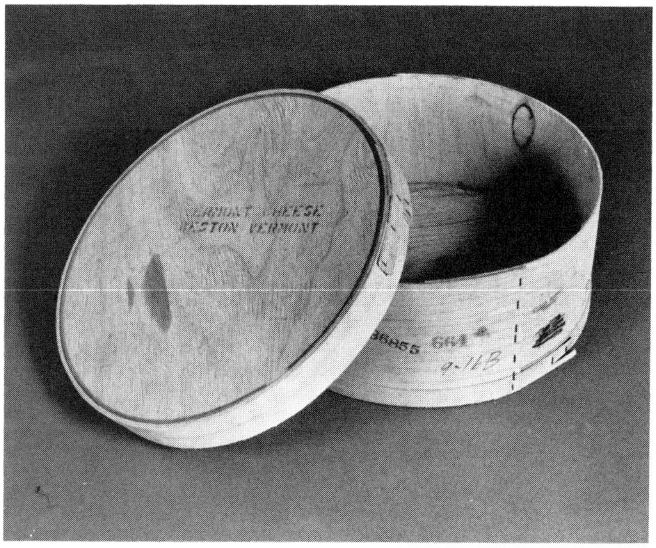

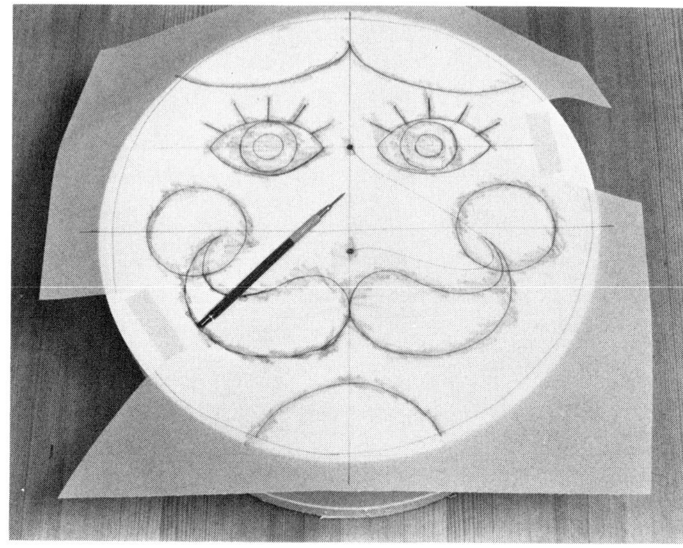

Probably the most annoying conflict that parents and children have revolves around picking up toys and keeping bedrooms in respectable condition. Any device that will make this chore entertaining should be a welcome one. This particular block-and-toy organizer started life filled with cheese and was found in a Vermont cheese shop. These large round wooden containers are seen often as they are manufactured for the shipment of cheeses.

The gimmick here is that the top of the box also becomes a plaything. The nose, made of pliable cord, is also the handle for opening the box. Children can have fun changing the shape of the clown's nose.

These boxes are made of extremely rough and therefore splintery wood. Begin by sanding the surface with a heavy-grit sandpaper. Apply several coats of white latex paint. The design is a simple one and done mainly with a compass. Trace the design onto the box top. Drill two holes for the cord that will create the nose-pull. Next fill in the areas with

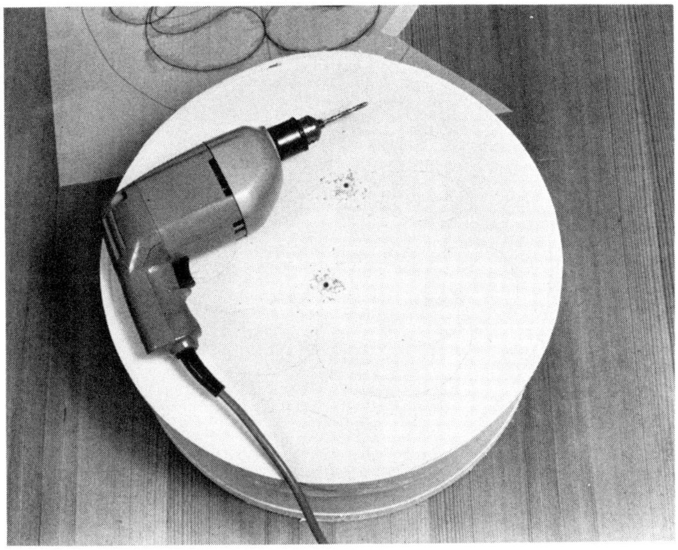

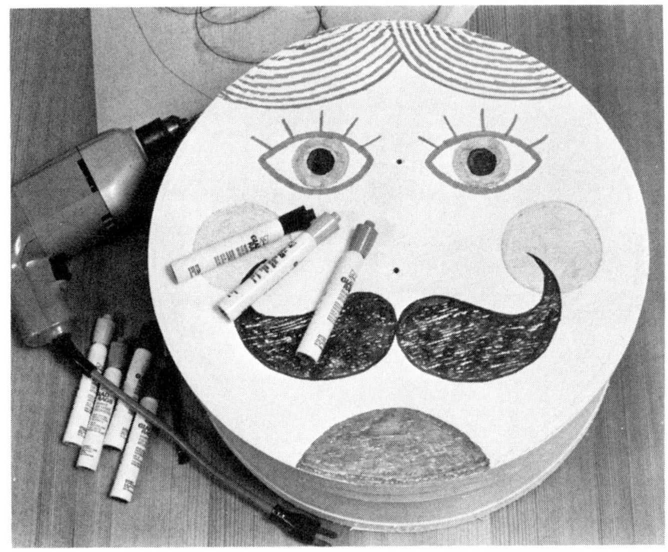

Trace design onto top of box.
Drill holes for cord.
Fill in design with waterproof markers or paint.

colorful markers. If you feel confident enough, the children might enjoy helping with this project.

Spray paint the bottom portion in a bright color. The band around the top of this box was painted with acrylic in a contrasting color. Next, coat the entire box with high-gloss polyurethane varnish. This will protect the design as well as give the box a shiny finish. The inside can be spray painted and coated with varnish as well, or lined with vinyl wall covering or plastic self-adhesive shelf paper.

Thick macramé cord in a bright purple color was used here for the handle. The Army & Navy stores carry a supply of cord, less expensive than what you would find in craft shops. A thick piece of rope or knitting yarn can also be used, but the yarn is not as good because it isn't as strong.

To secure the handle, thread each end through the top of the drilled holes and make a knot on the underside. Check the length of the cord to see how it falls and to make sure there is enough for the children to play with before cutting.

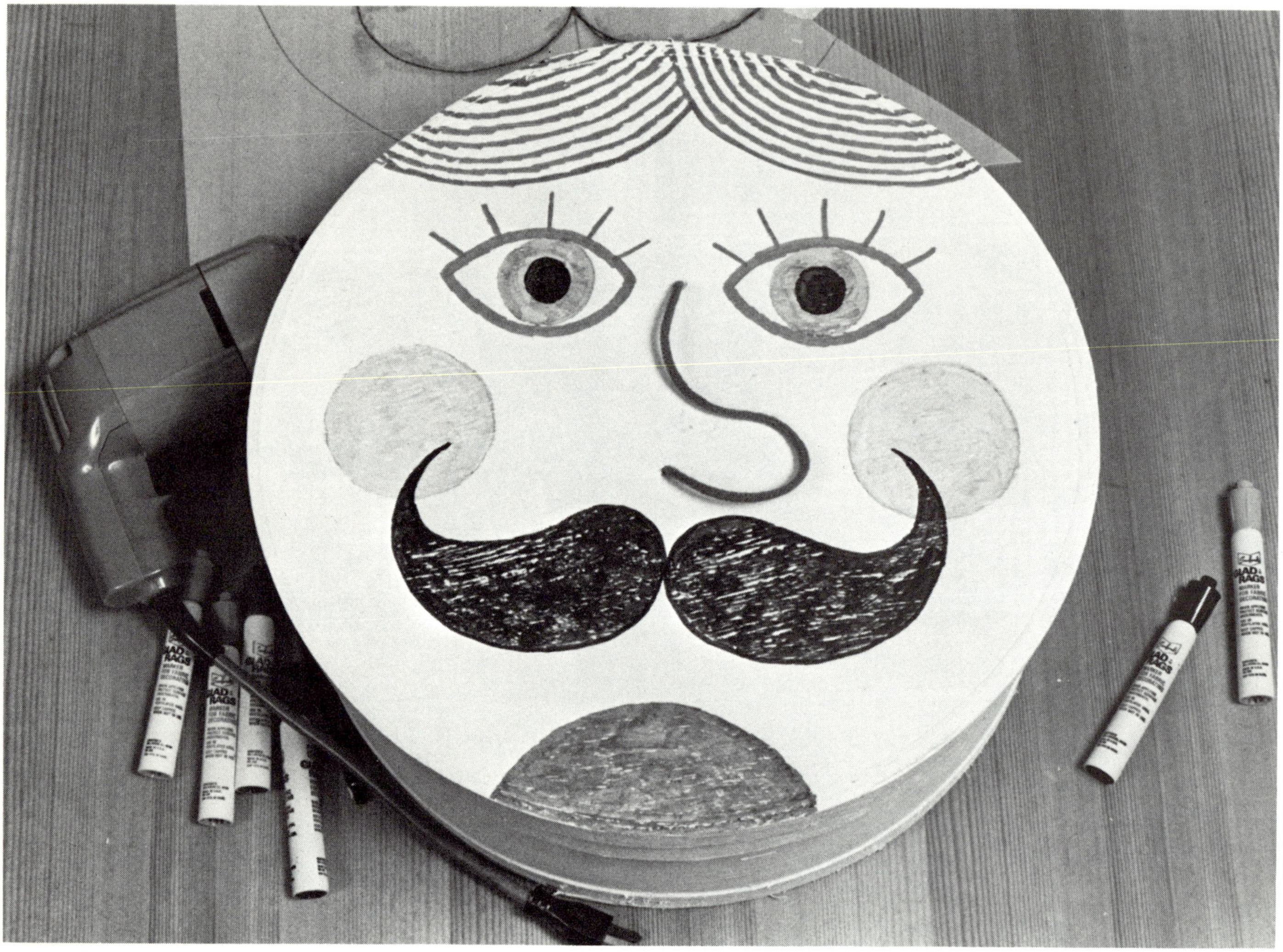

Make different noses by rearranging cord handle.

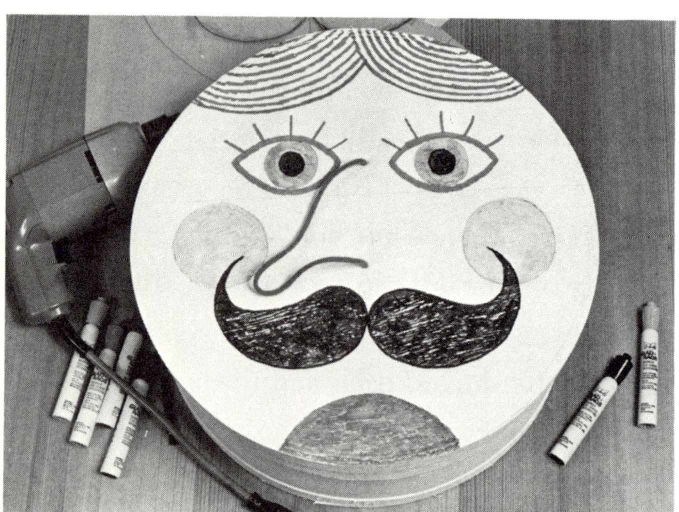

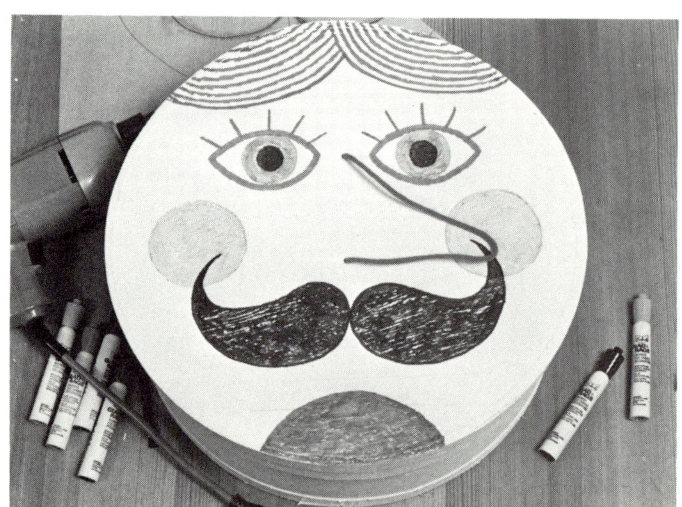

CUT IT OUT

One of the ways that I like to dress up a cigar box is with decoupage. In this way you can choose the design to fit your decor, and the size of the box is perfect to work on.

Decoupage is a craft that originated in the eighteenth century, and the word means applied cutouts. The designs are not painted onto the surface but rather cut out from paper. You might find a picture in a book, on a greeting card, or on wrapping paper. Magazine paper is too thin and should not be used. The print from the other side of a picture from a magazine will show through once the design is pasted to the box. At this point it will be too late to undo the error. Decoupage prints are sold individually in craft shops along with the other supplies needed.

Begin by painting the outside of the box. I used spray enamel paint in a bright yellow color. Or you can substitute acrylic paint, which is applied with a flat brush. It will take several coats to cover the cigar paper so that the words don't show through. When the paint is dry, sand lightly with a fine-grit paper to create a smooth surface.

Select pictures that are appropriate for the size and shape of the box. Cut the design out with fine cuticle scissors. Be sure to cut away all excess paper around the design so that it won't look messy when glued to the background. Arrange the pictures in an appealing way. Try changing the layout and stepping back to scc how it might look better. When you have decided on the final arrangement, glue each element in place with white glue. Wipe away excess glue around each cutout with a slightly damp sponge. Let the cutouts dry for a few minutes.

Next, you must protect the surface with varnish. This can be done with spray varnish or by hand with regular indoor

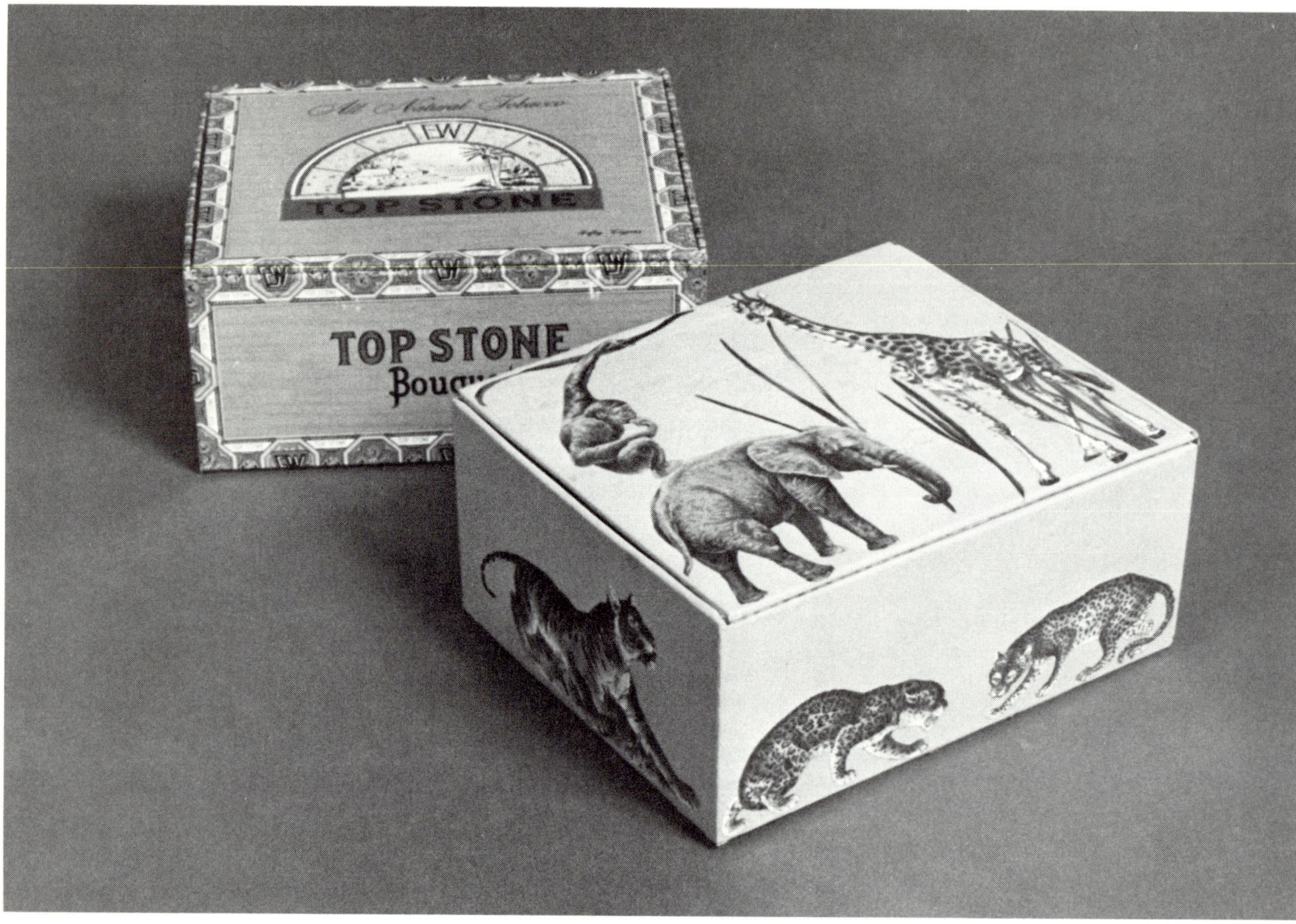

wood varnish. Prop the lid open slightly with a toothpick so that it won't get stuck shut. Spray a coating evenly over the entire box. If you are using varnish from a can, it should be applied with a ½-inch flat varnish brush. Brush the varnish over each side and the top of the box. Hold the box up to the light as you do this. Since the varnish is clear it is often easy to miss whole sections. Draw your brush in only one direction. The varnish should never be applied thickly. Each coat should be as thin as you can apply it. I prefer to use the canned varnish because it gives a better finish even though the spray varnish dries more quickly, is easier to use, and you needn't buy a brush and cleaner. However, it does have a very unpleasant odor and you must take care to avoid drip marks caused by uneven spraying.

Each coat of varnish must dry thoroughly before reapplying. The spray varnish will take an hour or more to dry. The canned varnish should dry all day. However, the brushed-on varnish is equal to two or three spray coatings. Either way, the box will require three to five coats of varnish to sufficiently cover the prints.

When the outside is finished, paint or line the interior. Wallpaper, wrapping paper, self-adhesive paper, fabric, or tape can be used to create a pretty inside. I never feel that a box is finished until I have lined it. Felt or suede cloth are very good materials for the lining as no hemming is required and they are both thick and cushiony for fragile objects.

This project makes a nice gift as it is practical and can be designed in a personal way. Select the designs that best relate to the use of the box or the taste or interests of the person who might receive it. Another suggestion for personalizing the box is to use photographs to cover the top. Pressed flowers can also be used, but you should then cover them with the spray varnish and several extra coats will be needed. For an elegant lining consider plush velvet or a brocaded fabric.

ICE CAPADES

The large metal paint buckets that hold a gallon of paint make good, inexpensive ice buckets. This one is shiny aluminum and, when filled with ice, the outside becomes cold and frosty. If you use it in a rather formal setting, it will almost look like an elegant silver ice container. When not in use for ice, have it double up as a plant holder. The thin metal handle is sturdy and perfect for hanging on a gutsy hook.

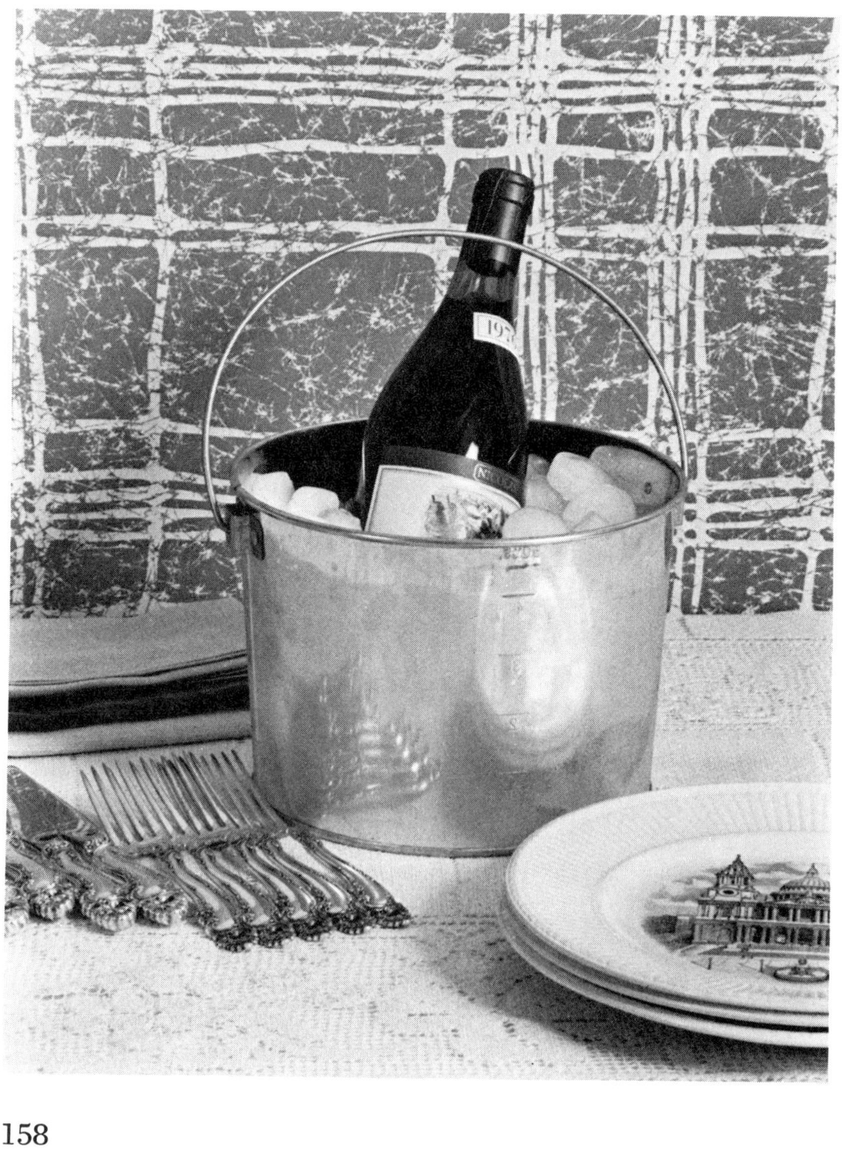

COMMON CARRIERS

TOOL UP

Bags, bags, and more bags. Government-issued materials are always contained in something, usually in heavy-duty burlap or canvas bags. A utility bag shaped like a flight bag, but smaller, sports a strap for easy belt attachment. A dunk bag is made of lightweight rugged nylon mesh with a drawstring. It is used to wash canteen items, as a tote bag, gadget bag, fish bag, campsite food storage bag, ball bag, and for cooling beverages in a stream. A musette bag is made of heavy-duty duck and divided with inner compartments. It has a rear outside pocket and side pocket, adjustable back straps that convert to shoulder use, front tabs with eyelets, and can be used as a schoolbook bag. A smaller version is the belt pouch bag, which is 7″ × 3½″ × 3″ and comes in assorted colors. This water-repellent nylon bag is used by hunters, fishers, skiers, hikers, and campers because it has handy clips and loops for attaching to a belt. An all-purpose favorite that will probably always be around is the G.I. duffel bag with its sturdy web handle and shoulder strap. This bag is perfect for storage and travel. It can even be dyed a color more exciting than the standard olive green. And there is the lightweight version of this, the laundry bag with brass grommets and cotton draw-rope. These can be dyed, painted with a design, stenciled, and hung in the closet for storage of blankets or for what it was originally intended, dirty clothes. Aside from all the bags that I've mentioned, there are many, many more, and a well-equipped Army & Navy or surplus store worth its stripes will have a huge assortment. Whatever your need, there is certainly a bag to fit it at less than half what you will pay elsewhere. Best of all, it will be unique.

The smaller bags that are intended for attachment to a belt have a lot of versatility. I like to hang them on hooks in the kitchen for wooden spoons and so on. But this little one is perfect as a bike tool carrier and there is ample apparatus to attach to the handle bars. I have come across the same style made slightly larger and it is fine for holding three tennis balls. This summer I intend to have one knapsack on the rear of my bicycle for a tennis racket and another on the front to carry the balls. With my leather French map-case for necessities (see page 162), I'll be all G.I.-decked out.

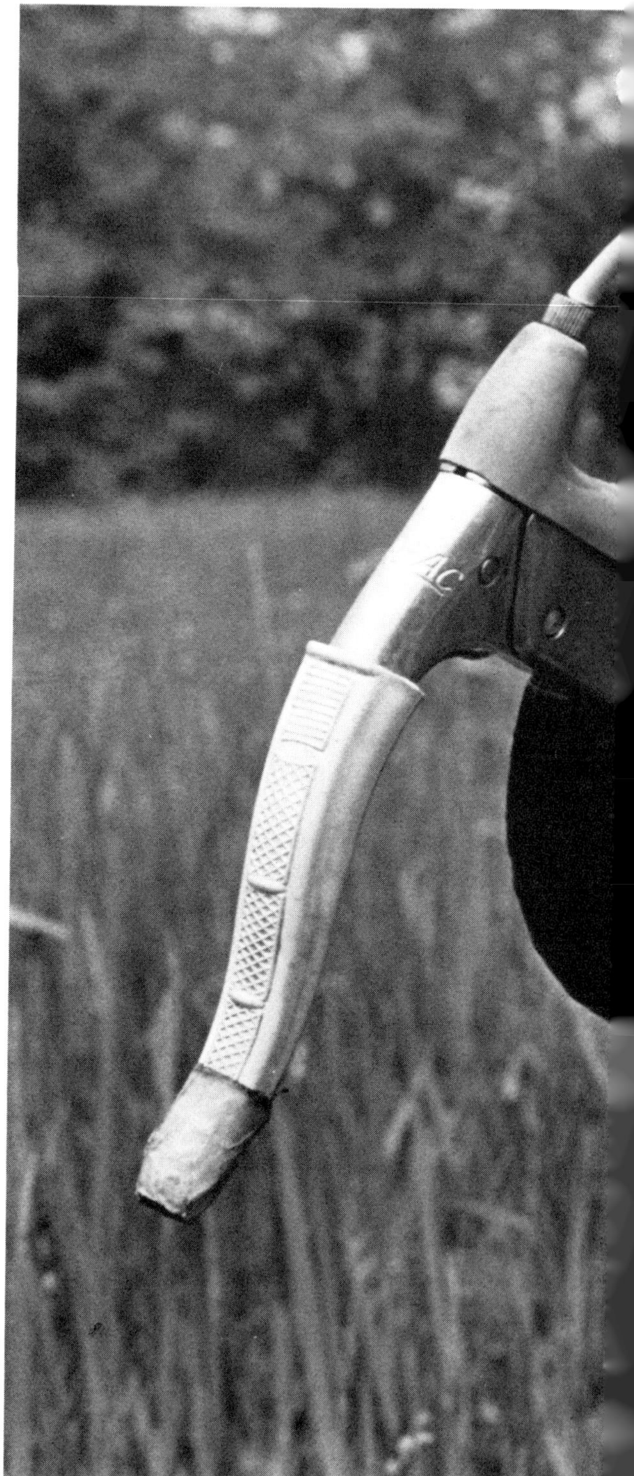

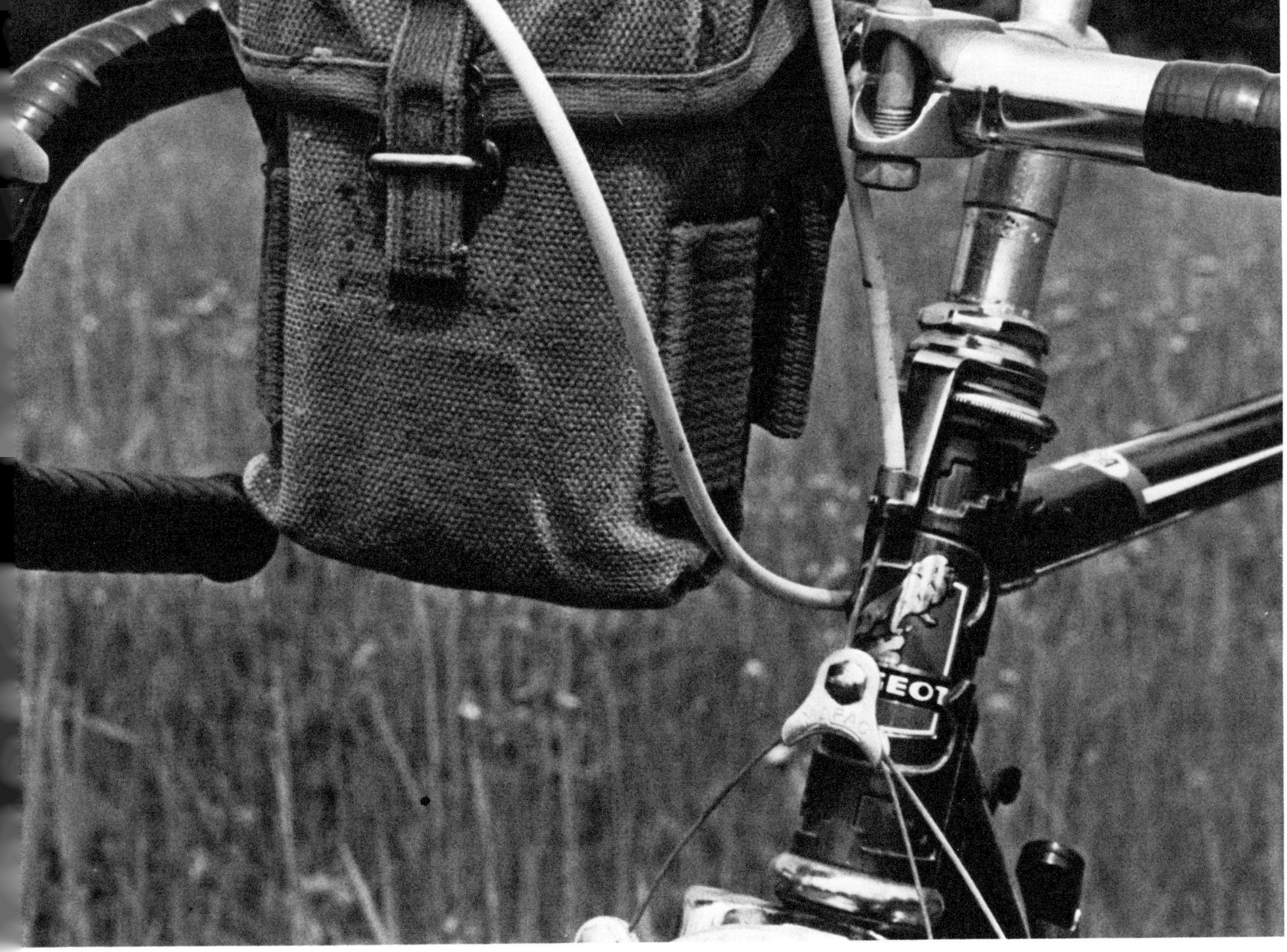

UNCOMMON CARRIERS

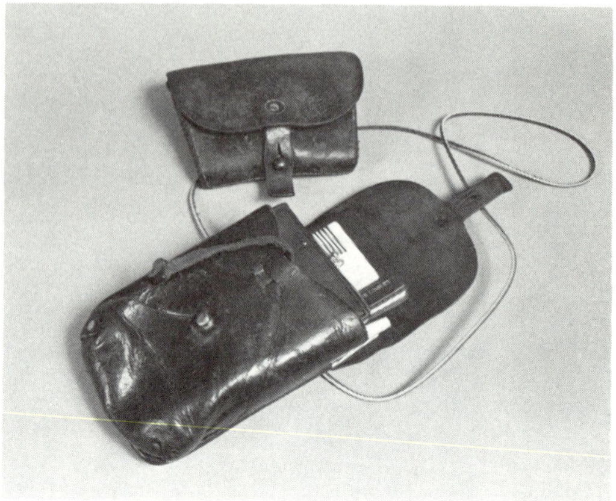

Leather cases made for maps and cartridges make convenient purses. The long pouch is called a French map-case and has a lot of good features. As these cases are well worn, they are, by now, beautifully softened. There is enough room to fit a wallet, comb, checkbook, and pen. With a tight squeeze a lipstick and address book might fit as well. In other words, just the bare essentials. The flap, which is the closing, fits down and catches on a brass knob. In addition, there is a leather thong laced in the front. This piece extends inside the case and when it is pulled up, the contents are lifted for easy access. The back sports a wide, thick leather piece that is secured by four brass buttons and is used to attach the case to a belt. If you prefer, a leather thong or strip can be tied through this back piece in order to create a shoulder strap. Adjust it to the length that is most comfortable.

These cases can be found in many shapes and sizes although they are all rather small, part of their appeal. Some have a divided compartment that makes the carrying space limited. I have had mine for years and it is soft and smooth from use. Many of these cases can be used as is, others will need some work. If you find that yours is dull, clean it up with soap and water and wax it with a paste made especially for leather. You might want to darken a light-colored leather. This can be done with shoe dye or polish that is brushed on, left to dry slightly, then rubbed into the leather until no excess can be wiped away. For extra satin patina, spit on the pouch and rub away with a soft cloth. Soldiers claim that a spit polish is the best way to shine leather boots, and it works just as well for the map-case purse.

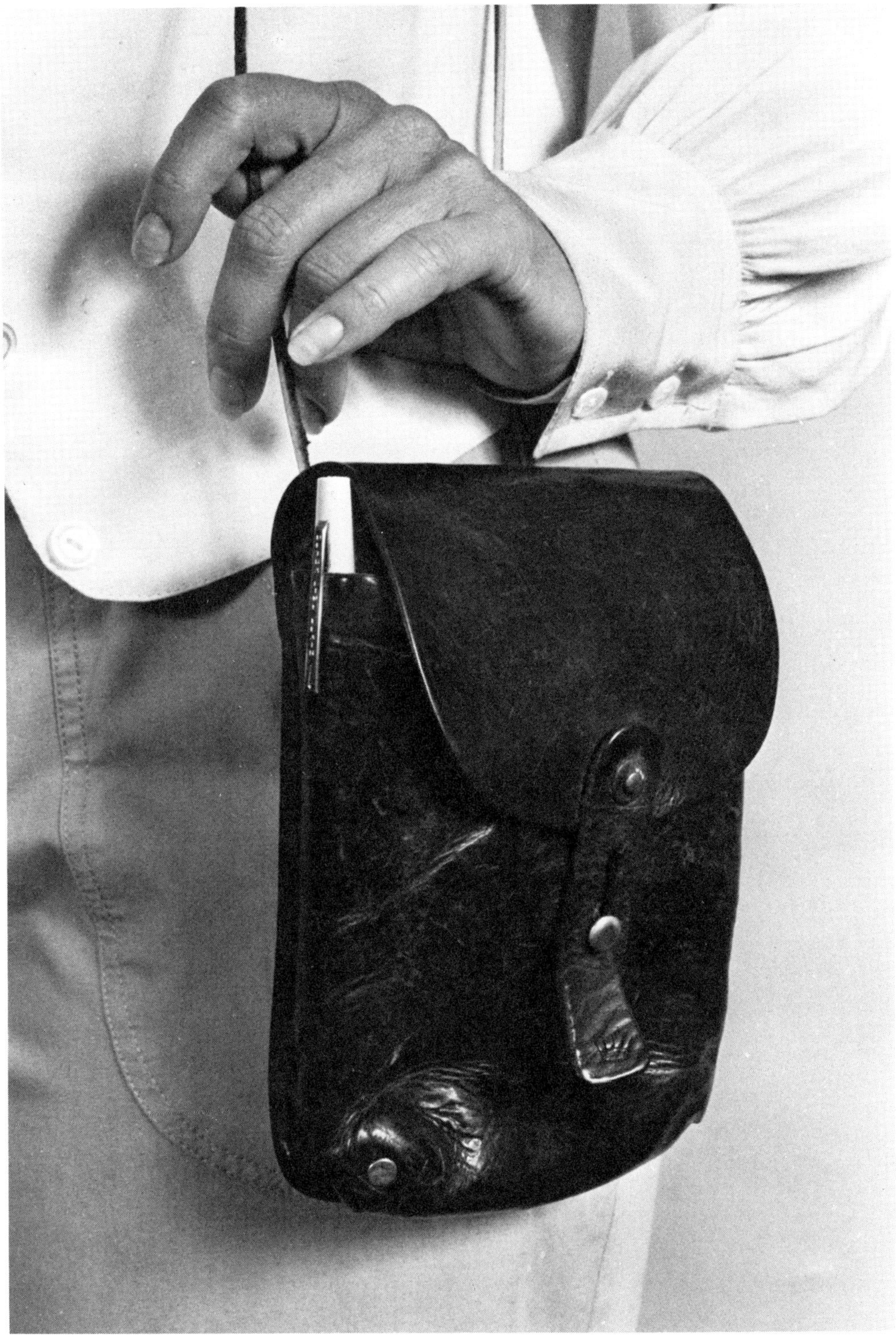

HOLD THE NEWS

The versatile canvas water bucket, suggested as a planter on page 122, can also be used to hold magazines and newspapers. Although collapsible when not in use, the bucket will hold its shape rigidly when pulled open. Bolts of fabric, balls of yarn, or household items could also be kept in the bucket. Or hang one on a hook in the closet to use for holding mittens, scarves, hats, and so on. If you want a handy closet organizer, hang several on a low closet pole and fill each with socks, underwear, and other small items. This is most helpful in a child's closet. For small toys, such as blocks, cars, stuffed animals, and even books, the water buckets make clean-up a cinch. And, if you are a tennis player, use one to hold cans of balls. If you have several buckets, try stenciling each person's name on a different color one, or the name of the item that each will contain.

Old-fashioned galvanized buckets are also available. If you can't find used ones in antique or junk shops, reproductions are made and sold through mail-order companies. Those huge milk cans that we often see converted into umbrella stands and outdoor planters can now be ordered easily also. Watering cans, cylinder scoops, spitoons, ice cream containers, washtubs, water pails, kettles, pitchers, and various other pails come in a wide assortment of sizes and have as many uses. These items are so common that we can easily overlook them as creative sources for home decorating. Almost any container is a possible candidate for conversion, so don't be hasty to discard anything.

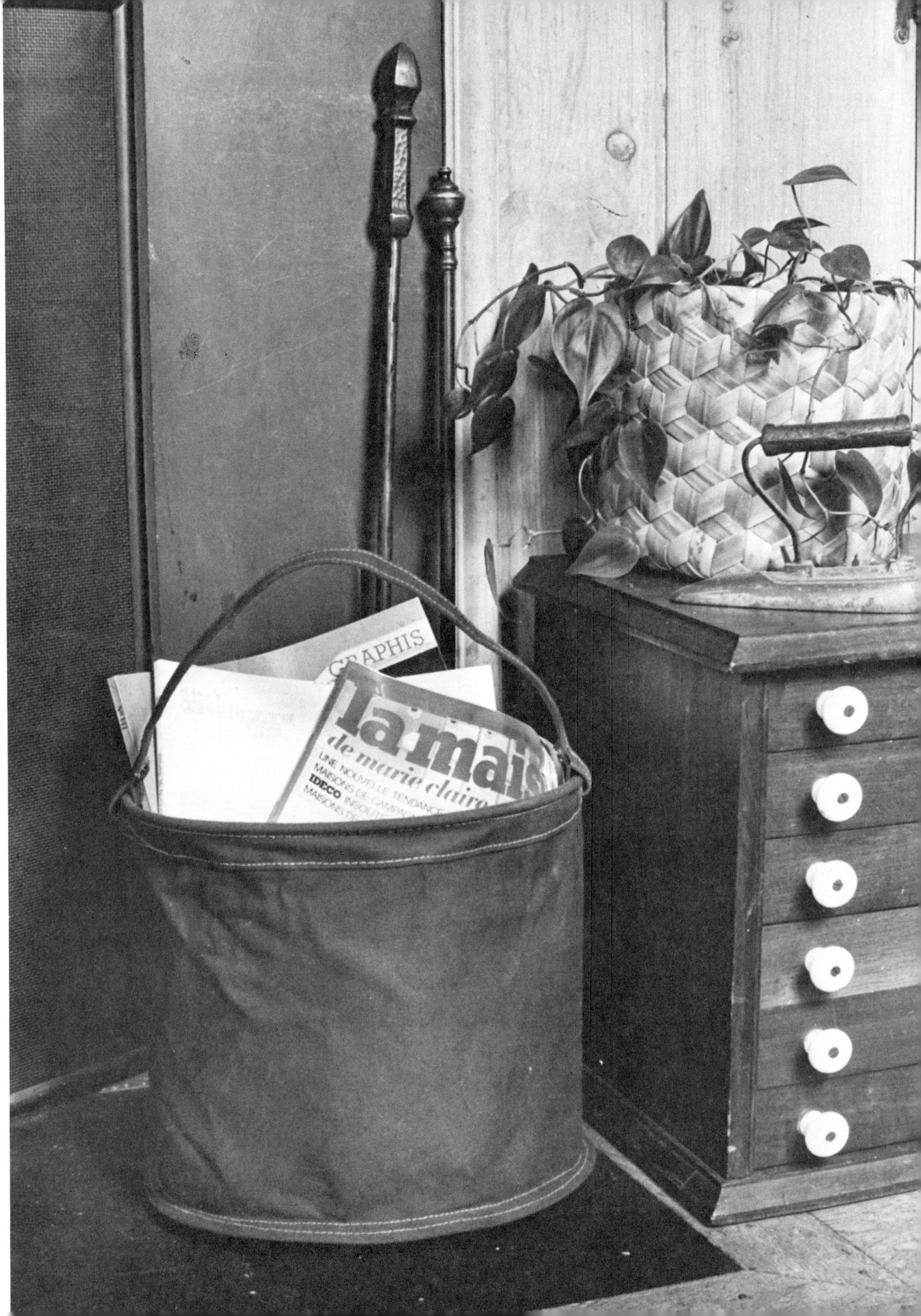
GRAPHIS
UNE NOUVELLE TENDANCE
IDECO

FISHING FOR A COMPLEMENT

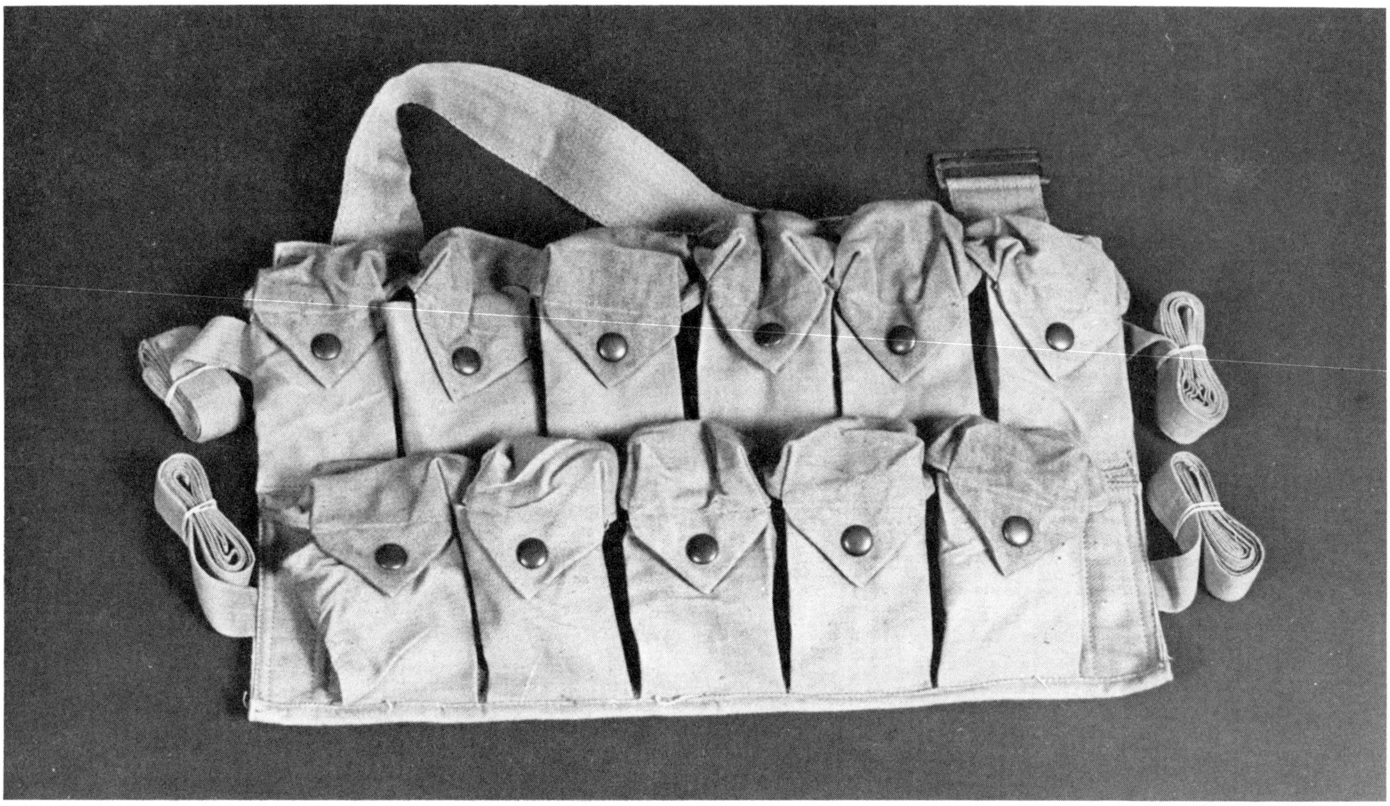

A cartridge belt has eleven flat-top, snap-shut pockets. Anything that is small and can be organized into the compartments can be readily available and safely stored. It is an ideal fishing tackle carrier and has always been popular with fisherpeople, hunters, campers, and sportsmen and women. In the home, small spice bottles could be stored in each pocket, and the straps used for attaching to the waist could be utilized for wall hanging. The heavy canvas is olive green, but a bright purple, red, or yellow fabric dye eliminates the drabness immediately. The material can also be decorated with fabric paint, or each pocket can be stenciled with a number or word. For this you will need acrylic paint and a stipple brush.

PACK IT IN

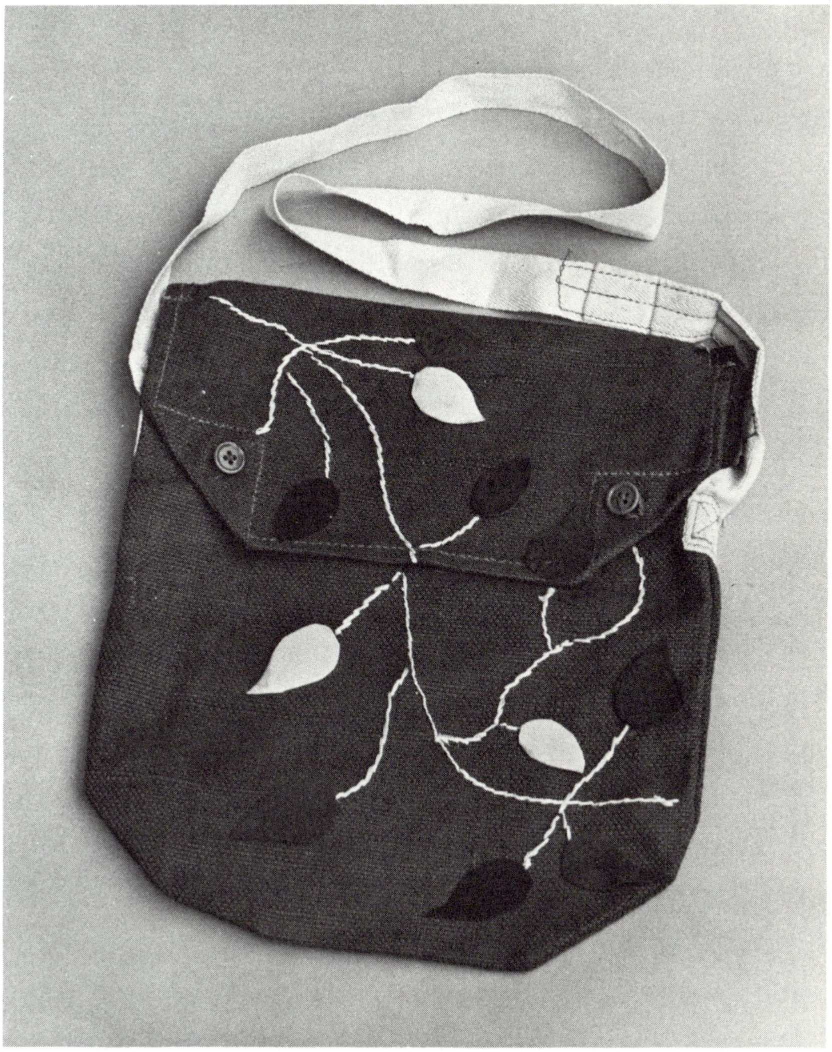

Burlap bags come in little sizes, big sizes, and every size in between. Probably the single most popular item that can always be found in abundance in Army & Navy and surplus or camping stores is a bag for anything. And, they have to be the best-looking, most versatile carry-alls around. Well made, with reinforced stitching everywhere, each has a shoulder strap or some means for attaching to a belt, bike handles, waist, or anything else you can think of. The Army seems to have over-designed everything to insure efficiency, compactness, and serviceability, and the many carrying bags are probably the best example of this. Everything on the bags either buttons, snaps, or buckles and it doesn't take much imagination to find a use for all of them. The green burlap bag can be used as is or decorated with a variety of craft techniques. In this case, a branch was embroidered across the front and small leather leaves were applied. Each leaf is a different autumn color. They were cut from scraps so that they fit at the ends of the branches.

Begin by roughly drawing the design on a piece of paper. Then copy it in pencil on the bag. Choose a design that is not too complicated and can be done freehand. Select a contrasting color for the thread and embroider the branches first. The embroidery thread and needle are available in notions stores or the five-and-ten. Next, cut out the leaves. Turn each piece over and spray the back with fabric adhesive. Place the leaves onto the bag and press down with your palm. They will adhere securely and no sewing is necessary. Another design suggestion is to use interesting buttons in place of the leather leaves. Find buttons that are unusual and vary in size. Use rickrack trim in place of the embroidery if you don't want to do much sewing. This can be put on with the fabric adhesive as well.

MAIL-ORDER SOURCES OF SUPPLIES

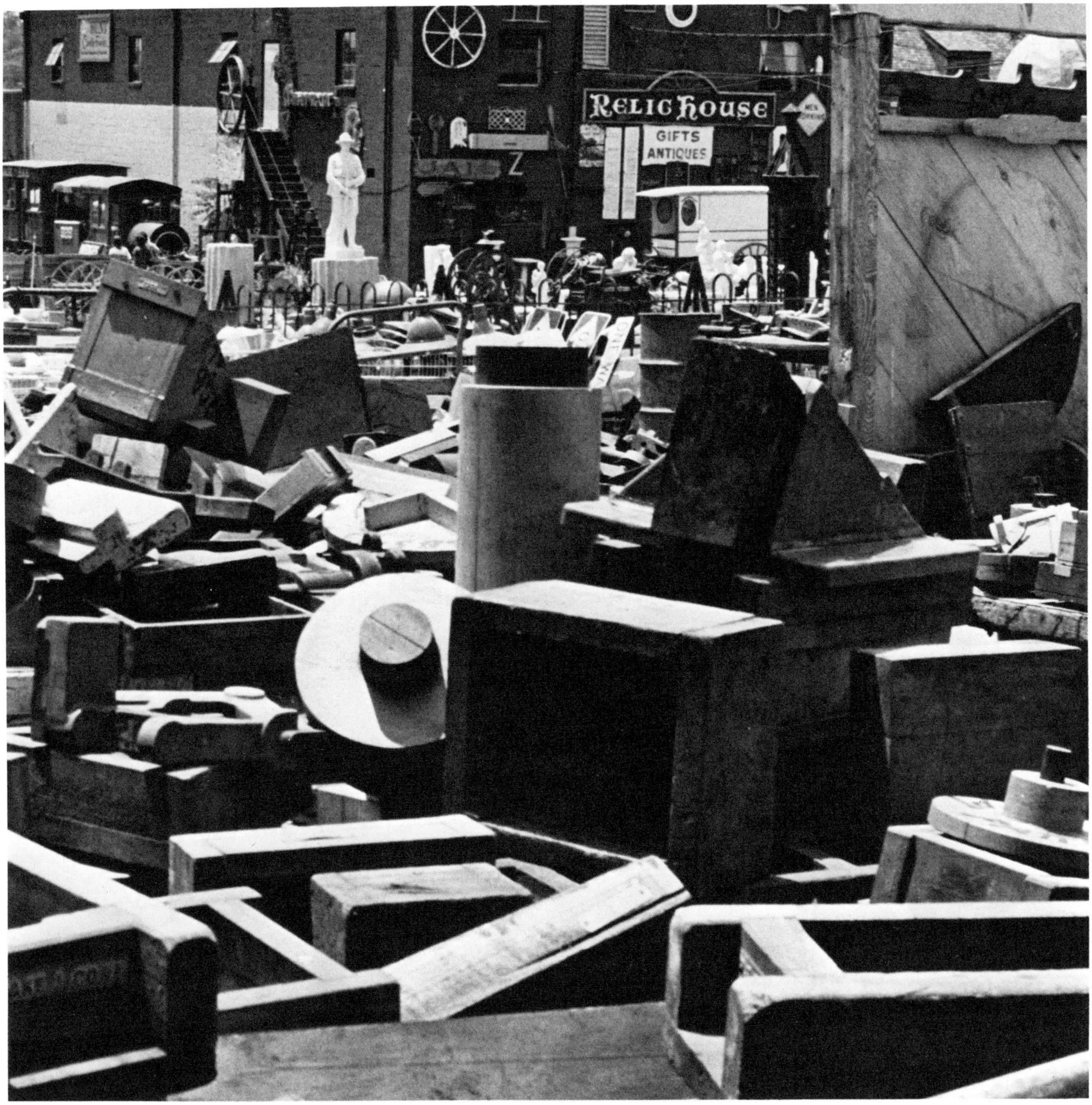

The following companies have catalogs and provide mail-order service.

Army & Navy Stores

Army & Navy Supply Corp.
1938 Third Ave.
New York, N.Y. 10029

Hudson's Army & Navy Store
105 Third Ave.
New York, N.Y. 10003

Uncle Dan's Surplus Store
Dept. MYP
3350 W. Bryn Mawr
Chicago, Ill. 60607

Weiss & Mahoney Inc.
142 Fifth Ave.
New York, N.Y. 10011

Art Supplies

Charrette
31 Olympia Ave.
Woburn, Mass. 01801
This company will send you a fabulous catalog chock full of wonderful materials for all your art and crafting needs. The Corbu stencils, Fome-Cor, mounting and illustration board, miter box, compass, and fourteen different frames including the Gallery Clips come from this source.

Barrels and Kegs

Cordell Enterprises, Inc.
1622 W. Morse Ave.
Chicago, Ill. 60626

The Cracker Barrel
527 Narberth Ave.
Haddonfield, N.J. 08033

Spaulding & Frost Co. Inc.
Fremont, N.H. 03044

Baskets

Dell-Co Imports
Box 1593
Laredo, Tex. 78040

Fran's Basket House
89 W. Main St.
Rockaway, N.J. 07866

Blankets

Mover's blankets:

Village Stripper Antiques
519 Hudson St.
New York, N.Y. 10014

Navy blankets:

The above Army & Navy stores

Boating and Marine Equipment and Hardware

A.G.A. Correa
P.O. Box 401
Wiscasset, Me. 04578

This company has a catalog available for ordering unusual and hard-to-find marine hardware and fittings, as well as gift items.

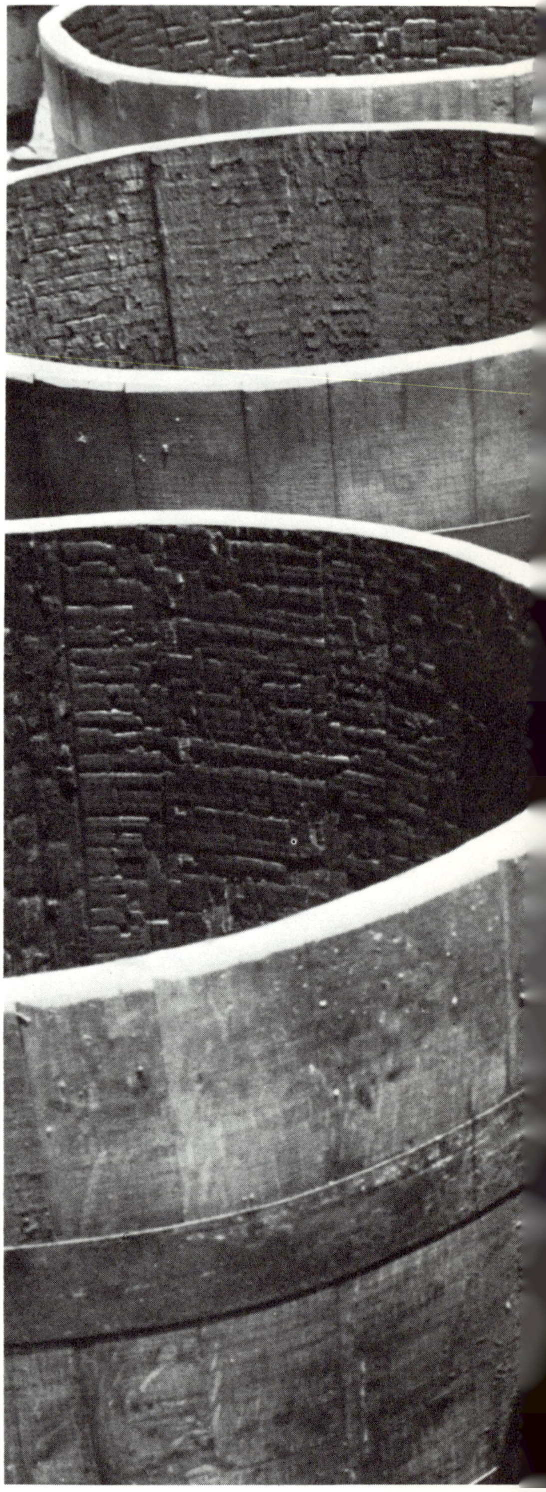

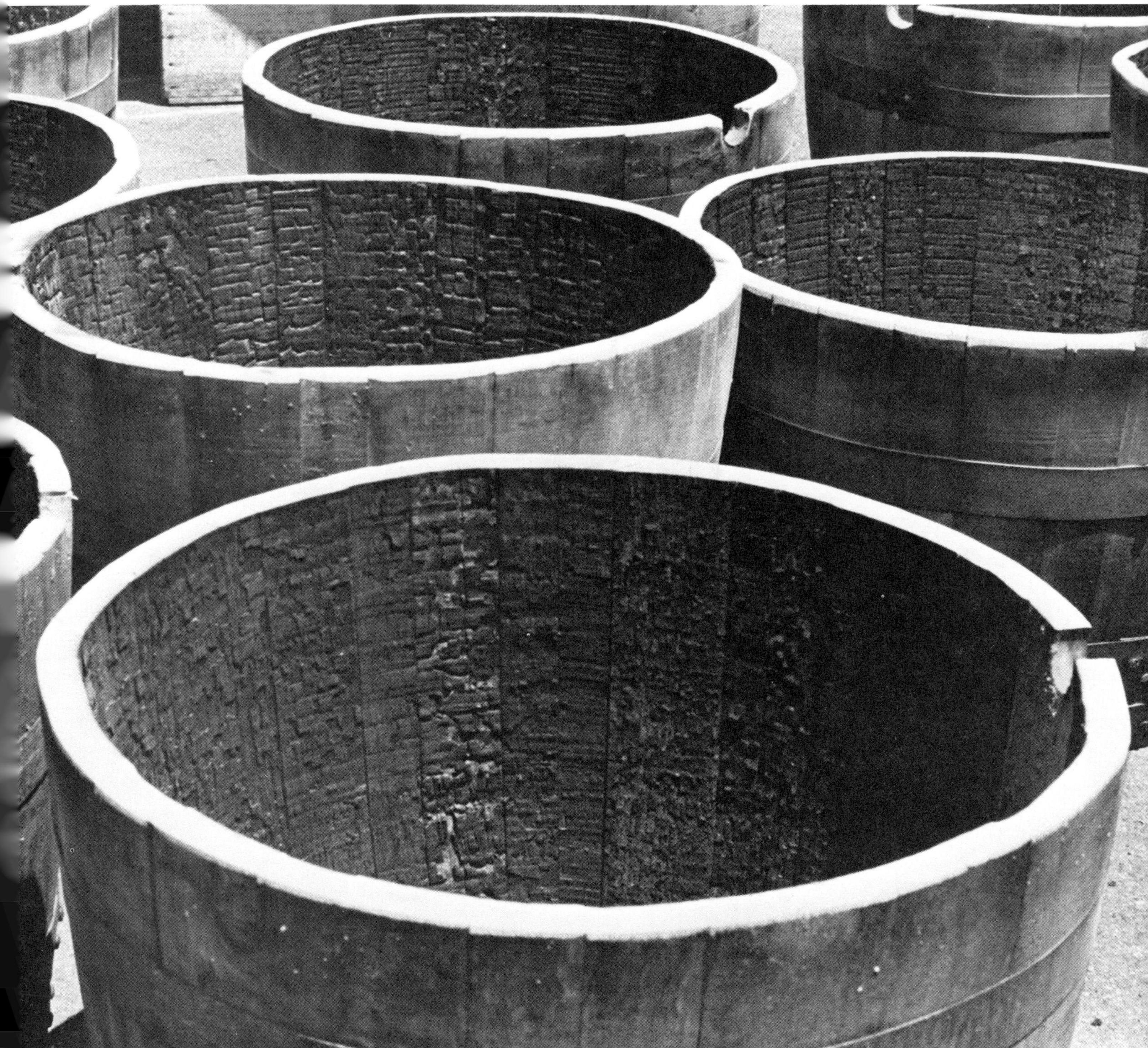

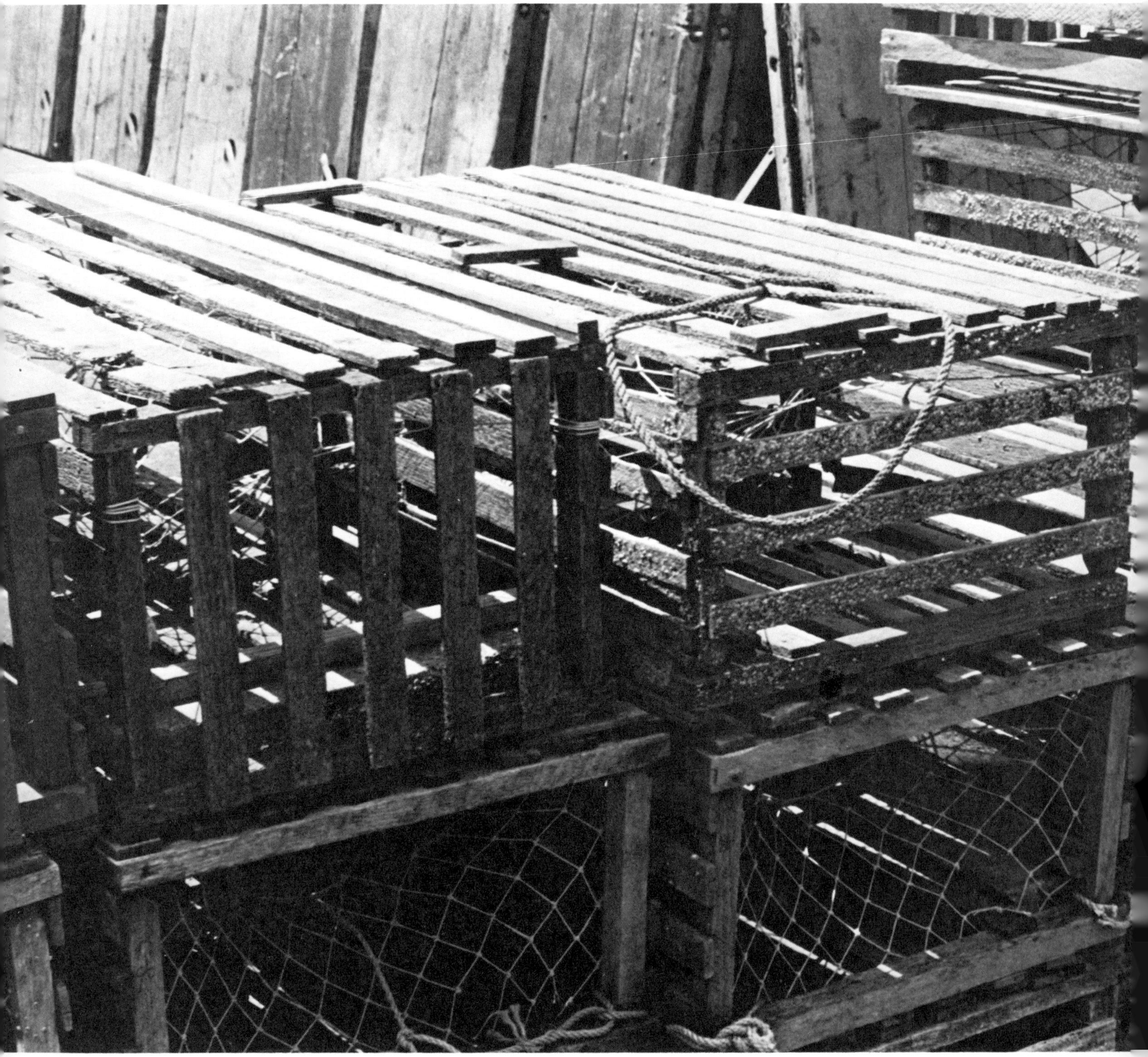

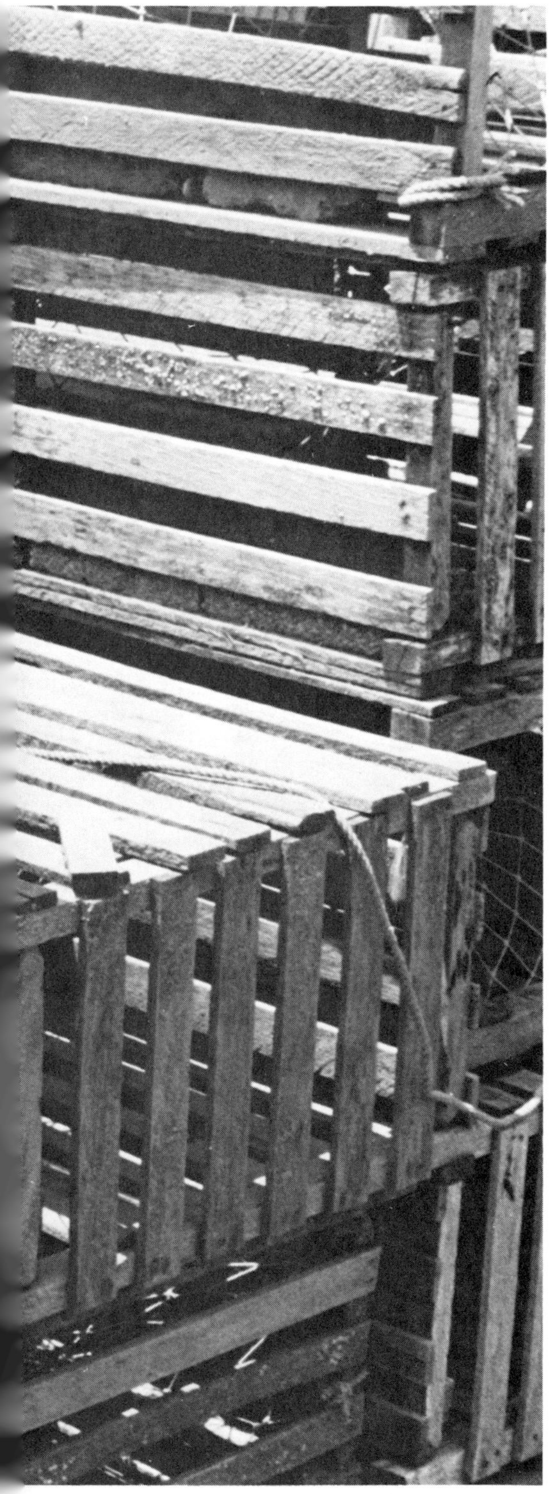

Goldberg's
202 Market St.
Philadelphia, Pa. 19106

West Products Corp.
140 Greenwood Ave.
Midland Park, N.J. 07432

Chicken Coops

Cordell Enterprises, Inc.
1622 W. Morse Ave.
Chicago, Ill. 60626

Clothing, Camping, and Hunting Gear

Eddie Bauer
Box 3700
Seattle, Wash. 98124

L. L. Bean, Inc.
454 Main St.
Freeport, Maine 04032

Cooking and Camping Equipment

Recreational Equipment Inc.
Box 22088
Seattle, Wash. 98122

The Smilie Co.
575 Howard St.
San Francisco, Calif. 94105

Catalog 10¢. They carry simple utilitarian objects, all size cooking pots, canteens, lanterns, camp beds.

Crates, Baskets, Tubs, and Buckets

The Cracker Barrel
527 Narberth Ave.
Haddonfield, N.J. 08033

Frames

Charrette
31 Olympia Ave.
Woburn, Mass. 01801

Kulicke Frames Inc.
636 Broadway
New York, N.Y. 10012

Catalog $1.

General Surplus

Army & Navy Surplus Stores Corp.
1938 Third Ave.
New York, N.Y. 10029

Volume Distributors
40-17 24th St.
Long Island City, N.Y. 11102

Government Surplus

Palley Supply Co. Inc.
2263 E. Vernon Ave.
Los Angeles, Calif. 90058

Catalog $1. This is the largest government-surplus store in the country, with seven and a half acres of government and industrial goods. If you can't find it elsewhere, you can probably get it here. Not all items listed in the catalog.

Latches, Hooks & Fixtures

Latham's Corner
Rt. 68, Box 103
White Creek, N.Y. 12057

Lockers

Lyon Metal Products
2444 Morris Ave.
Union, N.J. 07083

Ask for local dealer information.

Mail-Order Houses

J.C. Penney Co. Inc.
1301 Ave. of Americas
New York, N.Y. 10019

Montgomery Ward
Chicago, Ill. 60607

Mother's Truck Store Catalogue
Box 75
Unionville, Ohio 44088

This store sells old-time implements that are hard to find.

Sears, Roebuck and Co.
Dept. 139
2650 E. Olympia Blvd.
Los Angeles, Calif. 90051 (West Coast)

4640 Roosevelt Blvd.
Philadelphia, Pa. 19132 (East Coast)

Ask for their Farm and Ranch catalog also.

Whole Earth Truck Store
558 Santa Cruz Ave.
Menlo Park, Calif. 94025

They distribute the *Whole Earth Catalog*, which is $5 and lists camping equipment that is hard to find.

Maps

Geological Survey Maps
Washington, D.C. 20242

A folder describing topographic maps and symbols is available on request.

Hammond Inc.
12 East 41st St.
New York, N.Y. 10016

Rand McNally & Co.
10 E. 53rd St.
New York, N.Y. 10022

Metal Ware

Dell-Co Imports
Box 1593
Laredo, Tex. 78040

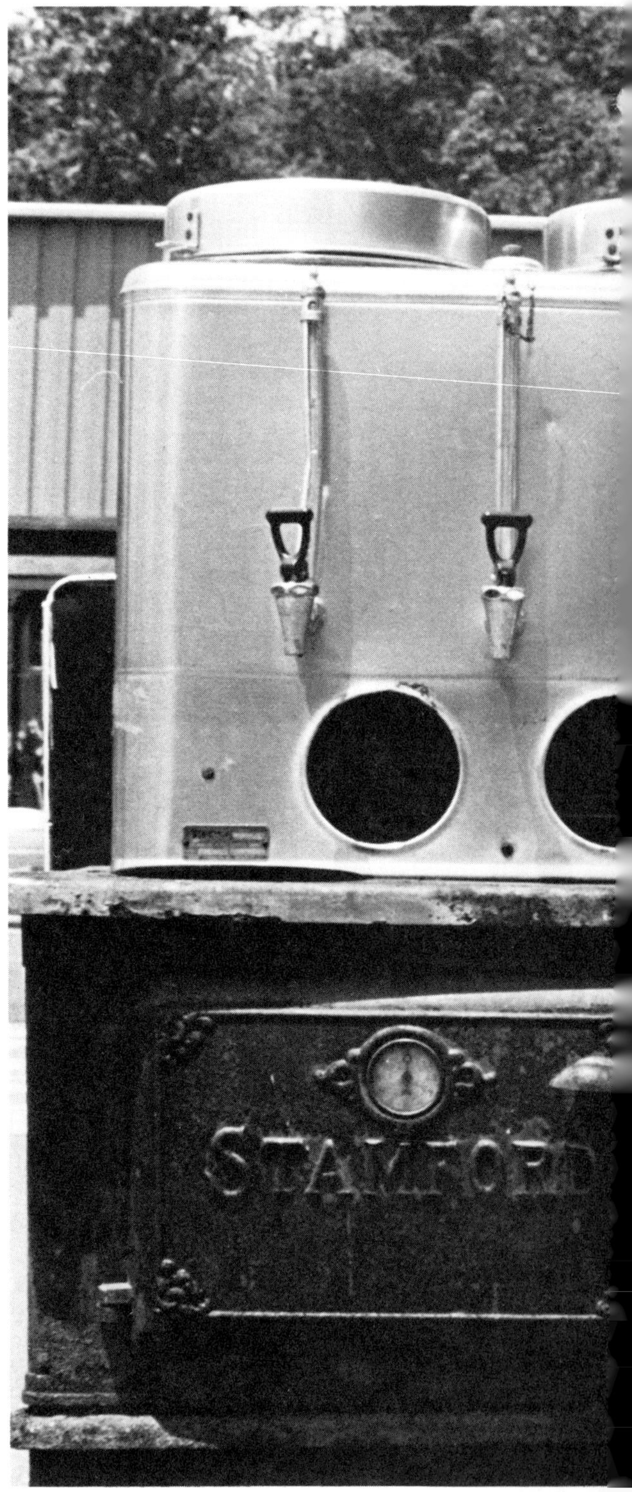

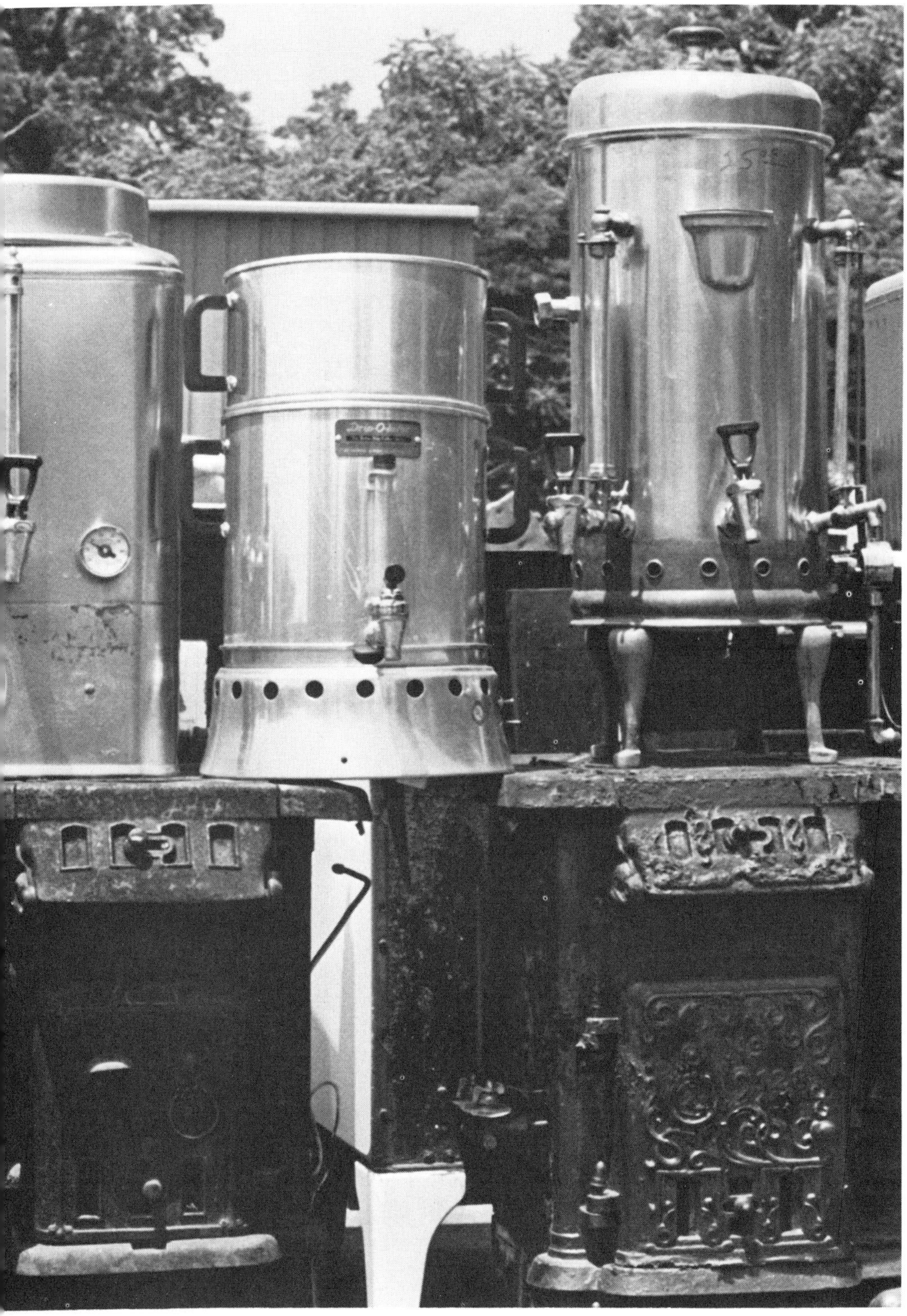

Military Clothing

I. Buss & Co.
50 W. 17th St.
New York, N.Y. 10011

Natural Food Stores

Byrd Mill
Box 5167
Richmond, Va. 23220

Raul C. Laing Apiaries
8448 Chestnut Ridge Rd.
Rt. 77
Gasport, N.Y. 14067

Pine Boxes

Spaulding & Frost Co. Inc.
Fremont, N.H. 03044

They carry boxes of all sizes with and without cushion tops.

Posters

New York Botanical Gardens
Bronx, N.Y. 10458

Their full-color folder shows the beautiful botanical posters that are available at reasonable cost. Most are $6.

Triton Gallery Inc.
323 W. 45th St.
New York, N.Y. 10036

This gallery specializes in theater posters, reasonably priced at between $3 and $5.

United House Wrecking

328 Selleck St.
Stamford, Conn. 06902

If you can't find what you're looking for anywhere else, no request is too bizarre, no item so unusual that the Lodato family of United House Wrecking hasn't carried it, doesn't have it, or can't locate it. No catalog available, but a folder will be sent on request.

Product Information

All wallpaper used for background or in crafting projects is washable, vinyl Wall-Tex provided by the Borden Company. Krylon spray paint and varnish and Elmer's Glue-All, also from Borden's, was used where mentioned.

The fabric spray adhesive is 3M "Scotch" Brand Spra-Ment and the sandpaper is 3M WetorDry or 3M Press N' Sand.

Presstype and Letraset press-on letters are available in art supply stores and extensive catalogs are provided to choose a style and size from.

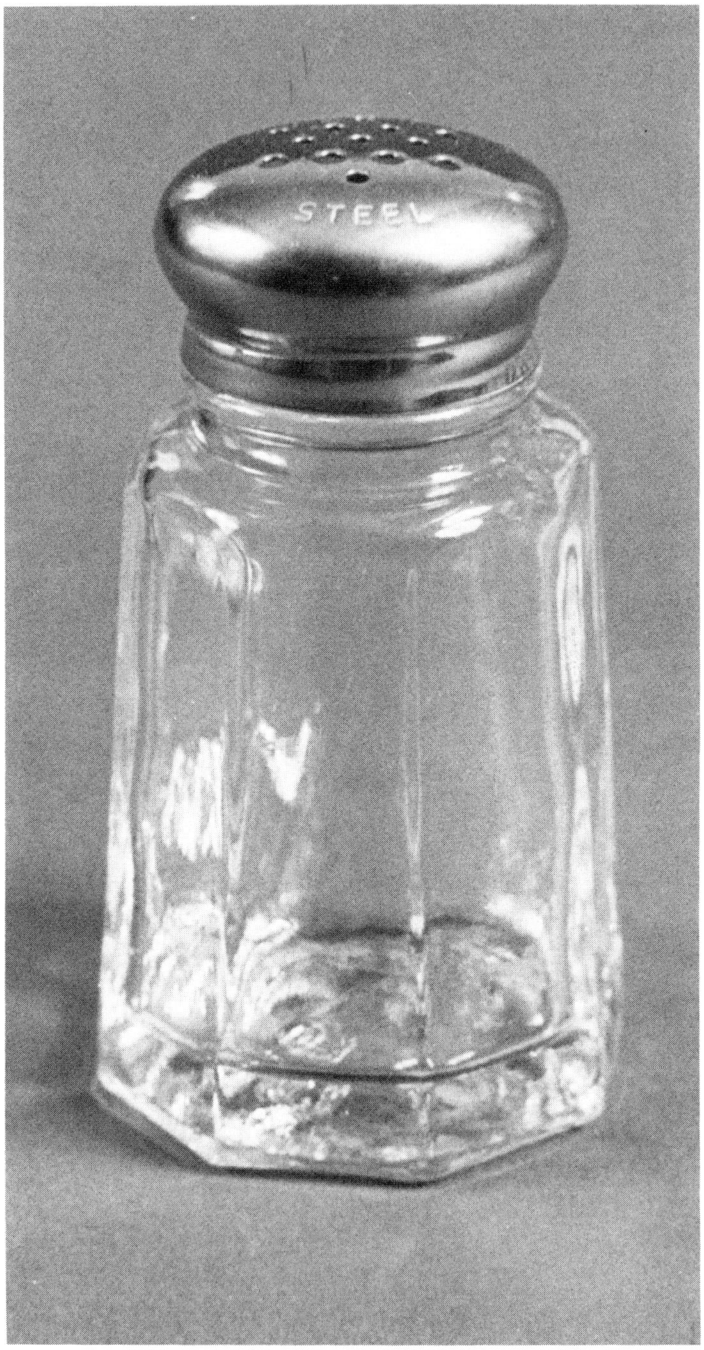